D0855555

Systemic Religious Education

BT
207
L64

13.36

Systemic Religious Education

TIMOTHY ARTHUR LINES

Religious Education Press
Birmingham, Alabama

13585

Copyright © 1987 by Religious Education Press
All rights reserved

No part of this publication may be reproduced, stored in a retrieval system, or transmitted, in any form or by any means, electronic, photocopying, recording, or otherwise, without the prior written permission of the publisher.

Library of Congress Cataloging-in-Publication Data

Lines, Timothy Arthur.
  Systemic religious education.

  Includes bibliographies and index.
  1. Christian education.   I. Title.
BV1464.L56   1987   207   86-20383
ISBN 0-89135-057-8

Religious Education Press, Inc.
Birmingham, Alabama
10 9 8 7 6 5 4 3 2

Religious Education Press publishes books exclusively in religious education and in areas closely related to religious education. It is committed to enhancing and professionalizing religious education through the publication of serious, significant, and scholarly works.

To
DEBBIE

30   2071

30. 2071

Contents

Preface

I shall be telling this with a sigh
Somewhere ages and ages hence:
Two roads diverged in a wood, and I—
I took the one less traveled by,
And that has made all the difference.[1]
                                    Robert Frost

The fall and early winter of 1984 turned out to be one of those revelatory times when—at least in retrospect—things began to come together for me as a religious educator. Frankly, at the time I felt more as if I were coming apart than coming together, but such are the dynamics of growth and maturity. Let me list a few of my activities during those months as evidence of how my perspective on religious education is a bit different from more traditional views.

For approximately twenty hours a week I was a chaplain at Central State Hospital just outside the city limits of Louisville, Kentucky. I served in an acute ward of the adult psychiatric unit, where the average patient stay was something like three weeks. I observed dozens of people flow in and flow out of the hospital, some of them making return visits. I sat there in the ward hour after hour with no identifying mark to broadcast that I was a chaplain: no name tag, no uniform, not even a clerical collar. The only objective difference between me and other persons in those chairs was that I possessed a key that allowed me in and out of the locked ward. At first I guarded the key carefully, since it was

1

my one symbol of "okayness." The longer I sat, listened, talked, and watched, the less I felt that I had the need or even the right to use the key. My rigid views of health and normalcy underwent some rapid alterations. I came to consider that chaplaincy a very significant experience in religious education.

Three times a week I taught in the School of Christian Education at The Southern Baptist Theological Seminary in Louisville. I faced thirty-five bright, inquisitive seminarians for an hour at a time, and together we wrestled with understanding "behavioral foundations." It was not long before I learned that teaching is much more than the delivery of prepared lecture notes. I consider my interaction with those students a highly revealing religious education event.

Throughout the week I was associate minister for a church in the suburbs of Louisville. I taught Sunday School, made pastoral visits, and led worship services. I also experienced the deep personal relationships that create an authentic church "body." I value that experience as a truly religious education experience.

One night a week my wife and I co-led a group in a marriage enrichment seminar. It had an impact on our marriage, on our individual lives, and considering reports from others in the group, on other lives and marriages as well. You guessed it: I consider that a religious education event.

In the midst of these other activities I was involved in psychotherapy, both as a therapist and as a client. A Pandora's box of emotional, physical, and spiritual issues was opened to examination. I experienced growth, healing—and yes, significant religious education.

All of this was in tandem to writing a dissertation on the theory of religious education. Surely no one would deny that the experiences I have described would have some connection to a conceptualization of religious education. The discipline of doing research and of formulating sentences about a theory of religious education was in itself a religious education experience.

This fragmentary biographical confession is offered as my way of bringing authentic religious education into focus. When was I "doing" religious education? To put it more pointedly, when was I *not* doing religious education? I have more than a little difficulty in separating and isolating religious education from the welter of life experience; in fact, I cannot and will not.

My professional credentials may be important to some. Ministerially, I was ordained in 1977 and have served in parish ministries since 1969. These positions have ranged from associate pastor to minister of education, to minister of youth, to minister of music. Academically, I possess several graduate degrees. I have a Master of Divinity degree with a major in historical theology; an interdisciplinary Master of Science degree in Systems Science; and a Doctor of Education degree in religious education and administration. While I do not deny the value of professional experience or academic degrees, I doubt that they are valid proof of my authenticity as a religious educator. That should explain why I began by relating some of my personal experiences and should also be a clue to my concept of the future of religious education.

The thesis of this book is that religious education can become more effective and more mature if it is done from a systemic perspective. This thesis has four elements: (1) the systemic perspective is composed of a paradigm, a worldview, models, and simulations; (2) a systemic paradigm can be developed from the study of open systems; (3) a systemic worldview is emerging that is conducive and amenable to the overall systemic perspective; (4) systemic models of religion, education, and religious education can be constructed which reflect the systemic paradigm and which organically interrelate and cybernetically influence the systemic worldview.[2]

The structure of the book follows the four elements of the thesis. The initial discussion relates to the concept of perspectives. A variety of perspectives are explored, culminating in the introduction of the systemic perspective. The focus then shifts to a development of paradigms and to how open systems theory provides the basic orientation to the systemic paradigm. Worldviews become the next consideration, with the primary contribution being a description of an emergent systemic worldview. Finally, systemic models are proposed. Individual chapters express possibilities for systemic religion, systemic education, and systemic religious education. Not only do these models relate to the systemic paradigm and the systemic worldview, but they are also interactive with and interdependent upon each other.

The chapters should be read in consecutive order and not in piecemeal fashion. The worst approach would be to flip to the final chapter and expect it alone to explain systemic religious education. The book is a systemic whole and the argument unfolds throughout. Each chapter builds upon the previous ones, with systemic religious education coming as a result of the discussion of the entire book.

This book is not a tirade against either religion or science. It is just the opposite. The book is an attempt to integrate religion and science in a way that informs both and improves both. I am firmly convinced this can and must happen. Every day I find that I must work at integrating my professional identity as social scientist, minister, counselor, educator, and administrator.

The truth is that this book is neither a final statement of my thought nor an absolute declaration of the systemic perspective. It *is* a statement of who I am presently and of the way I perceive the future of religious education. I have every intention of continuing to grow, mature, and transform. I have every expectation that religious education will do the same. The goal of this book is not so much to present a full and complete conceptualization of religious education as it is to propose a fresh perspective, to suggest some different ideas, and to stimulate some creativity in the field of religious education.

Much confusion and frustration can be avoided if it is clear that this book addresses religious education and not specifically Christian education. While it is possible that in the future I may propose a theory of systemic Christian education, this book deals with systemic *religious* education. Religious education from a systemic perspective is broad, inclusive, and nonparticularistic. This effort is a movement toward integration and synthesis rather than toward isolation and exclusivism.

Words of thanks and appreciation come to mind in a flood, and in no way could I express them to all who are deserving. Many have read at least parts of the manuscript and have made helpful comments, bringing expertise from such diverse fields as physics, philosophy, and sociology as well as religious education. These people include Ernest White, Ralph Hardee, Daniel Aleshire, John Dillon, Charles Breslin, Robert Hoye, and David Britt. Ernest White has been my mentor and close friend, and much of my introduction to holistic perception I credit to him. David Britt has read the entire manuscript, giving me not only feedback but support and encouragement. Typing has been done competently and helpfully by Gaylyn Bishop, Debbie Lines, Maureen Odiam, and Beverly Scherzinger.

Heartfelt gratitude is sent to my students over the years for having struggled with me as I have tried to make each course "systemic." The entire faculty of the School of Christian Education at Southern Seminary has cheerfully put up with a seemingly endless stream of papers dealing with systems theory and religious education at various phases of development. William Rogers, Dean of the School of Christian Education, deserves special thanks for his patience, since I was continually running back to the library checking on "one last footnote" while serving as Assistant to the Dean.

This book is dedicated with love, honor, and respect to my wife Debbie. Anyone who could endure all these years of listening to me describe everything as a "systems problem" surely deserves more than a book dedication, and indeed it is the least I owe her. She continues to help me learn the systemic lesson of how two become one.

Louisville, Kentucky   TIMOTHY ARTHUR LINES

NOTES

1. Robert Frost, "The Road Not Taken," in *Robert Frost's Poems,* ed. Louis Untermeyer (New York: Washington Square Press, 1971), p. 223.
2. Since this book is a theoretical one, actual simulations are not described or tested. Systemic simulations are the next logical step in the development of the systemic perspective and would provide more than enough material for another book.

Chapter 1

Perspectives

I remember, I remember,
The fir trees dark and high;
I used to think their slender tops
Were close against the sky:
It was a childish ignorance.
But now 'tis little joy
To know I'm farther off from heaven
Than when I was a boy.[1]

Thomas Hood

Maturity is an essential component of healthy human development and a desirable consequence of growth, but it is often a disturbing experience. Maturity requires modifying patterns of behavior and thought that may have once been appropriate but are no longer so. What a child may accept to be reality, an adult may find to be fantasy at best and falsehood at worst. Maturity is that slow process of releasing the known and grasping for the unknown. Maturity produces a depth of perception that may provide fewer final answers but does produce better questions.

This chapter explores perspectives that permit better questions. A perspective is a particular viewpoint of understanding, and this brief glance through some of the religious education of the twentieth century reveals a deepening maturity, albeit a maturity necessarily fraught with disturbance, pain, and disagreement. Differences are to be expected in a field so multifaceted and diverse, but sufficient cohesion needs to be present in order to identify religious education as a recognizable field. The presentation of

7

perspectives seeks not only to spotlight the confusion and the chaos but to raise some possibility of order and understanding.

The middle course of becoming both unique and part of society is no easy road. A maturing individual encounters pitfalls at every turn, and in like manner religious education needs constant awareness as it matures. One danger is hermitic isolation. This occurs when one becomes afraid of others while also being so involved in personal interpretations and activities that the "outside" world fades into insignificance. Communication with the environment becomes unnecessary, since the truly valuable events are internal. Fear and anxiety sever contact with one's surroundings. Maturity is distorted when an individual becomes a misanthropic recluse.

The opposite danger on the road toward maturity is sycophantic dependency. Rather than developing a strong sense of worth and self-esteem from within, the dependent personality turns to external sources for identity. A person with a weak ego and overwhelming approval needs attaches to another person for sustenance, unable alone to become a self-supporting entity. Maturity is stunted when a person becomes a life-draining parasite.

Religious education can become isolated or dependent in its attempt at maturity. Rigid, thick boundaries that "protect" it from the environment will lead to irrelevance, self-involvement, and death. Inadequate self-understanding and structure will result in domination, subsumption, and dissolution. Neither of these aberrations creates a healthy maturity and an adult identity.

Maturity lives in the struggle for balance between the extremes. A variety of perspectives brings into focus both mistakes of the past and possibilities for the future. Mature vision requires honesty about what has transpired and commitment toward what needs to happen. One of the motivations for this book is to increase the health and maturity of religious education by pointing out dangerous tendencies from its past and by proposing some alternatives for the future. This is started by showing with requisite clarity the present situation through a multiplicity of perspectives. Those included in this chapter are: an overall perspective; theological perspectives; historical and theoretical perspectives; individual perspectives; and a focused perspective.

AN OVERALL PERSPECTIVE

The terms and concepts introduced in this section serve to give an overall perspective to the direction taken in this book. Each of the elements of religious education receives more definitive treatment in later chapters, but here the basic parameters are sketched for clarity and integrity. This book not only analyzes and explains, but proposes and advocates. It is only honest to be open about some of the foundational presuppositions that shape the contours of the discussion. This brief overview raises those presuppositions to the level of awareness for all to note and to take into account throughout the book.[2]

Most importantly, this book seeks to be *systemic*. As is said *ad infinitum* (and possibly *ad nauseum*) throughout the book, religious education should be approached, defined, understood, and experienced from a systemic perspective. Full detailing of what "systemic" means is reserved for later in the book, but suffice it to say here that systemic refers to the organic interrelatedness and interdependence of dynamic entities incorporating a whole. Religious education need neither be so isolated as to reflect only narcissistic interests nor be so dominated as to serve an imperialistic discipline.[3] Religious education from a systemic perspective searches for, attempts at, and creates ways of increasing health and interface among a variety of fields and disciplines.

Another key point is that the subject is *religious* education. No particular type of religion (such as Christianity), no specific division of a religion (such as Catholicism), and certainly no special denomination of a religion (like Southern Baptists) is the focus of the book.[4] The objective of the book is to integrate rather than to divide. The focus is on the essence of religious education that has applicability beyond cultural and ethnic boundaries, reaching to the very depths of humankind.

Additionally, the subject is religious *education*. As James Michael Lee has said so succinctly, "Education is the broad process whereby a person learns something."[5] Such a definition signals the intimidating but highly significant task ahead.

A familiar element of religious education is *nurture*. Horace Bushnell gave it classic articulation in the seminal work *Christian*

Nurture.[6] If Bushnell was the father of modern religious education,[7] then nurture has been a part of the religious education movement from its inception. Nurture is the caring, feeding, supporting, and sustaining aspect of religious education. Without the dimension of nurture, the relational and communal nature of religious education would be greatly diminished. Nurture suggests that the maturation process is at least in part a socialization process. Iris Cully wrote: "A person could be self-educated but he [or she] could not be self-nurtured."[8] The religious education envisioned in this book is not simply a cognitive activity but is designed to address holistic maturation. Cognition is one aspect of maturity but so are such processes as relation to society, emotional health, and integrity. These processes need the nurturing presence of others for growth and expansion.[9]

Closely related to nurture is *development.* Development denotes ever-increasing depth and complexity. Nurture without development results in parasitic and dependent behavior. Religious education as described in this book moves toward interdependence and interrelationship.

For useful and positive development, *intentionality* is an essential ingredient. A guiding purpose is requisite for religious education, protecting it from random activity and providing it with a raison d'etre. Intentionality directs the shaping of religious education through nurture and development. Conscious direction and choiceful behavior give power and force to religious education. When there is intentionality, there can be an evaluation of the progress (or lack of progress) made toward an objective. Identifiable results are possible when purpose is clearly stated and terms of achievement are made explicit.

Religious education as conceptualized in this book includes emphasis on both *integration* and *differentiation.* Integration is movement toward unity and harmony through holistic incorporation of multifaceted elements. Differentiation is the creation and nourishment of variety to meet individual and/or corporate needs and to reflect the impact of situational variables. Prolonged emphasis on either integration or differentiation ultimately produces unhealthy conditions. Integration pushed to dominance brings sameness, uniformity, and rigidity. Differentiation allowed to run rampant creates fragmentation, disorientation, and chaos.

A dynamic balance between the two gives religious education the freshness and vitality it requires, while it keeps the coherence and intelligibility it needs.

Another key to understanding religious education is *interaction*. It is dynamic, not a static entity. Religious education cannot be identified with a particular religious educator, with a specified methodology, with an articulated philosophy, or with an inspirational (or inspired) book. Religious education is interaction: a process in which the aforementioned variables may function but which are not the primary consideration. Consider a dance. To observe only the dancer's feet, or to concentrate exclusively on the music, or to respond to the pulsating rhythms alone is to miss the totality. The dance is an experience, a fusion of pattern, sound, and emotion. As the poet said:

> O body swayed to music, O brightening dance,
> How can we know the dancer from the dance?[10]

Transformation is the final aspect of religious education as discussed from the overall perspective of this book. Healthy change, in the sense of intentional development toward maturity, is a basic reason for doing religious education. Without change, religious education—indeed any kind of education—has no meaning or value. Religious education that only seeks to maintain the status quo is not the subject of this book. Granted, maintenance is necessary for survival, but mere existence is not sufficient justification for the continuance of religious education. Religious education in its authentic form is continually transforming individuals, groups, institutions, societies—*and itself.*

THEOLOGICAL PERSPECTIVES

The theological perspectives within the religious education movement of the twentieth century provide a striking context of history. This is not to say that religious education is a creation of the twentieth century, as even a cursory study of the history of religious education immediately reveals.[11] It is not to say that a theological perspective is necessarily the "proper" way to understand religious education. It is to say that a brief overview of the ebb and flow of the various theologies through the recent history of religious education can be instructive and illustrative. It shows the near-sightedness of a strictly theological perspective and reveals the current state of confusion about theology[12] in the field of religious education.

The determinative issue for religious education during most of the twentieth century has been theology.[13] Arguments were devoted to the *kind* of theology, to be sure, but the discussion revolved around theology nonetheless. First was the assumption that a "liberal" type of theology was the necessary foundation. Second was the challenge to liberal theology from a more conservative brand of theology called "neo-orthodox" theology.

The issue at present is whether theology of any stripe is actually the determinative issue.

The Liberal Perspective

The term "liberal" applied to the theological perspective dominant early in the twentieth century gains relevance only in retrospect. In its day,[14] liberal religious education based on the foundation of liberal theology *was* religious education.[15] There were opponents, certainly, primarily those whom Harrison Elliott identified as Fundamentalists;[16] but on the whole, for one to be a religious educator was to be a liberal in theology. The salient points of the liberal position were summarized from a historical vantage point by Roger Shinn: the Bible was regarded as a record of humanity's search for God; sin was understood as ignorance or misunderstanding; justification was received through doing good works; history was a recitation of divine movement; and the hope of the future was to be found in earthly fulfillment.[17]

A more contemporaneous description of the tenets of liberalism was rendered by H. Shelton Smith.[18] Although Smith was writing to challenge the liberals, his effort served to give explication of the movement in question. He identified four "major tendencies" which he found stemming from the thought of the nineteenth century.[19] First was *divine immanence,*[20] where the idea of God was understood less as transcendent and distinct from the human order and more as inherent and continuous with the human process. Second was *growth,*[21] which Smith explained as having three facets:

(1) growth of religion in the individual; (2) growth of religion in the race; (3) growth as a mode of achieving individual and social change.[22]

Third was the innate *goodness of man* [persons],[23] meaning liberal theology tended to deemphasize the depravity of humanity and focused instead on societal ills. Fourth was the *search for the historical Jesus*.[24] Smith pointed here to the effort to create a biography of Jesus that resulted in making Jesus function more like a "twentieth-century modernist" than a first-century rabbi.[25]

Perhaps the definition that captured the essence of liberal religious education was the one proposed by George Albert Coe in 1929. Coe did as much as anyone to shape liberal religious education,[26] and he defined it this way: "It is the systematic, critical examination and reconstruction of relations between persons, guided by Jesus' assumption that persons are of infinite worth, and by the hypothesis of the existence of God, the great Valuer of Persons."[27] The resonance of Smith's four points echo throughout Coe's definition.

Harrison Elliott saw the formation of dissent regarding liberalism and tried to dissipate it with his 1940 book, *Can Religious Education Be Christian?*[28] Elliott stated that the purpose of his book was "to discuss the educational rather than the theological issues,"[29] yet he spent his time primarily debating theology. Elliott answered the question posed in the title of his book by saying that religious education *could* be Christian *if* the term "Christian" were interpreted according to experiential (read, liberal) definitions.[30] Far from closing the issue and dissipating the challenge, Elliott actually opened the door for a forceful rejoinder. H. Shelton Smith's response[31] was not long in coming.

The Neo-Orthodox Perspective

The year 1941 brought H. Shelton Smith's book *Faith and Nurture*. Smith began his penetrating analysis of the then-current status of religious education with this statement: "That the modern movement in Protestant religious education is confronted with a crucial decision in its theological orientation can hardly be denied."[32] From the first Smith made clear that the argument was about theology. His challenge took the form of a pointed

question: "Shall Protestant nurture realign its theological foundations with the newer currents of Christian thought or shall it resist
those currents and merely reaffirm its faith in traditional liberalism?"[33]

It immediately became clear that Smith was rejecting liberalism, and was supporting the "newer currents," which came to be
called "neo-orthodox" theology. The tone of Smith's book was
polemical[34] in that it pointed out the weaknesses and inadequa-
cies of liberalism. As Smith himself admitted, he did not design
the book to propose a new program of religious education practice.[35] He was content to expose the deficiencies of the older
system and to leave the new constructions to others.

What was neo-orthodoxy? William Hordern observed that the
term "neo-orthodoxy" was in truth only a blanket expression for
a wide variety of positions and beliefs.[36] Some of the other names
by which it was known are instructive. It was labeled "crisis
theology" since it came face-to-face with facism, world war, and
mass destruction.[37] "Reformation theology" was used to denote
heritage to the principles of the Protestant reform movement of
the sixteenth century.[38] The rubric "Barthianism" resulted from
the leadership and influence of Karl Barth on the theological
formulations.[39] The term "neo-orthodox" was what Kendig Cully
called a direction pointer:[40] It signaled an affirmation of a traditional (orthodox) type of Christianity but was expressed in
fresher, more vigorous forms (hence, *neo*-orthodox) than had
been done in the recent past.

The four points that H. Shelton Smith used to critique liberalism are easily turned into descriptions of neo-orthodoxy. In a
sense, the neo-orthodox tenets were polar opposites to liberalism.[41] Instead of stressing the immanence of God as did the
liberals, the neo-orthodox theologians emphasized the transcendence of God. God was understood to be "wholly-other"[42] from
humanity, separate from earthly culture. Where liberals saw
growth and progress throughout human history, the reformers
saw human tragedy and societal failure. Against the innate goodness of persons came awareness of the dark side of humanity:
Humans are depraved and sinful, and salvation must come from
beyond the bounds of mortals. The search by liberals for the
"Jesus of history" became the quest by neo-orthodox theologians
for the "Christ of faith."

The message of neo-orthodoxy was that humanity could not save itself. The dream of the liberals to bring about the Kingdom of God on earth (primarily through religious education) was no longer tenable in the face of harsh realities. Hope turned to a sovereign God, who stood outside the realm of human reason and understanding, and who would bring the fulfillment of the cosmic purposes without human assistance.

There was no doubt that religious education had to be recast in the face of such challenges, and there was no dearth of persons who rushed to the task. Kendig Cully wrote that "the church throughout Christendom has been benefiting ever since from the response its educational theorists have been making in the effort to move into new directions."[43] Much attention is given in this chapter and throughout this book to a few of these attempts to reconstruct religious education. Yet to identify the issue as a movement from one theological bias to another is far too simplistic.

An Environmental Perspective

The force of the neo-orthodox criticisms upon religious education cannot be attributed solely to the theological arguments, however well-done they were, by H. Shelton Smith, Karl Barth, or any other theologian. Currents "outside" the spheres of theology and religious education were demanding attention. In discussing the development of the Religious Education Association during the period of the early 1940s, historian Stephen Schmidt made this observation:

> National and international events moved toward World War II. The rise of German national socialism, the advent of Hitler's challenge to Western civilization, and the systematic slaughter of the Jews were actions that did not respond to reason or group discussion methods. The R.E.A. as well as other educational associations stood on the sidelines of human history. Religious education had neither skills nor sufficient moral force to prevent a world-wide holocaust. Old slogans of the "brotherhood of man and the fatherhood of God" appeared as ill-chosen descriptions of inhumane horrors. The entire liberal legacy seemed bankrupt.[44]

To understand either theology or religious education from a perspective of "ivory-tower" isolation is to misunderstand them.

Liberal theology and liberal religious education were not separate from the environmental and historical context in which they were formed. Understanding must include such events as "The War to End All Wars," Prohibition, and women's suffrage. Neo-orthodox theology and the consequent revolutions in religious education cannot be fathomed apart from the happenings at Pearl Harbor, Dachau, and Hiroshima. Authentic theology and religious education are never self-contained islands, floating independently and serenely apart from the rest of society.

To understand theology and religious education as locked into a symbiotic *folie à deux* is also to misunderstand them. The assignment to theology as the determinative issue in religious education is a confusion of theology with the much larger environment of religious education. C. West Churchman defined the environment as that which is "outside" the entity or process under discussion.[45] Theology is "outside" religious education in the sense that theology and religious education are not synonymous. Theology is thus part of the *environment* of religious education. Religious education is influenced by theology because theology is an environmental factor, but theology is also influenced by religious education by virtue of the function religious education plays in the environment of theology.[46]

It is the intention of this book to develop an environmental perspective of religious education and not to stop with a myopic theological perspective. More pointedly, the discussion in this book is an environmental discussion and not strictly a theological one. Theology may have a voice in the religious education pursued in this book, but it does not have a solo.

HISTORICAL AND THEORETICAL PERSPECTIVES

There are any number of ways to express the historical and theoretical dimensions of religious education. To a large extent, the theological and environmental perspectives just reviewed presupposed a certain degree of historical and theoretical understanding. Rather than to attempt any kind of comprehensive study of how modern religious education has grappled with its history and theory, three perspectives are offered as examples of the ways religious education has been approached. The first focused on theory with a minimum of historical correlation. The second is similar to the first, but used theoretical divisions based on theological formulations. The third is chiefly helpful for its historical viewpoint, but included theoretical considerations.

Harold William Burgess

One of the most influential books in the recent history of religious education has been *An Invitation to Religious Education,* by Harold William Burgess.[47] While not actually endorsing a theory[48] or presenting a new one, Burgess has done the difficult but invaluable task of injecting conscious awareness of theory into the psyche of religious educators. His thesis for the book was "to respond to the widely recognized need to deal with the matter of theory in the field of religious education."[49] Probably the most shocking result of reading *An Invitation to Religious Education* is the dawning awareness that religious education has fumbled along for such a long time without adequate attention to its theoretical underpinnings.

Burgess postulated four different approaches within religious education. Drawing from the germinal work of Harrison Elliott,[50] Burgess described a traditional theological theoretical approach, a social-cultural theoretical approach, and a contemporary theological theoretical approach.[51] The fourth approach was called a social-science approach from the writings of James Michael Lee.[52]

Each of these four approaches was analyzed according to several categories: the aims of religious education; the content; the role of the teacher; the place of the student in the process; the function of the environment; and the means of evaluation for religious education.[53]

One of the more revealing aspects of the book is the explanation of how religious education is perceived in each theoretical stance.[54] The traditional theological approach, represented by such educators as Frank Gaebelein, Lois LeBar, and Josef Jungmann, concentrated on the transmission of the salvific message to the student. George Albert Coe, W. C. Bower, and Ernest Chave were cited as examples of those in the social-cultural approach. They gave their attention to society and to the individual's participation in society for creation of the ideal social order.

The contemporary theological approach of Randolph Crump Miller, Lewis Joseph Sherrill, and James D. Smart aimed at a sense of community and belongingness within the church body. James Michael Lee's social-science approach deemphasized theological concerns and attempted to change the behavior of the student along religious lines. Burgess observed that it was his own belief that the social-science approach was the best of the alternatives for the future of religious education.[55]

Certainly one could quibble with some of the shades of interpretations by Burgess or with his placement of representatives, but the point is not so much the precise divisions as the concept. Burgess provided some organization to the field of religious education and to the theoretical constructs of religious education. This enables religious educators to make judgments about the various theories while it clarifies the importance of theory in religious education.

Ian P. Knox

Above or Within?, a book by Ian P. Knox,[56] was published one year after Burgess's work and was meant to be a companion volume to it. For whatever reason, it has not received the same degree of attention from the religious education community, but it is still a useful tool for understanding the field. Knox obviously patterned his book after the one by Burgess but made a unique contribution in the process.

Knox was concerned primarily at the point of theory, rather than practice. Echoing Burgess, Knox emphasized how "religious education as a field needs to pay a great deal more attention to theory."[57] The reasoning for that was twofold.[58] First, analysis of the theoretical framework would clarify and strengthen the individual theory in question. Second, consistency of practice growing out of theory would be enhanced. With such a view in mind, Knox did his study by using the same category system of aims, content, role of the teacher, the student, the environment, and means of evaluation that Burgess had developed.[59]

Where Knox provided his primary contribution, though, was in his introduction of the concept of "metaperspective." This he defined as "a personal panoramic template or pattern through which people filter their experiences and by which they assign meanings which make sense of the realities that confront them."[60] The metaperspective is that which persons use to synthesize all their personal experiences and their interpretations into a particular overview. As Knox said, in a real way "people . . . see what their metaperspective allows them to see."[61]

The heart of Knox's book was the demonstration of the concept of metaperspective. This was done through a continuum, using the polarities of natural and supernatural understandings of revelation. Evidence was presented as to how certain metaperspectives translated into religious education theory and practice.[62] The research question was: "Does adopting a certain metaperspective on the natural/supernatural relationship bear an affinity with a certain religious education theory and the practices which may follow from that theory?"[63] Not surprisingly, the conclusion of the study confirmed the question:

> The evidence uncovered seems clearly to indicate that when applied to six areas crucial to religious education . . . there is indeed a strong affinity between a religious educationist's religious education theory and the theological metaperspective out of which the particular theorist works.[64]

Knox deliniated three positions. When the supernatural was made superior to the natural, the metaperspective was considered to be "transcendist."[65] Religious educators placed within this area were Josef Jungmann, Johannes Hofinger, and James D. Smart.[66] Where the natural was ascendent over the supernatural, the term "immanentist" was employed.[67] Representatives were George Albert Coe, Gabriel Moran, and James Michael Lee.[68] The third position was meant to be an intermediate one, called the "integrationist."[69] This was a somewhat experimental and questionable stance that Knox proposed, and even he seemed uncomfortable with its degree of success. His decision as to whether this third position's theorists actually held the other two positions in equilibrium was equivocal: "Sometimes they do and sometimes they don't."[70] Knox used Randolph Crump Miller, Lewis Joseph Sherrill, and Marcel van Caster as examples.[71]

The important points that Knox made were the value of theory and the influence of metaperspectives. While his success at fully delineating three metaperspectives was dubious, Knox did provide some framework for the field of religious education.

Kendig Brubaker Cully

The Search for a Christian Education—Since 1940, by Kendig Brubaker Cully, continues to be of value to religious education, even though it was published in 1965 and is now somewhat dated and limited in its categories regarding subsequent theorists.[72] For the purposes of this book, three points of interest emerge.

First, Cully provided contemporary religious education with a historical perspective from which to view and understand the present. As described earlier in this chapter, Cully divided religious education into essentially two parts, with 1940 as the "watershed."[73] The period up to 1940 focused on George Albert Coe, W. C. Bower, George Betts, and Henry F. Cope.[74] The "significant event" of 1940 was the publication of Harrison Elliott's *Can Religious Education Be Christian?*"[75] An answer to Elliott came the next year with H. Shelton Smith's *Faith and Nurture* providing leadership for "a debate which would last long and move into as yet unforeseen channels."[76] Beginning with Smith's book, Cully described the "beginning of a new era in Christian education."[77] This broad sweep of historical vision is valuable in giving the present day some handles for analyzing the recent past.

Second, Cully proposed some categories or types of religious education that grew up after 1940. He developed eight groupings of religious educators writing at the time of his publication.[78] While the specific designations are not important here, it is instructive to see the effort to impose a degree of order over the chaos. He attempted to bring some unity and synthesis to the fragmentation.

Third, Cully clearly gave evidence of the lack of direction in religious education since 1940. Maybe the most significant factor of the book was its title. Religious educators, cut off from the roots of liberal theology, have tried to make their way anew.[79] Cully said that "religious education has been rediscovering its identity,"[80] and he viewed the return to biblical theology (neo-orthodoxy) and the ecumenical movement as unifiers in the attempt.[81]

It could be debated as to whether religious education is more settled today than it was at Cully's writing, but he did focus on a key point. He said: "The Christian search for an education produces in any generation whatever kinds of education are required and indicated by the things most surely valued and believed in various companies of those called Christian."[82] When the term "Christian" here is broadened to include all of religion, the issue is even more crucial. What is of value? What is determinative? These questions resonate throughout the rest of this book in search of an answer.

INDIVIDUAL PERSPECTIVES

Regardless of the amount of attention paid to theological currents, historical trends, and theoretical groupings, it is still true that individuals play an unmistakable part in the development of the field. While of course it is impossible to consider every individual religious educationist,[83] four are here discussed as representing individual contributions. These four were chosen eclectically from the recent history of religious education activity as a sampling of the kinds of work and types of approaches that have taken place. These four serve the additional purpose of helping to distinguish the particular perspective developed later in this book.

James D. Smart
James Dick Smart was best known during his long career as Professor of Biblical Interpretation at Union Theological Seminary in New York, a position he held for over ten years, serving into emeritus status. It is highly significant to note that Smart approached the study of religious education as a theologian and biblical interpreter. Perhaps his most used book, and seemingly the most relevant to religious education, was *The Teaching Ministry of the Church*,[84] yet this teaching emphasis was not the central focus of his efforts. A survey of his other writings[85] gives evidence that he understood religious education to be but one part of a much larger process.

That broader context was given explication in a later book by Smart, *The Rebirth of Ministry*.[86] It was in this book that Smart expressed his concern for the entirety of Christian ministry and provided his conceptualization of religious education as a part of a whole. His fear was that "in all our churches both the ministry and the Christian congregation have lost much of their essential biblical character."[87] His real concern was for the totality of the functioning of the Christian church and its integration in a biblical faith. The recurring phrase for this was a recapturing of the "apostolic ministry."[88]

The concept of "apostolic ministry" was essential to his consideration of religious education. Smart's explanation of the phrase was: "simply the ministry of Jesus Christ being continued, expanded, and carried ever farther afield in the world as Jesus Christ lives and speaks and acts redemptively through his ministers."[89] In this light, his "redefinition" of the goal for religious education became much more meaningful:

> That which is done in the educational program of the church today should be a valid continuation of what was done by Jesus with his disciples, then by those disciples with the people to whom they ministered, and by the Early Church with Jews and Gentiles who found their way into it.[90]

In other words, whatever the church does—including religious education—should be a continuation of what Jesus and his disciples started. This apostolic ministry was the unifier for Smart's understanding of the ministry of the church.

Smart's dissatisfaction was clear when he wrote: "We must confess frankly that in the contemporary church we sin deeply against this principle of the unity of the ministry."[91] He believed the apostolic ministry was being abandoned in religious education and elsewhere in ministry: "Whether we are preachers or pastors or teachers, our ministry must be the whole ministry of Jesus Christ."[92]

In the most basic analysis, when Smart wrote *The Teaching Ministry of the Church,* he was not simply addressing religious education and its practices. He was illustrating a larger problem and providing a larger solution. His most telling statement came in the conclusion to that book. He formulated the problem of religious education in this fashion: "At every point it has become evident that it is a theological problem."[93] The clear message was that whatever problem exists in the church is in essence a theological problem; the solution, then, must be a theological solution.

In summary, Smart did address the educational ministry of the church, but that was not his central concern. Smart dealt primarily with theology, and his approach to religious education was through a theological perspective.

Randolph Crump Miller

The figure of Randolph Crump Miller looms large in any understanding of religious education from the 1950s to the 1980s. The chronicler Stephen Schmidt wrote that Miller "influenced the development of the entire American Protestant religious education as a movement."[94] Through his voluminous writings, in his long tenure as editor of the journal *Religious Education,* and as Horace Bushnell Professor of Christian Nurture in the Divinity School at Yale University, Miller has been an incarnation of "mainline" Protestant religious education understanding. It was significant, then, when he described his search for a "clue" to the theory of religious education. He wrote: "I found the answer in theology."[95]

The Clue to Christian Education[96] was published in 1950, during the movement to neo-orthodox patterns of thinking. His key sentence was this:

> The clue to Christian education is the rediscovery of a relevant theology which will bridge the gap between content and method, providing the background and perspective of Christian truth by which the best methods and content will be used as tools to bring the learners into the right relationship with the living God who is revealed in Jesus Christ, using the guidance of parents and the fellowship of life in the Church as the environment in which Christian nurture will take place.[97]

Vital was his use of "relevant theology," which he later defined as "truth about God in relation to [humans]."[98] Also, Miller emphasized "right relationships," where theology was not as much mere content as a tool to be used in developing those relationships. Whatever the qualifications, however, Miller's foundation was theology.

The Theory of Christian Education Practice[99] followed *The Clue to Christian Education* by thirty years, but the theological stance remained firm. In the preface Miller said: "Christian education is a theological discipline and method."[100] The opening sentence of the text was: "The primary resource for understanding Christian education is the theological position implicitly or explicitly held."[101] While *The Clue to Christian Education* was distinctly neo-orthodox in tone and *The Theory of Christian Education Practice* was built upon process theology, the basic orientation was unyielding. Religious education was primarily and fundamentally approached through theology.

James Michael Lee

Against the stream of theological approaches, James Michael Lee has propounded the social-science approach to religious instruction[102] throughout his writings.[103] He forthrightly and unequivocally rejected theology as the sole basis for religious education. In the first of his trilogy of theoretical books, *The Shape of Religious Instruction*,[104] Lee stated:

> The central point of this book is that religious instruction is a mode of social science rather than a form of theology. . . . Simply stated, the social science approach regards religious instruction as basically a mode of the teaching-learning process rather than an outgrowth of theology.[105]

Lee is a lay educator in the Roman Catholic Church, or in his words, he has a "religious education apostolate."[106] Just as there is no doubting his sincerity or his competency, so there is no denying his blunt push for revolution. A former professor at the University of Notre Dame, and now (partially as a result of his stance) "in exile" at the University of Alabama at Birmingham,[107] he has been relentless in his effort. He put it like this: "My social-science approach to religious instruction, just like my life, is constantly and consciously targeted to basically change fundamental theory and practice in religion teaching."[108]

Lee believes his approach will replace theology as the way to do religious instruction. In fact, he is convinced that this is already coming to pass.[109] Whether or not that happens, it is of great value to see what Lee has done for religious education. By introducing an entirely different approach through what Lee preferred to call a "macrotheory,"[110] he has brought into question the presuppositions used by theologians and religious educators. It is this clarifying function, along with the particular "social-science approach" he has developed, that makes Lee's work valuable. As Lee wrote in *The Shape of Religious Instruction:* "The social-science approach represents more than a basic direction for religious instruction. Fundamentally this approach is a worldview, a way in which a person meets, interprets, and integrates reality."[111]

Lee termed the subservience of religious instruction to theology[112] as the performance of a role as "messenger boy."[113] If the role has not been messenger boy, then religious instruction has been used only as a translator of theology.[114] Lee proposed that religious instruction become a mediator, "a new entity, composed of both theology and the practical order in a new ontological reality."[115] Thus Lee has carved out an entirely different role and function for the field of religious education than was possible through the theological approaches. He wrote: "As mediator, religious instruction does not stand between theology and practical life; instead, it fuses them together, empowering both."[116]

James Michael Lee has changed the field of religious education by providing a basic alternative to the theological approaches. Now the approach can be through theology or through the social sciences. In the opinion of Charles Melchert, these *are* the two fundamental choices: One can either start the approach to religious education through theology or through the social sciences.[117] Religious education is no longer simply a theological debate. Whatever stance one takes regarding Lee and his approach, the social sciences must now be recognized and evaluated by religious educators.

John H. Westerhoff III

John Westerhoff is an enigma. As one book tumbles after another, the reader is left with a lot of interesting thoughts but little substance or continuity. Westerhoff is not one to construct a careful, systematic framework for religious education. His goal is different. He is one to stir discussions, to animate people, and to generate ideas. He said of himself:

> Most content when skipping from one activity to another, I am like a farmer who plants a field and then goes off before the crop begins to break ground. Instead of staying around to see my vision come to fruition, I am off looking for new fields to plow.[118]

From one of his writings, a crop was harvested for this book. It may be that he would no longer support the ideas himself,[119] but he did introduce a stimulating proposal.

Westerhoff, in *Will Our Children Have Faith?*,[120] addressed a problem he believed faced religious education. He called the problem the acceptance of "the assumptions of the schooling-instructional paradigm."[121] This paradigm, an "agreed-upon frame of reference which guides [the church's] educational efforts,"[122] proceeded upon the notion that "whatever the church's needs, our typical solution has been to develop courses of instruction for the church's school."[123]

The solution to this problem, Westerhoff proposed, was "a community of faith-enculturation paradigm" for use in religious education.[124] His interest was in creating a nurturing and caring environment in which children of all ages could grow and develop into mature persons and complete Christians. He said of his idea that "our new paradigm must broaden the context of Christian education to include every aspect of our individual and corporate lives within an intentional . . . faith community."[125]

There is confusion over whether Westerhoff approached religious education from theology or social science. Evidence points both ways. Charles Melchert placed him within social science because of Westerhoff's emphasis on community.[126] James Michael Lee placed Westerhoff within the theological approach.[127] The evidence in *Will Our Children Have Faith?* placed Westerhoff in the theological stream, as he used liberation theology for his foundation[128] much as Randolph Crump Miller used process theology for the basis of his 1980 book. In this larger context, then, Westerhoff proposed no new alternative to the approaches of social science or theology; indeed, he fits quite comfortably into either, with the above indication of residence in theology.[129]

A FOCUSED PERSPECTIVE

Indications have been made throughout the chapter as to the particular focus of this book. A general outline was sketched in an overall perspective. The broad sweep of religious education was surveyed through theological perspectives, historical and theoretical perspectives, and individual perspectives. These have provided a contextual screen on which to project a focused perspective.

The focus of this book is a search for, an attempt at, and the creation of a transforming perspective toward religious education. It is a *systemic perspective:* an integrative, transdisciplinary, and dynamic venture that perceives religious education from a teleological[130] viewpoint. The systemic perspective uses the organism as its primary metaphor, where interrelated and interdependent elements interact to create a dynamic and transforming whole. The goal, then, is to develop religious education organismically.

It is not the intention of this book to dismiss either the current approaches to religious education or the historical contributions. The commitment and achievements of religious educators from a variety of sources are acknowledged and respected. The present attempt is to build upon the foundation of others and not to disparage them.

It is not the purpose of this book to present a developed "program" of religious education. A "full and final" presentation should not be expected. In the first place, a systemic perspective is dynamic and inclusive, hence never complete. In the second place, to be systemic is to gain synergy from a variety of resources. As Thomas Kuhn has said, this type of activity is "an intrinsically revolutionary process that is seldom completed by a single [person] and never overnight."[131] The function of this book is to help clarify the vision of religious education. It is not to do the work individually that is rightly the responsibility of the field of religious education.

The systemic perspective on religious education is complementary to James Michael Lee's social-science approach to religious instruction, but the foci are different. Lee concentrates on the teaching-learning act, while this book considers religious education in its broadest interpretation.[132] It is the beginning point that is common: Both proceed from a social-science approach.[133] The discussion that follows is not strictly from a theological perspective. Theology is discussed, to be sure, and even more importantly religion is considered,[134] but theology is not the determinative factor. What *is* determinative is explored through the systemic perspective.

NOTES

1. Thomas Hood, "I remember, I remember," in *The Poetical Works of Thomas Hood* (New York: James Miller, 1873), pp. 74-75.
2. This is inclusive of my own self-awareness. I make no claim to being an automaton. This kind of honesty gives me better understanding of my own beliefs.
3. The dominating discipline of the past has been theology. Now social science demands attention from religious education. My point is that religious education must make some intentional decisions about its own destiny.
4. It is true that I am a Protestant Christian, member of a church affiliated with the Southern Baptist Convention. I have no wish to deny this heritage, but neither do I wish to be blind to the influence my heritage exerts. At issue here is a much broader subject than any particular expression of religion.
5. James Michael Lee, *The Shape of Religious Instruction: A Social Science Approach* (Birmingham, Ala.: Religious Education Press, 1973), p. 6.
6. Horace Bushnell, *Christian Nurture* (New Haven: Yale University Press, 1888). This work was originally published in its final form in 1861.
7. There is a strong case for this. For example, see John M. Mulder, "Introduction," in Horace Bushnell, *Christian Nurture* (reprint edition; Grand Rapids, Mich.: Baker Book House, 1979), p. vii ff.
8. Iris V. Cully, "Christian Education: Instruction or Nurture," *Religious Education* LXII (May-June, 1967), p. 259.
9. Nurture applies to individuals as they mature, as well as to groups of people. I am suggesting that religious education has responsibility for both individual and corporate maturity. The same processes apply.
10. William Butler Yeats, "Among School Children," in *Immortal Poems of the English Language,* ed. Oscar Williams (New York: Simon and Schuster, 1952), pp. 493-494.
11. For example, consult Lewis Joseph Sherrill, *The Rise of Christian Education* (New York: Macmillan, 1950). Other examples abound.
12. James Michael Lee defined theology as "the speculative science investigating the nature and workings of God." Theology is an abstract and cognitive science. See James Michael Lee, *The Content of Religious Instruction: A Social Science Approach* (Birmingham, Ala.: Religious Education Press, 1985), p. 7.
13. See James Michael Lee, "The Authentic Source of Religious Instruction," in *Religious Education and Theology,* ed. Norma H. Thompson (Birmingham, Alabama: Religious Education Press, 1982), pp. 121-122.
14. I am referring here to the approximate time period of 1903 (birth of the Religious Education Association) to 1940.

15. For example, see George Herbert Betts, *The New Program of Religious Education* (New York: Abingdon Press, 1921), pp. 28-31.

16. See Harrison S. Elliott, *Can Religious Education Be Christian?* (New York: Macmillan, 1940), p. 10.

17. Roger L. Shinn, "Neo-orthodoxy," in *The Westminster Dictionary of Christian Education,* ed. Kendig Brubaker Cully (Philadelphia: Westminster Press, 1963), p. 463.

18. H. Shelton Smith, *Faith and Nurture* (New York: Charles Scribner's Sons, 1941).

19. Ibid., p. 19. Smith's point was that liberalism was based on an out-dated foundation.

20. Ibid., p. 5.

21. Ibid., p. 10.

22. Ibid.

23. Ibid., p. 14.

24. Ibid., pp. 17ff.

25. Ibid., p. 19.

26. Stephen A. Schmidt called George Albert Coe one of the principle architects of the Religious Education Association. See Stephen A. Schmidt, *A History of the Religious Education Association* (Birmingham, Ala.: Religious Education Press, 1983), p. 22.

27. George Albert Coe, *What Is Christian Education?* (New York: Charles Scribner's Sons, 1929), p. 296.

28. Elliott, *Can Religious Education Be Christian?* pp. 9-11.

29. Ibid., p. 11.

30. Ibid., p. 318.

31. It is not accurate to describe Smith's book *Faith and Nurture* as a direct reply to Elliott's book, but Smith's book does indicate a "simultaneous intimate grappling with identical phenomena." See Kendig Brubaker Cully, "Two Decades of Thinking Concerning Christian Nurture," *Religious Education* LIV (November-December, 1959), p. 482.

32. Smith, *Faith and Nurture,* p. vii.

33. Ibid.

34. Ibid., pp. viii-ix.

35. Ibid., p. ix.

36. William Hordern, *New Directions in Theology Today: Volume One, Introduction* (Philadelphia: Westminster Press, 1966), p. 16.

37. Ibid., p. 15.

38. Langdon B. Gilkey, "Neo-orthodoxy," in *A Handbook of Christian Theology,* ed. Marvin Halverson and Arthur A. Cohen (New York: World Publishing Company, 1958), p. 258.

39. See H. Shelton Smith, "Let Religious Educators Reckon with the Barthians," *Religious Education* XXIV (January, 1934), pp. 45-51.

40. Kendig Brubaker Cully, *The Search for a Christian Education—Since 1940* (Philadelphia: Westminster Press, 1965), p. 75.

41. See Gilkey, "Neo-orthodoxy," p. 257.

42. For further discussion, see Rudolf Otto, *The Idea of the Holy,* trans. John W. Harvey, 2nd ed. (London: Oxford University Press, 1950; reprint edition, 1973), p. 25 ff.

43. Cully, *The Search for a Christian Education—Since 1940,* pp. 24-25.

44. Schmidt, *A History of the Religious Education Association,* p. 108.

45. C. West Churchman, *The Systems Approach,* rev. ed. (New York: Dell, 1979), p. 35. It is important that this point not be misunderstood. "Outside" does *not* mean isolation or rigidity. It does imply identity and distinctiveness through appropriate boundaries.

46. See especially chapter 4 for more attention to this point.

47. Harold William Burgess, *An Invitation to Religious Education* (Birmingham, Ala.: Religious Education Press, 1975).

48. The evaluation was quite even-handed, although Burgess did state his preference for the social-science approach. This personal view did not color the analysis.

49. Burgess, *An Invitation to Religious Education,* p. 3.

50. See Burgess, *An Invitation to Religious Education,* pp. 13-14. Burgess was referring to Elliott, *Can Religious Education Be Christian?* pp. 1-11.

51. Burgess, *An Invitation to Religious Education,* p. 15.

52. Ibid., p. 14. Burgess referred to the social-science approach first being in book form in 1970. He was pointing to the book by James Michael Lee and Patrick C. Rooney, eds., *Toward a Future for Religious Education* (Dayton, Ohio: Pflaum Press, 1970).

53. Burgess, *An Invitation to Religious Education,* p. 13.

54. Ibid., p. 167. Particular chapters in the book by Burgess should be consulted for further discussion.

55. Ibid., p. 168.

56. Ian P. Knox, *Above or Within?: The Supernatural in Religious Education* (Birmingham, Ala.: Religious Education Press, 1976).

57. Ibid., p. 5.

58. Ibid.

59. Ibid., p. 11.

60. Ibid., p. 3.

61. Ibid.

62. Ibid., pp. 5-9. These pages give summary statements of the evidence.

63. Ibid., p. 7.

64. Ibid., pp. 148-149.

65. Ibid., p. 47.

66. Ibid., pp. 59-61.

67. Ibid., p. 48.

68. Ibid., pp. 89-92.

69. Ibid., p. 49.

70. Ibid., p. 143.

71. Ibid., pp. 123-126.

72. Cully found eight positions and devoted a chapter to each position. See each of the chapters for Cully's selection of representatives for the positions.

73. Cully, *The Search for Christian Education: Since 1940,* p. 25.

74. Ibid., p. 15.

75. Ibid., p. 17.

76. Ibid., p. 20.

77. Ibid., p. 23.

78. Ibid., p. 153ff gives a summary of Cully's historical perspective.

79. Ibid., p. 168.

80. Ibid., p. 169.

81. Ibid.

82. Ibid., p. 162.

83. Harold William Burgess defined a "religious educationist" as "a person who is expert in religious educational theory and practice, especially one who has written books or scholarly articles on theoretical matters in the field of religious education." Burgess, *An Invitation to Religious Education,* p. 16.

84. James D. Smart, *The Teaching Ministry of the Church* (Philadelphia: Westminster Press, 1954).

85. Other writings of James D. Smart show a focus on biblical interpretation and the role of the Bible within society. See, for example, *The Strange Silence of the Bible in the Church: A Study in Hermeneutics* (Philadelphia: Westminster Press, 1970); *The Interpretation of Scripture* (Philadelphia: Westminster Press, 1961); *The Cultural Subversion of Biblical Faith: Life in the Twentieth Century Under the Sign of the Cross* (Philadelphia: Westminster Press, 1977).

86. James D. Smart, *The Rebirth of Ministry* (Philadelphia: Westminster Press, 1960).

87. Ibid., p. 9.

88. See in particular chapter 1 of Smart's book *The Rebirth of Ministry.*

89. Smart, *The Rebirth of Ministry,* p. 37.

90. Smart, *The Teaching Ministry of the Church,* p. 84.

91. Smart, *The Rebirth of Ministry,* p. 85.

92. Ibid., p. 104.

93. Smart, *The Teaching Ministry of the Church,* p. 205.

94. Schmidt, *A History of the Religious Education Association,* p. 136.

95. Randolph Crump Miller, "How I Became a Religious Educator—Or Did I?" *Modern Masters of Religious Education,* ed. Marlene Mayr (Birmingham, Ala.: Religious Education Press, 1983), p. 70.

96. Randolph Crump Miller, *The Clue to Christian Education* (New York: Charles Scribner's Sons, 1950).

97. Ibid., p. 15.

98. Ibid., p. 201.

99. Randolph Crump Miller, *The Theory of Christian Education Practice* (Birmingham, Ala.: Religious Education Press, 1980).

100. Ibid., p. 2.

101. Ibid., p. 7.

102. Lee has chosen to use the term "religious instruction" to place the emphasis of his work on the teaching-learning act. See Lee, *The Shape of Religious Instruction,* pp. 6-8.

103. James Michael Lee's first book was *Principles and Methods of Secondary Education* (New York: McGraw-Hill, 1963). Even here a social-science viewpoint is in evidence. The first full explanation of the social-science approach was in Lee, *The Shape of Religious Instruction.*

104. The second of the trilogy by James Michael Lee was *The Flow of Religious Instruction: A Social Science Approach* (Birmingham, Ala.: Religious Education Press, 1973). The third was *The Content of Religious Instruction* (1985).

105. Lee, *The Shape of Religious Instruction,* p. 2.

106. James Michael Lee, "To Basically Change Fundamental Theory and Practice," in *Modern Masters of Religious Education,* p. 254.

107. Ibid., p. 315ff.

108. Ibid., p. 296.

109. Lee, "The Authentic Source of Religious Instruction," p. 122.

110. Lee defined a macrotheory as "an overall and global form of theory into which are inserted theories and subtheories of a lesser scope." Ibid.

111. Lee, *The Shape of Religious Instruction,* p. 3.

112. Lee called the misuse of theology the "imperialistic queen of the sciences." See Lee, "The Authentic Source of Religious Instruction," p. 146ff.

113. Ibid., p. 156. Also note Lee, *The Flow of Religious Instruction,* p. 3.

114. Lee, "The Authentic Source of Religious Instruction," p. 159.

115. Lee, *The Flow of Religious Instruction,* p. 17.

116. Ibid., pp. 17-18.

117. Charles Melchert, "The Future of Religious Education: The Commitment in Religion and Education," in *Emerging Issues in Religious Education,* ed. Gloria Durka and Joanmarie Smith (New York: Paulist Press, 1976), p. 90.

118. John H., Westerhoff III, "A Journey Into Self-Understanding," in *Modern Masters of Religious Education,* p. 118.

119. Ibid., p. 116. Westerhoff has said that none of his efforts are to resolve anything for "more than a moment."

120. John H. Westerhoff III, *Will Our Children Have Faith?* (New York: Seabury Press, 1976).

121. Ibid., p. 10.

122. Ibid., p. 6.

123. Ibid., pp. 8-9.

124. Ibid., p. 49.

125. Ibid.

126. Melchert, "The Future of Religious Education," p. 90.

127. Lee, "The Authentic Source of Religious Instruction," p. 149.

128. Westerhoff, *Will Our Children Have Faith?* p. 30ff.

129. Westerhoff said elsewhere that he understood religious education (his preferred term was "catechesis") to be a theological discipline, where "theological presuppositions provide the screen for understanding both theory and practice." See John H. Westerhoff III, "A Discipline in Crisis," *Religious Education* LXXIV (January-February, 1979), pp. 7-15; quote from page 11.

130. By "teleological" I mean purposeful, goal-directed behavior.

131. Thomas S. Kuhn, *The Structure of Scientific Revolution,* 2nd. ed. (Chicago: University of Chicago Press, 1970), p. 7.

132. James Michael Lee has indicated many times that religious education is inclusive of instruction, guidance, and administration. For example, see Lee, "The Authentic Source of Religious Instruction," p. 111.

133. Stated even more precisely, this book is an experiment in and an exploration of systems theory, which can be understood as one mode of the social-science approach. Chapter 2 is devoted to a more detailed explanation of systems theory.

134. See chapter 4 for a discussion of religion and its relationship to theology.

Chapter 2

Paradigms

Flower in the crannied wall,
I pluck you out of the crannies,
I hold you here, root and all, in my hand,
Little flower—but *if* I could understand
What you are, root and all, and all in all,
I should know what God and man is.[1]
                              Alfred, Lord Tennyson

How can religious education be done better?

That is the question every religious educator must confront, and the answers to it are cacophonous. While the assumption is nearly universal that it should and can be done better, the "how" is cause for ceaseless debate. This book is but one more attempt to find a better way to go about the process of religious education.

One possible approach is to understand religious education as a totally pragmatic and practical activity: Keep trying something until it works. The problem, of course, is that it is never clear what "works" without some criteria or framework for evaluation and guidance. In such an approach, nothing is ever done any "better," because comparison is impossible with no criteria. This pragmatic approach is not the one pursued in the following pages.

Another feasible approach is to develop a theoretical framework for religious education.[2] The previous chapter took note of a few of the attempts in the recent history of religious education

33

to take theory seriously. It is the theoretical approach that this book follows, especially since the field of religious education has had more than its share of casual and haphazard approaches. What follows is an attempt at a careful and comprehensive construction of a theoretical understanding of religious education.

Even from a theoretical perspective there are optional starting points. Social science and theology are the two primary options,[3] as was indicated in chapter 1. The systemic perspective can be understood as one way of doing social science and as such is compatible to the social-science approach to religious education. The traditional theological approach is not the starting point for a systemic perspective. The construction of a systemic theory of religious education seeks an even more fundamental place to start than is provided by theology. This foundation is created from a social-science approach.

No theory can adequately cover every position to everyone's complete satisfaction, and no claim is being made here to propose "the answer" to the problems of religious education. There is no claim here to resolve all of the conflicts between theoretical approaches. Such claims would be either naive or messianic. The theory offered is one designed to solve problems, but it creates others in the process. The hope is that at least better questions are formed even if no final solutions are found.

The purpose of this book, then, is to present religious education from a systemic perspective. The purpose of this chapter is to describe a systemic perspective: its elements, its genesis, its paradigm, and its theoretical foundations.

ELEMENTS OF THE SYSTEMIC PERSPECTIVE

The systemic perspective is composed of four principle elements: paradigm, worldview, model, and simulation. In this section these elements receive only an introductory treatment, since more complete discussions are given throughout the book. Attention is focused on the interaction and the mutual support that exists among the elements.

James Michael Lee has suggested that one of the possible reasons so few religious educators deal with theory is because the construction of a theory entails such sustained hard work.[4] He was surely correct in his evaluation of the difficulty of the task. This particular attempt from a systemic perspective is difficult initially because of the controversy over the starting point. It may appear that the selection of the elements and their appellation as "systemic" is arbitrary or capricious. That is not accurate, but some simple identification of the elements is necessary before the order and the interdependence of the elements become apparent.

Paradigm

A revolution is in progress, and religious education is becoming a part of it. Revolutions of this type reach beyond the borders of any one field or discipline, as Thomas S. Kuhn described in his book *The Structure of Scientific Revolutions*.[5] The current popularity and pervasiveness of the term "paradigm" can be largely attributed to Kuhn's book in which the linkage of revolution and paradigm was explained. Kuhn wrote that "scientific revolutions are here taken to be those noncumulative developmental episodes in which an older paradigm is replaced in whole or in part by an incompatible new one."[6] It is in this frame of mind that the systemic perspective (the systemic revolution?) is set forth, starting with the concept of paradigm.

To balance all this enthusiasm about revolutions and paradigms is the realization that there are also several difficulties in dealing with the concept of paradigm. One of the most serious is the mercurial quality of its definition. It begins to be a catchall for whatever an author has in mind at the time. Certainly Kuhn was guilty of imprecision, as Ian Barbour pointed out.[7] Kuhn originally defined paradigms as "universally recognized scientific achievements that for a time provide model problems and solutions to a community of practitioners."[8] A paradigm in this sense is a set of fundamental beliefs that serves to shape the direction of investigation and interpretation. A paradigm thus includes unique combinations of ontology, epistemology, and methodology.[9] In the same book Kuhn gave what seemed to be a different definition when he wrote that a paradigm is "what the members of a scientific community share."[10] In an article written years later, Kuhn introduced the terms "exemplar" and "disciplinary matrix" in an attempt to unravel the confusion over the understanding of paradigm but probably succeeded in only confounding the issue even more.[11] Increasing chaos over terminology has been created by various "Kuhnians" who have gone beyond what Kuhn wrote, yet who continue to cite him as their source.[12]

Another difficulty with the term is its relativity. There is a need for structure to understand structure. Kuhn recognized that "something like a paradigm is prerequisite to perception itself."[13] What one sees depends both on what one looks for, and on what one has previously experienced. In other words, there is no "tabula rasa" for the observer to start with. There must be an old paradigm to recognize a new one.

A third difficulty is that a new paradigm and its attendant revolution come about in response to a crisis. Without a crisis—a need for novelty—there is no reason to change the way things have been done in the past. The "way of the past" is what Kuhn called "normal science."[14] The new way of perception that causes a revolution he called a paradigm. Kuhn said: "Novelty emerges only with difficulty, manifested by resistance, against a background provided by expectation."[15]

It should be obvious by this time that, as important and as universally employed as the term is, no common acceptance exists as exactly how to understand the term "paradigm." Kuhn did prescribe two characteristics that are essential for the development of a paradigm: first, the attraction of adherents away from other models of inquiry; and second, an open-ended quality for solution of those problems addressed by adherents.[16]

The greatest criticisms of Kuhn's ideas have dealt with the topic of the incommenserability of new paradigms with the old, notably through Larry Laudan[17] and Imre Lakatos.[18] Both Laudan and Lakatos have proffered views that make the concept of paradigm more maturational and progressive than exclusionist, but the truth is that no final word has yet been spoken on the subject. Much more work remains to be done by philosophers of science to articulate the notion of paradigm.[19]

In this book, a paradigm is a shared example or pattern that serves a conceptual or methodological function. It is used here both for conceptualizing a foundational worldview and for constructing theoretical models.

Worldview

The term "worldview" is derived from the German *Weltanshauung,* loosely translated also as "world hypothesis"[20] or "world picture."[21] A worldview is a comprehensive set of assumptions and presuppositions about the ultimate reality of existence. It functions additionally as a "perceptual filter which can exclude data which would be incompatible" with the governing paradigm.[22] At issue here is not whether a person has a worldview; instead, at issue is what *kind* of worldview a person has.

A paradigm and a worldview are not synonymous. Although some read Thomas Kuhn as equating the two, he denied that accusation.[23] The elements of the systemic perspective include both a paradigm and a worldview: distinct but related parts of the entire perspective. It is difficult to conceive of one without the other. While it is true that the paradigm is the functional formulation of a pattern, it is just as true that every paradigm and observation are drawn from the assumptions and presuppositions about the nature of reality. Paradigms and worldviews are reminiscent of the old chicken-and-egg conundrum. No one really knows which came first because it depends upon your paradigm (or worldview)!

Considerable detail is given to the concept of formulating a worldview in the following chapter. Suffice it at this point to say that while there is an intimate relationship between paradigm and worldview, "paradigm" relates to a focused though abstract pattern while "worldview" relates to a comprehensive extrapolation of the paradigm to include an intelligible and unified (also abstract but often preconscious) understanding of reality as a whole.

Model

A worldview is an extrapolation from a specific pattern (paradigm) to a general mode of perception. A model is just the opposite direction from a worldview. A model is an extrapolation from a paradigm to an even more specific and limited activity or structure. It is a "symbolic representation of selected aspects of the behavior of a complex system for particular purposes."[24] It does not represent a one-to-one correspondence between reality and construct, but it is rather a "tool for ordering experience."[25]

Models are extensions by way of analogy.[26] Gerald Weinberg has written: "Every model is ultimately the expression of one thing we think we hope to understand in terms of another that we think we do understand."[27] In this book, the paradigm is that which "we think we do understand"; the model is that which "we hope to understand."

It is the work of constructing models from a new paradigm that Kuhn called "normal science." He observed that most scientists spend their lives "mopping-up" the results of a new paradigm by creating models that correlate and solve problems produced and made obvious by the paradigm.[28] In fact, he believed that most scientists neither know nor need to know the details of the birth of a paradigm.[29] The construction of models from the characteristics of the paradigm provides more than enough work to be done.

Although models are only representations of reality, they do provide an opportunity to explore the relationships among the components in a symbolic way. James Michael Lee wrote: "Model building is believed to be one of the most promising ways in which social science can make significant new discoveries and formulate more useful explanations."[30] In this book, properties of the paradigm and characteristics of the worldview provide the guidelines for the development of specific models. Models outlined in later chapters are of religion, education, and religious education. The models are not designed to be exhaustive representations, but rather to serve as applications of the paradigm and worldview.

Simulation

A simulation is an actual, concrete demonstration of a theoretical model. This is the normal province of scientific experimentation, observation, and evaluation. A simulation is the step in the systemic perspective which concretizes the theoretical framework.

Simulation is the one element of the systemic perspective that does not receive detailed attention in this book. Since simulation is a natural outgrowth of a model, it must be localized and specific. Because of the theoretical nature of this book, programatic simulations are not attempted. Simulation is the next step that would be taken for further development, verification, and demonstration of the systemic perspective.

GENESIS OF THE SYSTEMIC PERSPECTIVE

The basic outline of the systemic perspective is beginning to take shape. The elements of the perspective are paradigm, worldview, model, and simulation. The term "perspective" is employed as an inclusive designation for these four elements. Two basic questions now arise regarding the origin of the theoretical framework. First, where is the starting point for such an integrated and interrelated perspective? Second, why is it called a systemic perspective? These preliminary questions need some attention in order to find a sensible way to begin the discussion of the perspective.

Where to Begin?

The question of the point of origin for the systemic perspective is both essential and controversial. The approach this book pursues is first the development of the paradigm, then the formulation of the worldview, and finally the construction of specific models.

Some decision must be made about the order to be followed, since it is true that only one thing can be discussed at a time. In actuality, the paradigm and the worldview develop interactively, both historically and correlatively. A sharp division between them is neither accurate nor instructive. The division is made here for the sake of clarity and explanation.

Some believe that the worldview must come first. John Sutherland said that most paradigms come not from factual data, but from "axiological predicates derived from empirically transparent assumptions about the world and everything in it";[31] in other words, from the worldview. Of course, the problem is: Where and how did the worldview come about?

The systemic perspective as proposed in this book begins with the concept of paradigm and then moves to worldview. Stephen C. Pepper followed a similar path in his analysis of the idea of world hypotheses. Rather than paradigm, Pepper used the term "root metaphor."[32] He said: "By a root metaphor, I mean an area of empirical observation which is the point of origin for a world hypothesis."[33] It was from the analysis of the root metaphor that Pepper found the categories for the further development (or realization) of the larger hypothesis.

It is essential to see that the root metaphor, or paradigm, is based on observed, empirical data. That is the rationale for considering it first. This database provides a concrete starting place for construction of the theory. Pepper said:

> Herein lies the importance of a fruitful root metaphor. It is, to begin with, a small body of factual material as it stands. It guarantees at least an empirical start. . . . Its fruitfulness consists solely in its capacity to generate a set of categories with which careful reinforcement may prove relatively adequate for an unrestricted hypothesis.[34]

The root-metaphor idea is a reflection of the traditional analogical method for understanding the unknown.[35] Analogy goes from the known to the unknown. Since the paradigm or root-metaphor can be known empirically, then the worldview (world hypothesis) can be derived from the paradigm. As Stephen Pepper's maxim stated: "A world hypothesis is determined by its root metaphor."[36] Again the caution must be sounded: The paradigm may concretize the worldview in terms of categories and abstractions, but both are in coexistence and coevolution. In real life the seeming historical procession is not so neatly defined.

The answer to "where to begin?" is with the paradigm. The models for religion, education, and religious education follow both the development of a paradigm and the formulation of a worldview. Then models can be created that are functionally and structurally adequate.

This notion of adequacy is a major point, since it is the reason for such a detailed theoretical approach as the systemic perspective. James Michael Lee has described the construction of theory as "carefully establishing concepts and facts, and then systematically inserting these concepts and facts into those kinds of laws and theory which comprehensively explain the interactive variable relations among the concepts and facts."[37] This type of approach is distinct from the production of a tract (written to arouse action) and speculation (generated from cognitive reflection and inference).[38] Adequacy is the goal of a theoretical approach, but not the goal of either a tract or of speculation.

The present argument is that adequate models are developed by giving attention to purpose, to function, and to structure. The teleological dimension guides the construction of adequate models. This attention to purpose is attained if the development begins with the paradigm.

Why Systemic?

The perspective evolves from paradigm to worldview to model. But why call it the *systemic* perspective? It is the systemic perspective because the paradigm (root metaphor) is that of the open system: an entity "whose growth and survival depends on a constant interchange with environmental factors."[39] From the empirical data formulated about open systems, and subsequent construction of a general theory about open systems, a comprehensive and coherent worldview can begin to develop. Systemic models of religion, education, and religious education can then—and only then—be constructed which dynamically reflect and interactively influence the emerging worldview.

The empirical data and theory construction regarding open systems are relatively well-established. As in any effort at scientific research, progress is to be expected, but the basic conceptualization of open systems remains constant. It is in the extrapolation from the paradigm of open systems to a systemic worldview where flexibility is essential. The worldview is just emerging into reality. It can still be altered, shaped, and transformed.

How can the worldview be affected? Through the construction of systemic models. All elements of a system interact and interface with each other. As systemic models for religion, education, and religious education are introduced into the framework, changes within that framework are unavoidable. Change will not come by ignoring the paradigm, or by railing against the worldview, but through development of interactive and systemic models. In other words, it is necessary to become a part of the system in order to change the system.

The perspective is called systemic, then, because it is based upon the paradigm of open systems. It is at the point of paradigms that the theoretical framework is first addressed. All else that is meant by "systemic" must await the explanation and development of the systemic paradigm.

THE PARADIGM OF THE SYSTEMIC PERSPECTIVE

The paradigm of the systemic perspective is an attempt to impose order upon the bewildering mass of information flooding humankind.

At one end of the scale is the "macro-scope." The earth is spinning on its axis in space, yet it is orbiting its nearest star, the sun. Earth and its fellow-planets combine with the sun to make up a solar system. Yet the sun and its satellites are also moving in space, in a spiral pattern, with a mass of other stars called the Milky Way. The Milky Way is a galaxy, and a galaxy can contain from a few million to a few billion stars. And yet the Milky Way is just one of innumerable other galaxies, each one of which is moving away from every other galaxy.[40] How is the human being to comprehend all this data?

At the other end of the scale is the "micro-scope." Although no one has ever really seen one, an "atom" originally was defined as the smallest indivisible segment of reality. But physics has succeeded in "splitting" the atom since the 1940s. It is supposedly common knowledge that there are atomic nuclei composed of protons and neutrons, as well as orbiting electrons. But the latest research has shown even this to be a fantasy. There are no subatomic particles, no "things," only interface and interconnections; as Fritjof Capra said, the electron is real only in the mind of the scientist.[41] Can the human being really deal with this kind of complex information?

As incredible as it may seem, there is a way to conceptualize the macro-scope, the micro-scope, and all the territory in between. It is through the paradigm of *open systems*. The models for understanding are not yet complete: feverish activity for imposing order over galactic and atomic entities continues. It is the paradigm that is in place. This paradigm is introduced by way of definitions of systems and through an elemental typology of systems.

Definitions of Systems

There is an endless array of definitions for systems. The following attempt points out the particular emphases that various writers have made in their definitions. None of the definitions presented is essentially incorrect, just as none is necessarily contradictory. It is the focus of each that is different.

Gerald M. Weinberg made the chief criterion of a system that of perception. He selected the nontechnical approach by saying: "What is a system? As any poet knows, a system is a way of looking at the world."[42] He was giving attention to the fact that the important thing about a system is neither its isolation nor its ontological reality but its somewhat arbitrary emergence from the environment. He said elsewhere that a system means the "inside" and environment means the "outside."[43] This is the simplest level of definition, where a system is that which can be distinguished from a background. This process is chiefly a mental process, where the observer separates the "inside" from the "outside."

C. West Churchman chose to define a system as "a set of parts coordinated to accomplish a set of goals."[44] In this instance the emphasis is upon purpose and teleology. The reason for the "set of parts" being seen as a whole is the cooperation and integration among the parts to attain a common goal. Without the goal, the parts would remain differentiated but unrelated. The transforming factor is teleology.

Fritjof Capra gave consideration to the fact that a system must have integration to be distinguishable. He defined a system as "an integrated whole whose properties cannot be reduced to those of its parts."[45] One of the proverbs of holistic thinking is reflected in this definition by Capra: "The whole is more than the sum of the parts."[46] The methods of reductionism and analysis used to the exclusion of integration miss the characteristics of the system. The relational characteristics become apparent when the system is approached holistically.

A. D. Hall and R. E. Fagen offered a definition which is widely quoted and accepted. They stressed the importance of systemic relationships: "A system is a set of objects together with relationships between the objects and between their attributes."[47] This understanding of a system is close to that of Capra's, with the difference being a focus, not on the integrated whole, but on the interface and interdependence of the parts that make up the whole. This same emphasis was made by Ludwig von Bertalanffy in a simple definition: A system is a set of elements that stand in interrelation.[48] Again the focus is on the connections that bind the parts into a unity.

Russell Ackoff and Fred Emery devised a particularly definitive expression of a system: "a set of interrelated elements, each of which is related directly or indirectly to every other element, and no subset of which is unrelated to any other subset."[49] They made the point about interrelation but added the idea that when one element is affected, so is every other element. This illustrates the reason for introducing models of religion, education, and religious education into the overall structure of the emerging worldview: The models create change in the whole. However dramatic or effectual the change, it is still inevitable that change will result. Elsewhere Ackoff formulated three properties of systems that spell out the effect of a system's elements upon each other:

1. The properties or behavior of each element of the set has an effect on the properties or behavior of the set taken as a whole. . . .
2. The properties and behavior of each element, and the way they affect the whole, depend on the properties and behavior of at least one other element in the set. Therefore, no part has an independent effect on the whole and each is affected by at least one other part. . . .
3. Every possible subgroup of elements in the set has the first two properties: each has a nonindependent effect on the whole. Therefore, the whole cannot be decomposed into independent subsets. A system cannot be subdivided into independent subsystems.[50]

A system, in general terms, has interrelationships among its parts, is integrated and differentiated for a purpose, and is more than an aggregation of unrelated elements.

Types of Systems

A taxonomy of all the different types of systems is certainly beyond the scope and the intent of this section. The types of systems are limited to two: the closed and the open system.

The least interesting and most limited type of system is the closed system. In actuality, the closed system does not exist. A closed system is one which is totally independent and bounded from its environment, so that in reality such a system cannot exist over a period of time. As Kenneth Boulding observed: "In a totally closed system the input of one part . . . has to be the output of other parts."[51] This kind of existence can only be imagined by mental abstraction.

The central issue concerning a "closed" system, then, is its *degree* of closedness. A closed system is like a beautiful flower cut off in full bloom: It may appear to be alive and healthy, but its fate is sealed. Ludwig von Bertalanffy made a similar point when he said: "A closed system must . . . eventually attain a time-independent state of equilibrium, defined by maximum entropy and minimum free energy . . . where the ratio between phases remains constant."[52] Equilibrium is the absence of activity, or death.[53] Closed systems are of little interest because their future can be nothing other than a return to primordial chaos. This is a reflection of the Second Law of Thermodynamics which says a closed system always moves toward entropy[54] (dissipation) until the maximum and nonreversible equilibrium is attained.

The open system is much more promising. An open system is simply a system that *does* have import and export of material from the environment.[55] An open system can continue to grow, to become more complex, and to evolve because of the exchange process. The open system does not move toward equilibrium but toward a metabolism, or steady-state.[56] Rather than running down according to the Second Law of Thermodynamics, an open system can store up energy and regulate its output (at least temporarily).

Just as a totally closed system is a theoretical construct, so is the totally open system. A totally open system would be indistinguishable from its environment. The key is the degree of openness to the environment and the rate of exchange with the environment.

It is the *open* system that is the type of system employed as a paradigm for a worldview and for developmental models. This venture is not without precedent. Ludwig von Bertalanffy, the "father" of systems theory, said much the same thing: "The open-system model represents a fertile working hypothesis permitting new insights, quantitative statements, and experimental verification."[57] Since the open system is so important to the argument at hand, further detail is given to both the design and the characteristics of this type of system.

DESIGN OF THE OPEN SYSTEMS PARADIGM

The subject of a design for the open systems paradigm is by no means a settled one. Just as the reality of a system is in large measure a result of the conceptual ability of the observer, so the design of a system is understood differently by various systems theorists. One thing is clear: The design is made up of structure, function, and purpose. Beyond agreement on these three, the order, definition, and importance of each is highly debatable. Once again the problem is that of the "chicken-or-the-egg" variety.

Structure, function, and purpose are such interdependent and interactive concepts that it is difficult to tease them apart. Division of them is appropriate only for purposes of definition and explication. In actuality the three are dynamically interrelated.

Structure

The term "structure" refers to the pattern detected in time and space through which the input and output of the system flows. It is the "ordered set of interconnected operations performed by the elements of the system."[58] Analogically, structure is the representation which would appear if a "snapshot"[59] of the system were taken and the system frozen in time. Russell Ackoff said: "Viewed structurally, a system is a divisible whole."[60]

The activity called systems analysis[61] focuses primarily on structure. Here structure is the determinative factor, and the progression is from structure to function to purpose. As one group of analysts said: "If the system had a different structure, it would have a different function, and the same input function would have resulted in a different response."[62] To start with a particular structure, then, is to determine the process and the purpose of the system from the very first.

Function

The "function" of the system is the process and dynamic aspect of the system. Here the emphasis is not on the system's composition, but on how the system goes about its activity. Function is a focus on the flow-through, or transformation process, of the system: "A function is a mode of transformation of inputs into outputs or the rule by which the elements of the set of inputs are associated with elements of the set of outputs."[63]

Where the structure of the system can be caught in a snapshot, the function can be captured on time-lapse photography. The key is time. Structure can be found in synchronic time, while function is found in diachronic time. Russell Ackoff said that a system viewed functionally "is an indivisible whole in the sense that some of its essential properties are lost when it is taken apart."[64]

A focus on function is the activity of systems synthesis.[65] Here the desire is for a system to function in a particular way, and a structure is developed to allow it to function properly. Beginning with function allows a degree of creativity and flexibility to develop within structure but does not address specifically the teleological dimension of systems theory.

Purpose

Russell Ackoff and Fred Emery defined a purposeful system as

> one that can produce (1) the same functional type of outcome in different structural ways in the same structural environment and (2) can produce functionally different outcomes in the same and different structural environments.[66]

They were accenting one of the major points in distinguishing an open system from a closed one. An open system has equifinality: the ability to reach a desired state from differing initial conditions and by diverse paths. The opposite is true of a closed system, as Ludwig von Bertalanffy explained: "In any closed system, the final state is unequivocally determined by the initial conditions."[67] A closed system cannot be equifinal, but is deterministic. Bertalanffy continued: "This is not so in open systems. Here, the same final state may be reached from different initial conditions and in different ways."[68]

Open systems, with their "designed-in" purpose, have taken teleology away from vitalism[69] with its "deus ex machina" and put teleology into the hands of empiricism. The teleological dimension of open systems is not inserted (or delivered) from an external (or authoritarian) source but is an emergent and integral aspect of the whole. Purpose, as understood by the equifinality of open systems and by cybernetics,[70] allows science to investigate what had been strictly out of bounds. Bertalanffy did not let this go by unnoticed:

> What should be stressed, however, is the fact that teleological behavior directed toward a characteristic final state or goal is not something off limits for natural science and an anthropomorphic misconception of processes which, in themselves, are undirected and accidental. Rather it is a form of behavior which can well be defined in scientific terms and for which the necessary conditions and possible mechanisms can be indicated.[71]

The study of systems that begins with purpose makes the question "Why?" the central and primary consideration. The what (structure) and how (function) of open systems are fashioned to adapt and to evolve toward attainment of the emergent purpose of the system. In developing the models in later chapters (based on the paradigm of open systems), this teleological orientation is foundational. Purpose receives the initial attention, which allows the discussion of functions and structures to evolve naturally. Purpose, function, and structure become interactive and interdependent, each influencing and changing the other. In reality, all three design elements combine to create a dynamic, evolving, and transforming whole.

PROPERTIES OF THE OPEN SYSTEMS PARADIGM

The basic properties of the open systems paradigm are well-established and well-known. Already most of them have been discussed or referred to in the previous discussion, and the following chapter also makes extensive use of the characteristics. A brief listing of the properties serves to identify the basic elements and to complete the description of the paradigm. It is from these properties that a systemic worldview and systemic models are formulated.

The chief point of confusion about the characteristics relates simply to their classification and order. Ludwig von Bertalanffy was able to present the characteristics of open systems in as few as four categories.[72] Daniel Katz and Robert L. Kahn listed nine characteristics that clarified but expanded Bertalanffy's work.[73] Glenn Immegart and Francis Pilecki also used nine categories, though slightly different in arrangement from those of Katz and Kahn.[74] The point is that while the manner of presentation may vary, the elements themselves remain essentially the same. Open systems are given eight properties in the following section.

Holism

A characteristic of primary importance to all systems, especially open systems, is holism. Ludwig von Bertalanffy wrote: "The system therefore behaves as a *whole,* the changes in every element depending on all the others."[75] The one common element in all of the definitions of a system is the need for a system to be understood from a molar, rather than from a molecular, perspective. A system is not merely an aggregate[76] or a random collection of parts but is a unified and integrated entity.

The holism of the system is created by interactive and interdependent relationships among the various elements of the system. No part is isolated or independent from any of the others. Russell Ackoff's lengthy technical definition quoted earlier gave this issue great emphasis.[77] This was also the prompting for Ludwig von Bertalanffy's statement that "in the last resort, we must think in terms of systems of elements in mutual interaction."[78] It is the relationships among the parts that allow a system to be perceived as an irreducible unit.

Differentiation

At the same time that holism is kept in focus, it should be obvious that differentiation, or variety, is in the background. Without differentiation there would be no holism, only sameness and repetition. Without the holistic integration of the system, there would be no system, only differentiated but unrelated parts.

Holism (integration) and differentiation are two sides of the same coin.

John Sutherland defined differentiation as "increasing specialization of structure and function among system components."[79] One of the most interesting aspects of an open system is that it has the ability to evolve various structures and to perform different functions as it moves through time.[80] It is able to develop because of differentiation in structure and function but to remain recognizable while being true to its emergent purpose.

Differentiation is accomplished through both subsystems and suprasystems.[81] One of the frustrating (or delightful) aspects of systems research is that it is practically impossible to distinguish a single system because it is always dynamically interrelated to smaller and larger systems. Since the particular system under consideration is a human abstraction, it is permissible to have a degree of arbitrariness in the selection of the limits of the system. Glenn Immegart and Francis Pilecki phrased the thought this way: "Thus, just as all systems can analytically and practically be broken down into subsystems, all systems are, in fact, subsystems to a larger and more complex system."[82]

Boundaries

If it is difficult to distinguish a system from its subsystems and its suprasystems (and it is) then the heart of the problem is the boundary issue. A boundary permits a system to be distinguishable from the surrounding environment. A *permeable* boundary allows a flow into, through, and out of the system. If the boundary is so permeable as to be virtually nonexistent, the system loses its identity and dissolves into the environment. If a boundary is rigid and nonpermeable, then the system moves toward dissolution and equilibrium. The boundary issue is literally one of life and death. An open system, to remain an open system, cannot afford to be too open or too closed, and the boundary is the determinative factor.

A. D. Hall and R. E. Fagen defined the environment as "the set of all objects a change in whose attributes affect the system and also those objects whose attributes are changed by the behavior of the system."[83] C. West Churchman simply said that the environment is that which is outside the system.[84] The temptation would be to say, then, that the boundary separates the system from the environment. Such description would not be accurate, though, since the discussion is of *open* systems. Gerald Weinberg rightly saw that the boundary is not that which separates, but that which connects.[85] To so emphasize this property, he substituted the term "interface" for the term "boundary." Weinberg said: " 'Interface' is a more useful word than 'boundary,' for it reminds us to pay attention to the connection, and not just the separation, between system and environment."[86]

Because an open system has some degree of permeability, distinct boundaries between the organism and the environment are difficult to ascertain.[87] Closer and closer observation to a "boundary" reveals that it is not really a "thing": It is a connection, an interface. Classical science[88] was unable to deal adequately with this issue, because a boundary cannot be stripped from an open system and examined under a microscope. The boundary/ interface must be understood from the molar perspective. When boundary becomes an intelligible issue, then holism, differentiation, and environment are clear. They are not separate entities, but elements in dynamic interaction and continuous interchange.[89]

Dynamism

An open system is never static but dynamic.[90] This is accomplished by continual interaction with the environment, which can be broken into three processes. First, there is the input or inflow to the system from the environment. Second, there is the transformation process or the through-put:[91] What is received from the environment must be transformed into an appropriate form to be used by the system. Third, there is an output exported into the environment composed of both waste and product. These processes are continuous and cyclical.[92]

Since both the inputs and the outputs are related directly to the environment, an open system is said to have a dual role: to maintain itself as a functioning system and also to serve the environment.[93] It is clear that with a dynamic and interactive system, the system and the environment are continually being changed. The environment is changed by providing the system its resources and by receiving the output. The system is changed by the import of material from the environment and by the transformation of that material.

Equifinality

Equifinality has already been defined as the ability of an open system to reach a desired state from differing initial conditions and through a variety of means.[94] It is mentioned again because it is a property of every open system and because of the relationship the concept has to the environment. If the open system were not equifinal, it would be totally determined by the environment: Whatever the system imported from the environment would effectively determine the end product or output of the system. An open system *is* equifinal. Although resources from the environment vary, and these differences affect the functioning of the system, the system is still able to operate according to its guiding purpose. Because it is equifinal and teleological, an open system is able to adjust its structures and its functions in order to produce the desired output. An open system, then, is not deterministic but purposeful: It is equifinal.

The concept of equifinality can be carried one step further to *multifinality.* While equifinality does give emphasis to goal-directed behavior, it seems to imply that open systems pursue only one goal. The truth is that open systems are able to exhibit multifinality: the ability to pursue a variety of goals through differing initial states and by diverse paths. Though such complexity of purpose is difficult to imagine, reflection on the matter does affirm that such teleology is possible. In fact, an open system can exhibit *both* equifinality and multifinality by pursuing an idealized mission while concurrently achieving a number of correlative and progressive goals.

Feedback

How does an open system achieve its goals? It is through the process of feedback, both positive and negative. Feedback operates as the guidance process within an open system. A system monitors its output and is able to evaluate the information from the output to regulate both its rate of intake from the environment and its transformational activity.

This entire subject of feedback is the province of cybernetics.

Cybernetics research dates from the late 1940s when Norbert Wiener appropriated the Greek word for "steersman" into the English language.[95] A steersman on a ship knew the purpose, or course, of the ship's journey and governed the steering of the ship accordingly. If the ship was on course and no corrections were necessary, this was positive feedback. If the ship was detected to be going the wrong way—away from the desired goal—the steersman was able to determine the variance. This deviation from the goal was negative feedback. The negative (corrective) feedback was used to get the ship back on course. Cybernetics is the study of feedback, primarily corrective negative feedback, for all open systems.

Ludwig von Bertalanffy had negative feedback and cybernetics in mind when he said that purpose was no longer off-limits to the sciences.[96] Purpose understood as a goal state that can be approached quantitatively through the study of cybernetics gives the sciences an operational definition with which to deal. Negative feedback, and progress to a goal, can be measured and evaluated. Open systems opened the door to the introduction of purpose and teleological issues into science. No longer is purpose a metaphysical concept left to the imagination or to the vitalist.

Homeostasis

Closely related to feedback and cybernetics is the concept of homeostasis. Homeostasis was first developed into a discussion by Walter B. Cannon, a professor of medicine at Harvard in the 1920s.[97] Homeostasis refers to the ability of organisms (Cannon first took notice in humans) to maintain their own particular structure and function under a variety of circumstances.[98] In other words, even in an unstable environment an organism is able to maintain a degree of stability. In cold weather or in hot, the normal human body temperature is relatively stable at 98.6 degrees. The human body is homeostatic in that it maintains a constant body heat.

Homeostasis and feedback are related because homeostasis depends on feedback for the regulatory function. When the human body is too cold, this information (negative feedback) is processed and the person starts to shiver. The shivering motions are an attempt to increase metabolism and generate more heat. Homeostasis allows the human body, and all open systems, to maintain stability while undergoing dynamic and continuous change.

Growth

Ludwig von Bertalanffy said that one of the basic characteristics of an open system is organismic growth.[99] Growth is possible because an open system is moving toward *negative* entropy rather than toward entropy. It is the closed system that is doomed to increasing entropy, dissolution, and eventual equilibrium (heat death). An open system, through importation of material and resources from the environment, is able to build itself up and store those resources for its own survival (through homeostasis), and for growth and complexity.

Erwin Schrödinger, in the epochal publication *What is Life?*, described life as essentially negative entropy:

> Every process, event, happening . . . everything that is going on in Nature means an increase of the entropy of the part of the world where it is going on. Thus a living organism continually increases its entropy—or, as you may say, produces positive entropy—and thus tends to approach the dangerous state of maximum entropy, which is death. It can only keep aloof from it, i.e., alive, by continually drawing from its environment negative entropy. . . . What an organism feeds upon is negative entropy.[100]

An open system stays open through the accumulation of negative entropy. This accumulation not only allows the homeostatic function, but further development toward complexity and maturity.

FOUNDATIONS OF THE OPEN SYSTEMS PARADIGM

The eight properties of open systems, together with the definitions, typologies, and design elements of open systems, comprise the outline of the open systems paradigm. It remains to describe the foundations of the paradigm, and the story of the foundations for the open systems paradigm is the story of General Systems Theory.

The paradigm of open systems obviously did not leap into the consciousness of science unbidden or unsought. Its emergence was slow, painful, and disturbing to the whole of science. Thinking in terms of process, evolution, and holism has a long history, but the special focus of open systems can be more accurately pinpointed. Open systems theory is the work of the scientific field of research known as General Systems Theory.

General Systems Theory is a relatively new entrant into the scientific world. The most convenient date for its birth is 1954, when the actual Society for General Systems Theory was formed in Palo Alto, California.[101] As compared to the ancient disciplines of mathematics and physics, the relatively brief life span of General Systems Theory makes it a virtual infant. If it is an infant, though, it is growing fast. Research and literature are burgeoning at an astonishing rate. From its simple beginning as a theory of open systems, General Systems Theory is in full-scale development as a major contributor to the realignment of science.

What is General Systems Theory? There really is no simple answer to that question. As interesting and as seductive as the idea may be, an extensive survey of General Systems Theory is resisted. Only enough detail is provided here to explain how the open systems paradigm resulted from General Systems Theory. Since General Systems Theory is a newcomer to the scientific endeavor, it is experiencing an "identity crisis," and its outcome is by no means certain.[102] There are at least four ways to understand General Systems Theory: as a discipline, as a theory, as an ideology, and as a set of universal principles.

Discipline

Ludwig von Bertalanffy observed that the search for a scientific description of systems "has become a recognized discipline, with university courses, texts, books of readings, journals, meetings, working groups, centers, and other accoutrements of an academic field of teaching and research."[103] It is true that this may be the most visible and popular facet of General Systems Theory, and its name is Systems Science. This discipline is a "scientific exploration and theory of 'systems' in the various sciences . . . and general system theory as doctrine of principles applying to all . . . systems."[104]

Language needs to be handled carefully here. If there truly is an evolving discipline, then it is Systems Science. General System Theory is a much broader and a more inclusive field of study than is Systems Science. General Systems Theory is interdisciplinary and transdisciplinary, including but not limited to Systems Science.

General Systems Theory understood as a discipline is humorous but inadequate. It is humorous because one of the primary reasons for its development was to transcend the old categories of science and find a new approach. If General Systems Theory were to become a discipline, it would lose its claim to existence. The danger is very real, though, as Gerald Weinberg observed: "The general systems movement did not start out as a discipline but is probably ossifying into one."[105] It is inadequate because "discipline" misses the broad sweep of systems theory. A truly general theory cannot be contained in a discipline. Systems Science is a legitimate study, and may become a discipline for research, but it is not the totality of General Systems Theory.

Russell Ackoff was adamant that the systems movement not become ossified. He insisted that it "should remain a point of view."[106] Oddly enough, Ludwig von Bertalanffy can again be quoted to support this perspective argument as he said that the systems viewpoint is a new way of thinking.[107] This issue— whether General Systems Theory itself should become a discipline or remain a perspective—has been a major concern for systems theorists. The danger of "ossification" is on one side, but the danger of systems theory becoming nothing more than a cognitive activity is on the other side, as a self-study of the field said:

> There are significant discoveries and statements which have been and can be made about systems in general. . . . Further development can only be enhanced by efforts which attempt to provide codification, systematization and communicability of advances already achieved.[108]

In full awareness of the dangers, this book supports the argument that General Systems Theory best provides a perspective not to be limited to one discipline.

Theory

It would appear tautological to say that General Systems Theory is a theory, yet General Systems Theory is *not* a theory—at least not in the normal sense of theory as used in science. Again it was Ludwig von Bertalanffy who tried to sort out (or add to?) the confusion:

> The term "general system theory" was introduced by the present author [Bertalanffy], deliberately, in a catholic sense. One may, of course, limit it to the "technical" meaning in the sense of mathematical theory (as is frequently done), but this appears inadvisable in view of the fact that there are many "system" problems asking for a "theory" which latter is not at present available in mathematical terms. So the name "general system theory" is here used broadly, similar to our speaking of the "theory of evolution."[109]

Theory has been defined by Fred Kerlinger as "a set of interrelated constructs (concepts), definitions, and propositions that present a systematic view of phenomena by specifying relations among variables with the purpose of explaining and predicting the phenomena."[110] Conceptualizing a theory that would encompass *all* systems (truly a *general* theory) staggers the imagination.[111] As Kerlinger has framed the issue, the task would have at least three divisions. First would be the setting out of defined and interrelated constructs. Second would be the description of all the variables in the construct and the interrelations among all the variables. Third would be an explanation and prediction of the actual phenomena.

The construction of a general theory for systems of any type may be all but inconceivable, but James Grier Miller is an example of one who has offered an attempt at a general theory. He proposed a general theory of living systems in the monumental (and mammoth) *Living Systems*.[112] Miller identified seven hierarchical levels of living systems: cell, organ, organism, group, organization, society, and supranational systems.[113] His thesis was that "systems at all these levels are open systems composed of subsystems which process inputs, throughputs, and outputs of various forms of matter, energy, and information."[114] Miller then described nineteen subsystems that process some form of matter, energy, and information.[115] He then set out to quantitatively and empirically test the nineteen subsystems through examples in each of the seven levels of living systems. It was Miller's contention that this was the way to advance systems theory: to produce hypotheses and then confirm or disprove the hypotheses.

Miller has not won the argument. Very little has been done so far to advance "General Systems Theory" in this kind of verifiable, experimental activity. Very few have done any work on Miller's suggestions or his hypotheses.[116] The continued force of General Systems Theory, then, is not from the strict theory construction that the name implies. Its efforts are concentrated elsewhere—at least for the present.[117]

From the first, General Systems Theory has had more of an integrative intention than specific experiments and hypotheses allow. For example, Kenneth Boulding described the emergent General Systems Theory in 1956 as "a level of theoretical model-building which lies somewhere between the highly generalized constructions of pure mathematics and specific theories of the specialized disciplines."[118] Boulding went on to articulate General Systems Theory:

> In recent years increasing need has been felt for a body of systemic theoretical constructs which will discuss the general relationships of the empirical world. This is the quest of General Systems Theory. It does not seek, of course, to establish a single, self-contained "general theory of practically everything" which will replace the specific theories of particular disciplines. Such a theory would be almost without content, for we always pay for generality by sacrificing content, and all we can say about practically everything is almost nothing. Somewhere however between the specific that has no meaning and the general that has no content there must be for each purpose and at each level of abstraction, an optimum degree of generality.[119]

It is this "optimum degree of generality" that General Systems Theory seeks.

Ideology

The concept of "ideology" has had a long and controversial development. Its most familiar form has come through Marxism, but all kinds of meanings and shades of interpretation have grown up around the definition of ideology.[120] Whatever the definition, its usage raises the specter of propaganda, manipulation, and thought-control.

A constant and formidible critic of systems theory has been Robert Lilienfeld, a sociologist at City University of New York. He wrote a polemical history of the systems movement in *The Rise of Systems Theory: An Ideological Analysis.* In that book, Lilienfeld wrote that "systems theory is not a philosophy and is not a science; it is an ideology and must be considered as such."[121] He used Karl Mannheim's conception of ideology, which Lilienfeld defined as "an image of the world that seeks to maximize the social prestige and power of an interest group."[122] Lilienfeld's point was that systems theorists have set themselves up as "scientist-kings" who seek to rule the world through a "reason, conceptualization, and science" of their own making.[123] Lilienfeld wrote that in the final analysis systems theory "becomes as idealistic, utopian, and impractical as is any non-scientific teleological system, including magic, and is perhaps even less subject to testing and accountability."[124]

Such a bombastic description of systems theory gives more evidence of paranoia than scholarship, but Lilienfeld did raise some vital issues. First, systems theorists *do* have an "image of the world," but they are not alone in this. All humans have some image of the world—even sociologists. This subject of worldviews receives extensive attention in the next chapter of this book. Second, systems theorists are not trying to rule the world, but instead are trying to make sense of it and to integrate its diverse elements. A framework of understanding among humans surely need not be identified as a demonic or demagogic play for power. Third, Ludwig von Bertalanffy anticipated the charge of utopianism and defused it.[125] He explained that the movement toward a General Systems Theory is neither to dominate society through the sciences nor even to "perfect" it. The motivation is to improve society for the health of humanity in general and for the individual in particular. Fourth, General Systems Theory does not operate from the nineteenth century scientific understandings of reductionism and determinism, as Robert Lilienfeld seems to do. General Systems Theory is an influence for a dynamic, heuristic, and evolutionary conceptualization of science and of reality. It *is* scientific according to contemporary understandings of science;[126] it *is* subject to scrutiny;[127] and it *is* accountable, not only to science but to society as a whole.[128]

Principles

It has no doubt been noted that Ludwig von Bertalanffy has figured in every one of the preceding evaluations of a definition for systems theory. That has been no accident. Bertalanffy was the father of General Systems Theory and did a lot of generative writing. It should be for him to give the definitive statement of what General Systems Theory is.

Bertalanffy left evidence of the integrative nature of General Systems Theory. At one point he described the open system as a paradigm in much the same way that Thomas Kuhn had defined the concept of paradigm,[129] saying that he (Bertalanffy) saw the systemic viewpoint as representing a "novel paradigm in scientific thinking."[130] At another point, Bertalanffy expressed the belief that General Systems Theory was a herald of a "new worldview of considerable impact."[131] What was he trying to say? What is General Systems Theory: a viewpoint? a paradigm? a worldview?

Clarity comes with the recognition that terms such as "paradigm" and "worldview" were not given careful, definitive treatment until recently. It is unfair to force Bertalanffy's language into words that were not distinguished at the time of his writing. Bertalanffy's understanding of General Systems Theory can probably be best translated into current language this way: General Systems Theory is the bridge that brings the paradigm of open systems into contact with a worldview and with the concomitant models. This is possible through the discovery of principles:

> Thus, there exist models, principles, and laws that apply to generalized systems or their subclasses, irrespective of their particular kind, the nature of their component elements, and the relations or "forces" between them. It seems legitimate to ask for a theory, not of systems of a more or less special kind, but of universal principles, applying to systems in general.
>
> In this way we postulate . . . General Systems Theory. Its subject matter is the formulation and derivation of those principles which are valid for "systems" in general.[132]

In simplest terms, General Systems Theory is the scientific exploration for universal principles of wholeness.[133] These principles, in turn, provide the foundation for the overall systemic perspective.

PURPOSES OF GENERAL SYSTEMS THEORY

The purposes of General Systems Theory can be understood by looking at three areas. There is a statement of the aims of the systems movement. There is systems theory as a response to a societal and scientific crisis. There is systems theory as a framework for science. These three areas provide the background for understanding the universal principles sought by systems research.

Unity

One of the clear things in the systems movement is the statement of aims for General Systems Theory. This declaration was made by Ludwig von Bertalanffy, and it was simple and to the point. The goal was unity. The statement had five foci:

1. There is a general tendency toward integration in the various sciences, natural and social.

2. Such integration seems to be centered in a general theory of systems.

3. Such theory may be an important means for aiming at exact theory in the nonphysical fields of science.

4. Developing unifying principles running "vertically" through the universe of the individual sciences, this theory brings us nearer to the goal of the unity of science.

5. This can lead to a much-needed integration in scientific education.[134]

While these goals primarily refer to the long-sought unity of science, it is obvious that they radiate beyond the normal boundaries of science. General Systems Theory may have the potential for integration on an even larger scale.

Responsiveness

The paradigm of open systems and the move to the integration of the sciences is neither an accident nor the activity of idle thinkers. The systems movement is a response to the lack of an adequate theoretical framework for addressing societal crises.

The theoretical inadequacy was addressed by Ludwig von Bertalanffy as early as the 1920s. As a biologist, he found that the current mechanistic or vitalistic alternatives were not suitable to his empirical findings. He said he "became puzzled about the obvious lacunae in the research and theory of biology."[135] He began to advocate the organismic approach to biology, which sought to discover the principles of organization at various biological levels.[136] It was not long until he envisioned a General Systems Theory.

The move from a purely biological theory to a general theory was in response to a societal need. This need was expressed by Anatol Rapoport:

> The proliferation of disciplines, subdisciplines, and specialties threatened to fractionate the scientific community into mutually isolated conclaves unable to communicate with each other. Science threatened to become an avalanche of "findings" which in their totality no more add up to knowledge, let alone wisdom, than a pile of bricks adds up to a cathedral.
> The modern system point of view is a response to this threat.[137]

Gerald Weinberg gave a good insight into the problem. He noted that systems theory grew out, not of the failure, but of the success of classical science.[138] The older science had done such a good job of analysis, dissection, and reduction of everything to its basic elements that it needed help in putting it all back together again. General Systems Theory is a part of the attempt to integrate and to repair the damage of over-specialization.

Organization

Kenneth Boulding saw the true organizational potential of the open systems paradigm and developed it into a framework. This framework he called a "skeleton of science." Though Boulding wrote his ideas into an article in 1956, the ideas are still awe-inspiring and central to the purposes of General Systems Theory. His "skeleton" gave a structure to the aims of systems theory and a method to move toward the needed integration. He formulated "a framework or structure of systems on which to hang the flesh and blood of particular disciplines and particular subject matters in an orderly and coherent corpus of knowledge."[139] Boulding cited nine levels of complexity in his hierarchial organization.[140]

Frameworks level. This is the level of static structure which provides pattern and organization to the universe. Examples of static structure are found in the mental image of electrons orbiting around a nucleus and of planets orbiting around the sun. This elementary level suggests the structures that may appear if the system were "frozen" in time.

Clockworks level. This level reveals simple dynamics. Using the analogy of a clock, the universe can be understood as mechanical and predetermined motion. This is the orientation of Newtonian (classical) physics.

Thermostat level. It is at this level that the cybernetic function, or control and guidance mechanism, is detected. Information in the form of feedback is processed, and positive and negative determinations of the information are made possible.

Cell level. Here is the level of the true open system, in that a cell may have self-maintenance. In terms of biology, "life" is possible at this level, including self-reproduction.

Plant level. Here the living system experiences the possibility of the genetic-social experience, and the division of labor. Cells working together interdependently are able to have integration and differentiation, and hence the attainment of equifinality.

Animal level. The characteristics noticeable at this level are the emergence of increased mobility, teleological behavior, ability to structure information, and self-awareness.

Human level. Here the individual human resides, with abilities for speech, self-consciousness, and a sense of history (existence in time and space).

Social organizations level. At this level humans join together to form groups through human interaction. There is a sharing of values, emotions, and symbols.

Transcendental level. This is the level assigned to the abstract search for the ultimates, the underlying principles, and maybe even a general theory. The term "transcendent" here does not refer to that which is "out there," but rather to what is emergent and potentially present.

RELATIONSHIPS OF GENERAL SYSTEMS THEORY

Much has been said about General Systems Theory as an integrator and a skeleton of science, but it would be a serious mistake to understand the systemic movement to be limited to science. Because of its emphasis on general systems, the movement is seeking to move beyond the limits and barriers of disciplines. What Ludwig von Bertalanffy and his collaborators were about was the development of a "new way of thinking,"[141] applicable to the realm of science in particular but also to the broader environment in general.

The integration sought by the systemic perspective is an operational integration, and not an ontic integration. Operational integration is the establishment of a common perspective and a common process of activity that produces a holistic approach to understanding problems and devising solutions. Ontic integration is the belief that ultimately all things have the same mode of existence: that beneath the surface, all reality shares the same basic essence. This kind of ontic integration degenerates into a cognitive activity that understands reality as sameness and uniformity. General Systems Theory, in its quest for operational integration, is holistic, which requires both integration and differentiation. A systemic perspective gives focus to dynamic unity and harmony by celebrating diversity and binding it together in homeostatic balance.

Ludwig von Bertalanffy embodied this kind of interdisciplinary and transdisciplinary research. He was first and foremost a biologist, which explains his initial interest in organismic conceptions, but he was by no means limited to biology. He was a practitioner in such diversified fields as psychiatry, mathematics, physics, sociology, and philosophy. He was a "scientific generalist,"[142] and was able to see the need for development of other "scientific generalists." One of his explanations for his work was that it made "important headway toward interdisciplinary synthesis and integrated education."[143]

Since the "father" of systems theory was an integrator, it is no surprise that the theory itself is integrative. A brief survey of antecedents and parallel movements shows how General Systems Theory is but one manifestation of a greater evolution toward synthesis.

Cybernetics

The study of cybernetics can be dated from 1948 with the publication of Norbert Wiener's *Cybernetics*.[144] The resulting work on information theory, regulation, and computer technology gives evidence of its potency and relevance to contemporary society. Though a field large enough to more than occupy a person for a lifetime, cybernetics is best understood as a subsystem of the larger General Systems Theory. Cybernetics is the study of communication and the general theory of control, and this is characteristic of open systems.[145] The two (General Systems Theory and cybernetics) grew up interdependently, and without one the other could not have developed. Yet cybernetics is the study of feedback, which is only one part of the larger concern of systems theory.[146]

Structuralism

Ludwig von Bertalanffy acknowledged the close connection of Structuralism to General Systems Theory, citing Claude Lévi-Strauss and Jean Piaget in particular.[147] He termed Structuralism as parallel to his own findings. The greatest impact of the Structuralists has come to bear through sociology and educational psychology, where the interest in integration and structural similarities is evidence of the relationship to General Systems Theory.

It would appear that Structuralism is a parallel to some of the goals of General Systems Theory, but there are some significant differences as well. The greatest question comes at the point of integration. Depending on individual authors, there are indications that Structuralism may be a search for ontic integration rather than operational integration. If the pursuit of the "deep structures"[148] that lie beneath the surface is a way of saying that there is a fundamental uniformity in reality, then Structuralism parts ways with General Systems Theory. If these deep structures, though, are evidence of the development of general principles that interpret reality, then General Systems Theory is in consonance with Structuralism.[149]

Gestaltism

The term "Gestalt" is a German word loosely translated to mean "pattern" or "integrated form." A school of Gestalt-field psychology originated in Germany with such people as Kurt Koffka and Max Wertheimer, and the influence spread, especially to the United States. Gestalt-field psychology reacted strongly to the reductionistic and behavioristic methods of persons like E. L. Thorndike and John B. Watson. The Gestaltists turned their attention to perception and cognitive organization rather than to stimulus-response experimentation.[150]

Ludwig von Bertalanffy understood Gestalt psychology as a beginning toward an interest in open systems and toward a general theory but thought that the interest was not developed sufficiently.[151] He cited Wolfgang Köhler and Gordon Allport as related but comparatively superficial to the quest for the principles of unity.[152]

Organismic Philosophy

The philosophy of organism espoused by Alfred North Whitehead was another parallel to the work of Ludwig von Bertalanffy. Bertalanffy insisted that he developed his ideas independently of Whitehead and that the appearance of their ideas took place within the same year.[153] It could certainly be argued that the philosophical aspects of open systems have their roots in Whitehead, as well as in such related philosophers as William James, Henri Bergson, and John Dewey.[154] For example, Whitehead was in print with the first hint of his plan in *Science and the Modern World* in 1925, and his magnum opus, *Process and Reality,* was published in 1929. Bertalanffy stated that he publicly presented his ideas first in 1937[155] but published only after World War II.[156] It appears that the systemic ideas were "in the air" and that "the simultaneous appearance of similar ideas independently and on different continents was symptomatic of a new trend."[157]

CONCLUSION

Systems theory, as understood from the paradigm of open systems and from General Systems Theory, has contributions to make that can be developed in at least two ways. First, it is a tool of science in that it is an attempt to develop theoretical and empirical constructs that can be used to unify science and related philosophical explanations of reality. Second, it is but one manifestation of a multifaceted and evolutionary movement to impose order over the chaotic flow of history and experiential data. Systems theory cannot be removed from its historical and intellectual milieu: It must be seen as a contributor to a much larger reality.

These two aspects of systems theory are both utilized in the following chapters. The chapters that develop particular systemic models emphasize the theoretical and empirical constructs that are made possible through the development of the paradigm of open systems. The chapter that immediately follows uses the paradigm of open systems theory to explore the emergence of a worldview, of which General Systems Theory is a major, but by no means a sole, contributor.

In summary, the paradigm of open systems is a link in two directions. It can be followed to the development of theoretical models, or it can be followed to an emergent worldview. Steps are taken in the following pages to scout the territory in both directions. The more elusive path of worldviews is pursued first.

NOTES

1. Alfred Tennyson, "Flower in the Crannied Wall," in *The Complete Poetical Works of Tennyson,* ed. W. J. Rolfe (Boston: Houghton Mifflin, 1898), p. 274.

2. James Michael Lee defined "theory" as "a statement or group of statements organically integrating interrelated concepts, facts, and laws in such a fashion as to offer a comprehensive and systematic view of reality by specifying relatives among variables." James Michael Lee, "The Authentic Source of Religious Instruction," in *Religious Education and Theology,* ed. Norma H. Thompson (Birmingham, Ala.: Religious Education Press, 1982), p. 117. Also note the discussion by Lee about the purpose of his trilogy being "to provide a solid theoretical foundation for the field of religious instruction." James Michael Lee, *The Content of Religious Instruction: A Social Science Approach* (Birmingham, Ala.: Religious Education Press, 1985), p. 749ff.

3. This is clearly stated by Charles Melchert in "The Future of Religious Education: Commitment in Religion and Education," in *Emerging Issues in Religious Education,* ed. Gloria Durka and Joanmarie Smith (New York: Paulist Press, 1976), p. 90.

4. James Michael Lee, "To Basically Change Fundamental Theory and Practice," in *Modern Masters of Religious Education,* ed. Marlene Mayr (Birmingham, Ala.: Religious Education Press, 1983), p. 299.

5. Thomas S. Kuhn, *The Structure of Scientific Revolutions,* 2nd. ed. (Chicago: University of Chicago Press, 1970).

6. Ibid., p. 92.

7. See the discussion in Ian G. Barbour, *Myths, Models and Paradigms: A Comparative Study in Science and Religion* (New York: Harper & Row, 1974), p. 108 ff. Also see Thomas S. Kuhn, "Second Thoughts on Paradigms," in *The Essential Tension: Selected Studies in Scientific Tradition and Change,* ed. Thomas S. Kuhn (Chicago: University of Chicago Press, 1977), pp. 293-319.

8. Kuhn, *The Structure of Scientific Revolutions,* p. viii.

9. Ibid., pp. 4-5.

10. Ibid., p. 176.

11. Kuhn, "Second Thoughts on Paradigms," pp. 293-319.

12. This is described by Barry Gholson and Peter Barker in "Kuhn, Lakatos, and Laudan: Applications in the History of Physics and Psychology," *American Psychologist* 40 (July, 1985), p. 756 ff.

13. Kuhn, *The Structure of Scientific Revolutions,* p. 113.

14. Ibid., p. 10.

15. Ibid., p. 64.

16. Ibid., p. 10.

17. See, for example, Larry Laudan, "A Problem-Solving Approach to Scientific Progress," in *Scientific Revolutions,* ed. Ian Hacking (Oxford: Oxford University Press, 1981), pp. 144-155.

18. See especially Imre Lakatos, "Falsification and the Methodologies of Research Programs," in *Criticism and the Growth of Knowledge,* ed. Imre Lakatos and Alan Musgrave (Cambridge: Cambridge University Press, 1970), pp. 91-196.

19. See some directions for this in Gholson and Barker, "Kuhn, Lakatos, and Laudan: Applications in the History of Physics and Psychology," pp. 755-769, especially pp. 765-767.

20. See Stephen C. Pepper, *World Hypotheses: A Study in Evidence* (Berkeley, Calif.: University of California Press, 1942).

21. See. N. Max Wildiers, *The Theologian and His Universe: Theology and Cosmology in the Middle Ages to the Present* (New York: Seabury, 1982), especially p. 130 ff.

22. John W. Sutherland, *A General Systems Philosophy for the Social and Behavioral Sciences* (New York: George Braziller, 1973), p. 121.

23. This is an example of a "Kuhnian" idea. See Thomas S. Kuhn, "Second Thoughts on Paradigms," pp. 297-298.

24. Barbour, *Myths, Models and Paradigms,* p. 6.

25. Ibid.

26. James Michael Lee called a model "a kind of embodiment of a structural analogy." Lee also helped clarify the relationship of theory to model construction. See James Michael Lee, *The Shape of Religious Instruction: A Social*

Science Approach (Birmingham, Ala.: Religious Education Press, 1971), p. 158.

27. Gerald M. Weinberg, *An Introduction to General Systems Thinking* (New York: John Wiley & Sons, 1975), p. 28.

28. Kuhn, *The Structure of Scientific Revolutions,* p. 24.

29. Ibid., p. 246.

30. Lee, *The Shape of Religious Instruction,* p. 158.

31. Sutherland, *A General Systems Philosophy for the Social and Behavioral Sciences,* p. 12.

32. See the note in Stephen C. Pepper, *Concept and Quality: A World Hypothesis* (La Salle, Ill.: Open Court, 1966), p. 393.

33. Ibid., p. 3.

34. Ibid., p. 14.

35. Pepper, *World Hypotheses: A Study in Evidence,* p. 91.

36. Ibid., p. 96.

37. Lee, "The Authentic Source of Religious Instruction," p. 120.

38. Ibid., p. 119, provides a fuller discussion of these approaches.

39. John W. Sutherland, *Systems: Analysis, Administration, and Architecture* (New York: Van Nostrand Reinhold, 1975), p. 41.

40. For a fuller discussion, see Chapter Two in Jamal N. Islam, *The Ultimate Fate of the Universe* (Cambridge: Cambridge University Press, 1983), pp. 8-12; Igor D. Novikov, *Evolution of the Universe,* trans. M. M. Basks (Cambridge: Cambridge University Press, 1983), pp. 33-43; and Chapter One in Carl Sagan, *Cosmos* (New York: Random House, 1980), pp. 3-21.

41. For a fuller discussion, see Chapter Three in Fritjof Capra, *The Turning Point: Science, Society and the Rising Culture* (New York: Simon and Schuster, 1982), pp. 75-97.

42. Weinberg, *An Introduction to General Systems Thinking,* p. 52.

43. Ibid., p. 145.

44. C. West Churchman, *The Systems Approach,* rev. ed. (New York: Dell, 1979), p. 29.

45. Capra, *The Turning Point,* p. 43.

46. I have called this a "proverb" to call attention to the fact that while this statement does reflect some truth, it also reflects an over-generalization. This discussion about whether a whole is an absolute entity without divisibility, or whether a whole is a combination of elemental parts, has been and continues to be a controversial one throughout philosophy, social science, and natural science. It would seem that to emphasize one argument to the exclusion of the other is to be blindly dualistic. Neither is correct for every situation: A whole is both a unified entity and an entity composed of parts. Holism without differentiation is sameness; variety without integration is chaos. For a summary of this problem, see May Brodbeck, "Logic and Scientific Method in Research on Teaching," in *Handbook of Research on Teaching, Vol. I,* ed. N. L. Gage (Chicago: Rand McNally, 1963), pp. 44-93.

47. A. D. Hall and R. E. Fagen, "Definition of System," in *Systems Research for the Behavioral Scientist,* ed. Walter Buckley (Chicago: Aldine, 1968), p. 81.

48. Ludwig von Bertalanffy, *General System Theory: Foundations, Development, Applications,* rev. ed. (New York: George Braziller, 1968), p. 38.

49. Russell L. Ackoff and Fred E. Emery, *On Purposeful Systems* (Chicago: Aldine-Atherton, 1972), p. 18.

50. Russell L. Ackoff, *Redesigning the Future: A Systems Approach to Soci-*

etal Problems (New York: John Wiley & Sons, 1974), p. 13.

51. Kenneth E. Boulding, *Ecodynamics: A New Theory of Societal Evolution* (Beverly Hills, Calif.: Sage Publications, 1978), p. 85.

52. Bertalanffy, *General System Theory,* p. 125.

53. Equilibrium should not be confused with homeostasis. Equilibrium is the balance of opposing forces that results in inactivity. Homeostasis is steady-state: a constant or a positive ratio of exchange between the system and the environment, whereby the systemic character and relationships remain identifiable.

54. Entropy is movement toward dissolution, chaos, and death. Negative entropy is movement toward order, complexity, and life.

55. Bertalanffy, *General System Theory,* p. 121.

56. Ibid.

57. Ibid., p. 150.

58. Fernando Cortés, Adam Przeworski, and John Sprague, *Systems Analysis for Social Scientists* (New York: John Wiley & Sons, 1974), p. 8.

59. Sutherland, *Systems,* p. 24.

60. Ackoff, *Redesigning the Future,* p. 14.

61. Cortés et al., *Systems Analysis for Social Scientists,* p. 5.

62. Ibid., p. 20.

63. Ibid., p. 10.

64. Ackoff, *Redesigning the Future,* p. 14.

65. Cortés et al., *Systems Analysis for Social Scientists,* p. 5.

66. Ackoff and Emery, *On Purposeful Systems,* p. 31.

67. Bertalanffy, *General System Theory,* p. 40.

68. Ibid.

69. Vitalism is a doctrine that espouses the belief in an ontic division of body and soul. The "vital" element, the life-source, is separate and distinct from the physical reality.

70. Cybernetics is the study of evaluation, regulation, and guidance of a system, based on experience and goal-directed behavior.

71. Bertalanffy, *General System Theory,* p. 46.

72. Ibid., pp. 124-138.

73. Daniel Katz and Robert L. Kahn, *The Social Psychology of Organizations* (New York: John Wiley & Sons, 1966), pp. 19-26.

74. Glenn L. Immergart and Francis J. Pilecki, *An Introduction to Systems for the Educational Administrator* (Reading, Mass.: Addison-Wesley, 1973), pp. 39-45.

75. Bertalanffy, *General System Theory,* p. 66. The emphasis is from Bertalanffy.

76. The differences between aggregates and systems are discussed in Andras Angyal, "A Logic of Systems," in *Systems Thinking,* ed. Fred E. Emery (New York: Penguin Books, 1969), pp. 17-29.

77. The reference here is to the quote from Ackoff, *Redesigning the Future,* p. 13.

78. Bertalanffy, *General System Theory,* p. 45.

79. Sutherland, *Systems,* p. 36.

80. Equifinality is the ability to achieve a desired state from differing initial conditions and by diverse paths. Open systems also have the ability to perform multifinality: pursuit of a variety of goals by differing initial conditions and by diverse paths.

81. A subsystem is a subset of the identified system; a suprasystem is a larger environment of the specified system. For example, if the identified system is the United States, a subsystem would be the state of Kentucky and a suprasystem would be the United Nations.

82. Immegart and Pilecki, *An Introduction to Systems for the Educational Administrator, p.* 38.

83. Hall and Fagen, "Definition of a System," p. 83.

84. Churchman, *The Systems Approach,* p. 35.

85. Weinberg, *An Introduction to General Systems Thinking,* p. 147.

86. Ibid.

87. Capra, *The Turning Point,* p. 275.

88. "Classical" science is given definition in chapter 3. The term refers to Newtonian or pre-Einsteinian science.

89. Sutherland, *A General Systems Philosophy for the Social and Behavioral Sciences,* p. 37.

90. Bertalanffy, *General System Theory,* p. 88.

91. The term "through-put" is used by Katz and Kahn, *The Social Psychology of Organizations,* p. 20, but other writers use the term "transformation process." The terms are used interchangeably here.

92. Systems are referred to as "cycles of events" in Katz and Kahn, *The Social Psychology of Organizations,* p. 20.

93. Immegart and Pilecki, *An Introduction to Systems for the Educational Administrator,* p. 39.

94. Bertalanffy, *General System Theory,* p. 40. Bertalanffy used "final state," but I prefer "desired state" to give a processive, evaluative meaning to the definition.

95. Stafford Beer, *Cybernetics and Management* (New York: John Wiley & Sons, 1959), p. 30.

96. Bertalanffy, *General System Theory,* p. 46.

97. Ibid., p. 41. Also see Robert Lilienfeld, *The Rise of Systems Theory: An Ideological Analysis* (New York: John Wiley & Sons, 1978), pp. 15-16.

98. Ervin Laszlo, *The Systems View of the World: The Natural Philosophy of the New Developments in the Sciences* (New York: George Braziller, 1972), p. 41.

99. Bertalanffy, *General System Theory,* p. 136.

100. Erwin Schrödinger, *What is Life?: The Physical Aspect of the Living Cell* (Cambridge: Cambridge University Press, 1944; reprint edition, 1967), p. 76.

101. Bertalanffy, *General System Theory,* pp. 14-15. The name of the organization is now the Society for General Systems Research.

102. It is interesting to note the struggle for identity within the systems movement, especially in light of a similar struggle within contemporary religious education.

103. Bertalanffy, *General System Theory,* p. xvii.

104. Ibid., p. xix.

105. Weinberg, *An Introduction to General Systems Thinking,* p. 46.

106. A personal note written by Russell L. Ackoff to Roger Cavallo, recorded in *Systems Research Movement: Characteristics, Accomplishments, and Current Developments,* ed. Roger E. Cavallo (Society for General Systems Research, 1979), p. 8.

107. Bertalanffy, *General System Theory,* p. xviii.

108. For the complexity of the issue, see the whole report of Roger E. Cavallo, ed., *Systems Research Movement.* The quote is from page 8.

109. Bertalanffy, *General System Theory,* p. xix.

110. Fred N. Kerlinger, *Foundations of Behavioral Research,* 2nd ed. (New York: Holt, Rinehart & Winston, 1973), p. 9.

111. Ibid.

112. James Grier Miller, *Living Systems* (New York: McGraw-Hill, 1978).

113. Ibid., p. 1.

114. Ibid.

115. The critical subsystems of a living system were listed by Miller as reproducer, boundary, ingestor, distributor, converter, producer, matter-energy storage, extruder, motor, supporter, input transducer, internal transducer, channel and net, decoder, associator, memory, decider, encoder, and output transducer. See Miller, *Living Systems,* p. 3.

116. A notable exception is the Systems Science Institute at the University of Louisville, Louisville, Kentucky. The Institute was started by James G. Miller while he was president of the University of Louisville.

117. It is probably not correct to say that a truly "general" system theory will never evolve. If it does, it will be a long time in coming.

118. Kenneth E. Boulding, "General Systems Theory—The Skeleton of Science," *Management Science* 2, (1956); reprinted in *Society for General System Research Yearbook, Vol. 1,* ed. Anatol Rapoport (Society for General System Research, 1956), p. 11.

119. Ibid.

120. For an introduction to this historical development, see George Lichtheim, "The Concept of Ideology," in *The Concept of Ideology and Other Essays,* ed. George Lichtheim (New York: Random House, 1967), pp. 3-46.

121. Lilienfeld, *The Rise of Systems Theory,* p. 257.

122. Ibid., p. 3.

123. Ibid., p. 279.

124. Ibid.

125. Bertalanffy, *General System Theory,* p. 52.

126. See chapter 3 for what the term "contemporary science" means in more detail.

127. The report edited by Roger Cavallo is a serious example of self-study. See Cavallo, *Systems Research Movement.*

128. The interest of systems theory (and this book) is to integrate the society, and the only hope for this is wide participation. Systems theorists are not "scientist-kings," but are revolutionaries who want to expand the sciences to include feedback from the larger society.

129. Bertalanffy, *General System Theory,* p. 18.

130. Ibid., p. xviii.

131. Ibid., p. xvii.

132. Ibid., p. 32.

133. Ibid., p. xx.

134. Ibid., p. 38.

135. Ibid., p. 12.

136. Ibid.

137. Anatol Rapoport, "Foreword," in *Systems Research for the Behavioral Scientist,* ed. Walter Buckley, p. xxi.

138. Weinberg, *An Introduction to General Systems Thinking,* p. 3.

139. Boulding, "General Systems Theory—The Skeleton of Science," p. 17.
140. Ibid., pp. 14-16.
141. Bertalanffy, *General System Theory,* p. xviii. Bertalanffy was not referring here to a strictly cognitive approach. He was saying that new perceptions would lead to further investigation.
142. Ibid., p. 51.
143. Ibid.
144. Norbert Wiener, *Cybernetics: Control and Communication in the Animal and the Machine,* (Cambridge, Mass.: M.I.T. Press, 1948).
145. Beer, *Cybernetics and Management,* p. 7.
146. Bertalanffy, *General System Theory,* p. 17.
147. Ibid., p. xviii-xix.
148. See especially the model in Michael Lane, "Introduction," in *Introduction to Structuralism,* ed. Michael Lane (New York: Basic Books, 1970), p. 15. The entire book is a good source for understanding the conceptual background of Structuralism.
149. One way to trace the influence of Structuralism is through James Fowler, *Stages of Faith: The Psychology of Human Development and the Quest for Meaning* (San Francisco: Harper & Row, 1981). Fowler based his work on Lawrence Kohlberg, Erik Erikson, and Jean Piaget—Structuralists all. To evaluate Fowler's work is to evaluate the antecedents of Structuralism as well.
150. For a fuller discussion see Morris L. Bigge and Maurice P. Hunt, *Psychological Foundations of Education: An Introduction to Human Motivation, Development, and Learning,* 3d ed. (New York: Harper & Row, 1980), p. 277ff.
151. Bertalanffy, *General System Theory,* p. 11.
152. Ibid., pp. 11, 208.
153. Ibid., p. 12.
154. James Grier Miller said he was first oriented to the organismic conception by Alfred North Whitehead personally and that if Whitehead were writing today he would write about a "philosophy of system" rather than a "philosophy of organism." See Miller, "Preface," *Living Systems,* pp. xiii-xxi, especially p. xiii.
155. Bertalanffy, *General System Theory,* p. 90.
156. Ibid.
157. Ibid., p. 12.

Chapter 3

Worldviews

The tide rises, the tide falls,
The twilight darkens, the curlew calls;
Along the sea-sands damp and brown
The traveler hastens toward the town,
   And the tide rises, the tide falls.

Darkness settles on roofs and walls,
But the sea, the sea in the darkness calls;
The little waves, with their soft, white hands,
Efface the footprints in the sands,
   And the tide rises, the tide falls.

The morning breaks; the steeds in their stalls
Stamp and neigh, as the hostler calls;
The day returns, but nevermore
Returns the traveler to the shore,
   And the tide rises, the tide falls.[1]
             Henry Wadsworth Longfellow

To discuss worldviews is to discuss the dynamics of change.

The terms "worldview" and "change" sound so comfortable and so innocuous, yet they are only covers for the turmoil and turbulence underneath. This chapter deals with such fundamental issues and approaches that various authors have employed rather emotional language in their discussions of the topic.

Alvin Toffler, in his book *The Third Wave,* said that his focus on a different approach to civilization was "the single most explosive fact of our lifetimes."[2]

Lawrence LeShan and Henry Margenau took up the concept of worldviews by saying: "Our most pressing problems cannot be solved with the old world picture. We must either find a new way . . . of conceptualizing reality, or else go under."[3]

No less a world figure than Ilya Prigogine wrote that "we are in a period of scientific revolution . . . a period not unlike the birth of the scientific approach in ancient Greece or of its renaissance in the time of Galileo."[4]

The physicist Heinz Pagels echoed Prigogine, but took the thought a step further. He said: "We live in the wake of a physics revolution comparable to the Copernican demolition of the anthropocentric world—a revolution which . . . has left most educated people behind."[5] If it is proper to include religious educators within Pagels' category of "educated people," then this chapter is an attempt to get religious educators caught up with the revolution and to see what contribution religious education can make to it.

This chapter, then, addresses the all-important concept of worldviews. It is a logical outgrowth of the foundational discussion of paradigms and a preparation for the development of systemic models of religion, education, and religious education. After an orientation to the idea of worldviews, this chapter surveys historical formulations of worldviews, specifically from positions of theology and classical science. Upon this basis, the outline of an emergent worldview is sketched: the systemic worldview.

ORIENTATION TO WORLDVIEWS

One of the most influential books in the philosophy of science was Thomas Kuhn's *The Structure of Scientific Revolutions*.[6] Kuhn's operational definition of scientific revolutions was "those noncumulative developmental episodes in which an older paradigm is replaced in whole or in part by an incompatible new one."[7] The concept of paradigms was the subject of chapter 2, but of importance here is the *result* of paradigms and of paradigm shifts: revolution. Kuhn said that "during revolutions scientists see new and different things when looking with familiar instruments in places they have looked before."[8] In fact, Kuhn went so far as to say that "after a revolution scientists are responding to a different world."[9] In simple terms, a revolution is a change of worldview.[10]

Sometimes the methods and language of science are threatening to nonscientists, especially those in religious studies. Kuhn used a term that is quite familiar to people in religion. He used "conversion" as a synonym for the change from one worldview to another, saying that a "conversion experience" is at the very core of a scientific revolution.[11] In a very real sense, Kuhn's understanding of conversion differs very little from the understanding in religious circles. A conversion in a religious sense is also a revolution: a complete change of lifestyle, belief, and orientation to reality. It could be said that a "Christian conversion" is the adoption of a "Christian worldview," in the sense that a worldview is a way of interpreting and interacting with fundamental reality.

Milton Rokeach helped to clear up foggy notions of "belief" when he described five classes of belief.[12] Type A beliefs are primitive beliefs, which are seemingly beyond controversy since there is virtually 100 percent consensus about them. These are what Rokeach called "the 'basic truths' about physical reality, social reality, and the nature of the self."[13] They are beliefs simply taken for granted by society.

Type B beliefs are also primitive beliefs, but they do not rest on a social consensus. They rely on an individual's personal interpretation of an experiential encounter with the object of belief. As a result of this personal involvement, Type B beliefs are essentially incontrovertible (from the viewpoint of the experiencing individual). Type C beliefs are authority beliefs, where a person accepts the belief system of someone he or she trusts. Type D beliefs are derived beliefs, which are beliefs held because the source is reliable. Type E beliefs are inconsequential beliefs. This final type of belief is unconnected to the total system and is easily changed with little effect.

What Rokeach described as Type A beliefs are precisely the province of worldviews. Worldviews are influenced by personal encounters (Rokeach's Type B), but most important is the fact that worldviews are societal perceptions. They are the means of experiencing and interpreting reality that are shared by a community through a near-unanimous consensus, and it is this consensus that makes them so difficult to change. It takes a "revolution" to change a primitive Type A belief, and after such a revolution there really is a "new world" to live in and explore.

With this introduction to worldviews, another approach to the concept may prove helpful. It is drawn from science, but makes a literal interpretation of how to view the world. It can serve as an analogy for understanding the more abstract use of worldview.

Literal Worldviews

History and the passage of time allow the luxury of hindsight and insight. What may not be obvious in the present becomes plain with the perspective of years for reflection. It is difficult to come to grips with the current worldview, not just because it is so abstract, but because we are so completely immersed in it. It is much like a fish trying to determine what the ocean is.

"Worldview" as used in this book is a very broad and inclusive term, but it can also be used in a focused way. For purposes of illustration, worldview can simply be understood to imply the way the world—planet earth—is conceived as existing in space. Even this conceptualization has not been constant. It has gone through revolutions, from Ptolemy to Copernicus to Einstein.

The Ptolemaic universe. Claudis Ptolemy (second century A.D.) was the Alexandrian astronomer and mathematician whose name was finally connected to the geocentric theory of the universe. Interestingly enough, Aristarchus of Samos (c. 310-230 B.C.) postulated a heliocentric orbit for the planets, but his geometry would not cooperate and his idea was discarded.[14] Ptolemy made the scientific formulation[15] with the earth as the center of the universe. He wrote that "if one should next take up the question of the earth's position, the observed appearance . . . could only be understood if we put it in the middle of the heavens as the centre [sic] of the sphere."[16] He went on to say that "it can be shown how the earth can neither move in any one of the . . . directions, nor ever change at all from its place at the centre."[17] The Ptolemaic system placed the earth at the center, with concentric orbits of the moon, Mercury, Venus, the sun, Mars, Jupiter, Saturn, and the stars.[18]

This basic understanding of the universe was classical cosmology. There were three characteristics: the earth was at the center of the universe; the earth was spatially bounded; and celestial phenomena required a different kind of explanation from terrestrial phenomena.[19]

The Copernican perception. Nicolaus Copernicus (1473-1543) started a revolution because he viewed the world differently. He was acutely aware of the danger implicit in his new concept: He delayed the publication of it until he was near death and then proposed it as a hypothesis.[20] Copernicus used mathematics to show that the sun, and not the earth, was the center of the universe. He wrote:

> We therefore assert that the centre of the Earth, carrying the Moon's path, passes in a great orbit among the other planets in an annual revolution round the Sun; that near the Sun is the centre of the Universe; and that whereas the Sun is at rest, any apparent motion of the Sun can be better explained by motion of the Earth.[21]

Now the sun was postulated to have concentric orbits of Mercury, Venus, the earth and its moon, Mars, Jupiter, Saturn, and the stars.

What happened here? Did the sun, earth, and planets change relative positions between the lifetimes of Ptolemy and Copernicus? That is not likely. The more probable answer is that the worldview changed.

The Einsteinian revolution. Albert Einstein (1879-1955) came along in 1905 and confounded the scientific world with, among other things, his theory of relativity.[22] He showed how such fixed concepts as mass and time were no longer absolute but were relative to each other and to the speed of light.[23] Separate but related studies investigated cosmological implications of this relative universe. It is not "at rest," but rapidly expanding. The various galaxies are each receding from the other.[24] It is now believed that the earth is not simply revolving around a stationary sun. The sun itself is revolving in a galaxy, and that galaxy is also moving away from every other galaxy.

It is surely correct that the physical and spatial relationships did not change radically from the time of Copernicus to that of Einstein. What did change was perception. Copernicus and Einstein *saw* things differently from one another.

Symbolic Worldviews

Just as Ptolemy and Copernicus are only symbols for much combined understandings of the world, so is Einstein a symbol for a new worldview. As Heinz Pagels noted,[25] though it is not yet in the consciousness of many people, a new worldview is emerging and evolving. Another revolution is underway. As surely as the Ptolemaic and Copernican systems demanded a broader understanding of reality to suit the view of the world, the Einsteinian revolution is demanding attention. More than redecorating is needed: There must be a whole new construction.

It is apparent by now that the real question is one of epistemology: How do we *know?* This basic question of philosophy is certainly beyond the ability of the writer, and seemingly of most writers. But some kind of statement must be made on how to approach reality. This book employs the term "worldview" to denote the total system of conscious and preconscious presuppositions regarding reality. Several authors have expressed this concept in a variety of ways.

Kenneth Boulding. Kenneth Boulding's term for the concept was "image," appropriately discussed in his book *The Image.*[26] While he provided no simple definition for "image," it can be summarized in six segments.

First, the image is not a "thing," but a "pattern which invades the whole."[27] The image is a structure, a method of organization, which for Boulding meant "anything that is not chaos."[28]

Second, this structure is organic, which implies that it "follows principles of growth and development similar to those with which we are familiar in complex organizations and organisms."[29] No part of the image is independent from the other parts;[30] each is interdependent and contributory to the whole.

Third, the image governs the behavior of the imager.[31] The image creates the value system, and hence the behavior.

Fourth, the image does not deal with absolute truth, which would require an independent and "outside" reality. Boulding said he preferred not to use the word "knowledge," since it implies validity. He said: "What I am talking about is what I believe to be true; my subjective knowledge."[32] He denied the existence of "facts," but instead substituted "messages filtered through a changeable value system."[33]

Fifth, the image is not necessarily, or even ideally, a private matter. It is shared by society and creates society. It is continually revised and reworked by the community. It is more than mere ideas and thoughts: It is an agent of transformation. Boulding said: "The image not only makes society, society continually remakes the image."[34]

Sixth, Boulding dealt with how change in the image takes place. He found "an orderly development in the public image" that is reflected in history: "The change in the image comes in mutations, through a Ptolemy, a Copernicus, an Einstein."[35] His point was that ideas do not drop out of the sky but are formed from the fabric of existing ideas. A Copernican revolution is incomprehensible without the Ptolemaic (or some such) system to revolt against.

Taken in sum, these six points are a good way of understanding the use of the term "worldview" in this book.

Ninian Smart. Ninian Smart has long been concerned with the explication of religions and ideologies, which has resulted in his use of the term worldview. He said: "The English language does not have a term to refer to both traditional religions and ideologies; the best expression is perhaps *worldviews.*"[36] Smart used the term as a catchall to express the total belief system of a person. He continued: "But whether we have spelled it out to ourselves or not, each of us has a worldview, which forms a background to the lives we lead."[37]

Lawrence LeShan and Henry Margenau. Lawrence LeShan and Henry Margenau offered the term "alternate realities" for the concept of worldview. They said that "reality" as an absolute is a notion of the past. While "each individual is born into a culture, and its orientations and basic beliefs shape him [or her] and remain deeply rooted in his [or her] personality all his [or her] life,"[38] this is not the end of the story. They felt that "the assumption that there is one 'true' definition of *all* reality is outworn."[39] They proposed the term "alternate realities" to denote a composite of different approaches to understand the whole.

Gregory Bateson. Where Kenneth Boulding used "image," Gregory Bateson used "mind." Bateson defined it as "a single knowing which characterizes evolution as well as aggregates of humans."[40] The individual mind he described as a "pattern which connects."[41] The collective mind he called a "metapattern": a pattern of patterns.[42] This metapattern is not a fixed thing in itself; rather, it is a "dance of interacting parts."[43]

Summary

A review of how people image and conceptualize could go on interminably. The attempt here has been to provide a variety of ways to understand the same concept. The abstraction—called "worldview" in this book—defies complete definition. It is best approached through analogy.

To summarize, Heinz Pagels said: "The human mind abhors chaos, finding order even if there is none."[44] Constellations of the stars are a final example. In one sense, the "stars" are actually localized explosions, fireballs moving through space with little if any relation to any other body. Viewed from earth, these burning suns are specks of light in a black sky. Yet it is hard to deny, at least for Western persons in this millenium, that some of them form a pattern that looks just like a "Big Dipper." After the image is seen for the first time, every night it seems to stand out from all other specks of light. What is the true reality? Stars arranged in the pattern of a dipper? Dots placed in a dark sky? Fireballs flying through space? It is a matter of perception, of orientation, not unlike the idea called worldview.

DIVISIONS OF HISTORY

This section is an effort to clarify and sharpen the concept of worldview by surveying a few of the ways in which the history of thought has been divided. Such a task as an "overview of the history of thought" sounds presumptuous and impossible, and of course it is both. No one can adequately summarize history and then divide it up; but since that is true, then one more try cannot hurt too much. There are many precedents to cite.

The warnings offered by Alvin Toffler serve well here. He acknowledged the discomfiture that historians have at neatly dividing civilization. He said: "In attempting so large scale a synthesis, it has been necessary to simplify, generalize, and compress."[45] He accepted the possibility of losing detail in exchange for clarity. By opting for three large divisions, he provided periods of history easily handled conceptually. Other possibilities of division are innumerable. Toffler admitted: "One could, no doubt, chop the past . . . into 12 or 38 or 157 pieces. But, in so doing, we would lose sight of the major divisions in a clutter of subdivisions."[46] Toffler's method has been employed by others and is used here. Caveat emptor.

Following is how five contemporary authors have handled the ebb and flow of human history. The direction this book takes is added as a sixth, but related, attempt at dividing history.

A. Graham Ikin

A. Graham Ikin chose to treat all of human experience in four ages. He listed the Stone Age, the Iron Age, and the current Atomic Age.[47] His main interest concerned the creation of a future for humans that would be the Unitary Age. He stated his vision: "We must go to [humanity] in the Unitary Age, in which lesser values will be conserved and harmonised and the costly and destructive wars which mar our history will be left behind."[48] Ikin's hope for the future is not opposed to what this book identifies as an emergent *systemic* worldview.

Alvin Toffler

Alvin Toffler divided history into three metaphorical waves, in a book logically entitled *The Third Wave*.[49] The first wave he identified as an agricultural phase, stretching from 8000 B.C. to A.D. 1750.[50] The second wave he dated from approximately A.D. 1650, and it crested in the midst of the twentieth century. He called this the industrial civilization.[51] The third wave, named the postindustrial society, had its birth in the 1950s, and its life span is unknown. This future-orientation and prediction was the real subject of his book. Toffler, then, used primarily vocational categories for his "waves": initially, persons worked as farmers; next, they performed as industrialists and factory workers; and now people function primarily as technicians.

Russell Ackoff

Russell Ackoff closely paralleled Toffler's divisions in the book *Redesigning the Future*,[52] but Ackoff did not attempt to be so comprehensive. He understood the unfolding of history in terms of revolutions. The Renaissance, with all its turbulence and liberation, produced the Machine Age which in turn gave rise to the Industrial Revolution.[53] Using the 1940s as the demarcation point away from the Machine Age,[54] Ackoff said we are now entering the Systems Age with its accompanying Postindustrial Revolution.[55] He saw the future in terms of problems to be solved and exploited for the good of the human race. For Ackoff it was this process of either creating or solving problems[56] that would dictate the success of the incipient Systems Age.

Fritjof Capra

Fritjof Capra wrote: "As individuals, as a society, as a civilization, and as a planetary ecosystem, we are reaching the turning point."[57] Appropriately enough, Fritjof Capra entitled his 1982 book *The Turning Point*. His focus, though taking care to set the context,[58] was the current shift from a mechanistic view of life to a systems view of life. He used Newtonian and quantum physics as examples of the changes underway in science and then related changes from other spheres of civilization to illustrate the broader view. Capra mirrored Russell Ackoff in concentrating on the movement from one age to the next, but his emphasis was different. Where Ackoff was pragmatic about problem-solving and creation of a desirable future, Capra was philosophical and inclusive. Capra's book was more descriptive of worldviews and the need for change than prescriptive. He did not offer solutions or methods.

Ervin Laszlo

Ervin Laszlo is a systems scientist and a philosopher, so his categorizations of history were quite similar to both Russell Ackoff's and Fritjof Capra's. He contrasted the atomistic (reductionistic) view of classical science with the emerging systems view of reality.[59] Laszlo attempted a statement of a natural philosophy for science based upon this systems view of the world. He described the development of systems thinking in terms of emergence rather than outright revolution.[60] In a sentence that opens the door to the way this book addresses the concept of worldview, Laszlo said:

The systems view is the emerging contemporary view of organized complexity, one step beyond the Newtonian view of organized simplicity, and two steps beyond the classical worldviews of divinely ordered or imaginatively envisaged complexity.[61]

Conclusion

None of the authors mentioned in this section have an absolute claim to history and its divisions. None of the divisions are perfect, but all of them are helpful. The time has come for a statement of the way this book divides history. For the purposes here, history is divided into three eras. First, there was the era of a theological worldview, from prehistory until approximately A.D. 1543: the year Copernicus published his heliocentric theory of the universe. Second, there was the era of a classical science worldview, beginning with 1543 and continuing until approximately 1954. Third, since 1954, humans have begun the era of a systemic worldview. This third era dates from the formation of the Society for General Systems Theory (later renamed Society for General Systems Research). While these dates are more symbolic than literal, they do serve as imaginary dividing lines. The sections that follow give support for the creation of these three eras of dominant worldviews.

A THEOLOGICAL WORLDVIEW

One of the things that becomes apparent in the detection of dominant worldviews is that they are epigenetic. Each one grows out of a previous worldview. Though they may oppose or contradict each other, they are still in intimate interrelationship. A classical science worldview is incomprehensible without the background of a theological worldview; and the contributions of the theological worldview are never completely lost.

Another lesson to be learned is that as worldviews develop through history they become more complex, more definite, and more clearly stated. The theological worldview is quite amorphous and shadowy, given distinction only in hindsight and in contrast to succeeding worldviews. A notion of a "theological worldview" would have been utter nonsense to a person like

Thomas Aquinas. That simply was the way to perceive reality. For this reason, the theological worldview can be dealt with briefly and summarily. It is the contrasting classical science worldview that requires closer analysis.[62] The religious worldview can be outlined in five categories.

Simplistic

Ancient and medieval people sought a simple fundamental reality to explain everything. For some it was a substance; for others it was a principle; for most it was a god (or gods).

Cha'im Perelman discussed the philosophical school at Miletus in the fifth and sixth century B.C., represented by Thales, Anaximander, and Anaximenes.[63] While present-day thinking tends to ignore their efforts at understanding the universe, they were in a sense laying a foundation for all philosophy and its satellite of science. Thales argued that the fundamental reality was water and that all things could be returned to their original liquid state.[64] Anaximander created the term "apeiron": the "unlimited," or "chaos" from which reality emerged.[65] Anaximenes postulated that air, or more accurately *psyche* (soul, wind, force), was the deepest reality.[66]

Plato and Aristotle preferred to employ rational concepts in their explanations rather than physical realities. Plato understood there to be Ideas or Forms beyond the material stuff of the universe and that these universals were the true essences.[67] Aristotle, while rejecting Plato's Forms, still talked of First Cause and the Unmoved Mover, and understood movement to be from potentiality to actuality.[68] Aristotle had a somewhat different view of the senses than did Plato. Aristotle's doctrine was best expressed in "nihil in intellectu quod non prius in sensu" (there is nothing in the mind which was not first in the senses), meaning that while the senses are the starting place for knowledge, all reality is not sensory. The highest realities were believed to be beyond (meta) the physical (hence, metaphysics).[69]

Most people simply turned to the gods for answers. The Greeks looked to Olympus, the Romans created a Pantheon, and the Jews and Christians opted for One God. There were many efforts to reconcile the gods and philosophy, and Christianity made a special effort to make sense of it all. Yet the fact remained that for the large part the concept of a transcendent being (or beings) was invoked to explain the physical and metaphysical origins.[70]

Divinely Ordered

Alfred North Whitehead referred to the struggle Galileo Galilei (1564-1642) had with the theologians of his time.[71] Galileo was a scientist and a theorist and as such was deeply interested in "why" questions.[72] The difficulty between Galileo and the theologians was that while Galileo was looking for a physical "why," the theologians were expecting a metaphysical "why." The imperialism of the theological worldview insisted that Galileo's physical and theoretical answers had to align with the theologians' predetermined metaphysical answers.

This rigidity was symptomatic of the theological worldview. Scientific theory and laws that lead to theory were of little importance to the theologians, since God, the gods, or at least some principle beyond mortal influence was at work. Transcendence created, directed, and controlled. Further exploration into the "how" of things was useless. The point to life and learning was to fulfill the divinely appointed function for humans. The theological worldview took the "how" for granted, by way of divine origin and direction, and emphasized the "why" by informing the people of their appointed place in life.

Deductive

Another story about Galileo gives insight into the theological worldview.[73] Galileo invited the professor of philosophy at Padua (Galileo also taught there) to look at the satellites of Jupiter through a telescope. The philosophy professor refused. Why did he refuse? He knew that they did not exist. How did he know? He knew because seven was the divine number, and therefore only seven heavenly bodies would exist in God's universe. Since moons around Jupiter would raise the total of heavenly bodies beyond seven, there were obviously no moons around Jupiter. The professor's logic was fine. The result was wrong.

The professor was following the formally correct usage of a syllogism. An example of a syllogism is:

All men are mortal.
Socrates is a man.
Therefore Socrates is mortal.

In a syllogism, a specific answer is deduced from the general principles. The grave danger, of course, is that if the general principles are wrong, the deduction must be wrong—regardless of the beauty of the logic.

The theological worldview used deduction to the exclusion of induction. Deduction is the key to theory and to all of science, but deduction must reflect the use of induction. Induction has value in the development of a valid base for the establishment of general principles. Induction leads to deduction. The theological worldview gave virtually no attention to induction, since the general principles were assumed to be divinely ordained, predetermined, and assured.

The hierarchy of truth[74] devised by Thomas Aquinas (1225-1274) was the great synthesis of Aristotelian and Christian thought. This effort by Aquinas represented an attempt to keep scientific observation acceptable but in its proper (inferior) place. Of the three steps on the ladder, truth discovered through observation of nature was the least valuable. Second was knowledge and truth gained by the use of reason and the development of the human mind. The third and highest form of truth was revelation. This was information gained from transcendence which was logical, permanent, and unchanging.[75] Truth received by revelation was incontrovertible, and all other truth had to conform to it.

Structural

The hierarchy of Thomas Aquinas reflected the overall hierarchical understanding of the theological worldview. The world was viewed as a hierarchy of successive tiers, where everything had a place, a purpose, and a structure that allowed for divine fulfillment.

The obvious example is the rigid physical view of the universe which was taught. The geocentric view of Claudius Ptolemy[76] was fully accepted by the theologians, not so much for its indisputable observational data but for its logic, rationality, and common sense. The only sensible understanding seemed to be an immovable earth, with sun, stars, and planets in worshipful orbit.

If the view of the universe was geocentric, even more was it anthropocentric. Humans were the crown of creation; they were the final fulfillment of the created order.[77] Whatever the value of nature, at best it was for the help and pleasure of humankind. Didn't God[78] create humanity to have "dominion" over nature and to subdue it?[79] Didn't God form persons by his own *nephesh*?[80] Humans were not thought to be gods, but neither were they believed to be animals. Humans were in their proper place—above and separate from the natural order, ranking just below divinity.[81]

The top of the hierarchy was divinity. Not a part of the created order, the idea of transcendence drew a line between human and divine. Either as a principle or as a personification, the creator was literally above and beyond the creation.[82]

The theological worldview was structural also in the sense that it was static: "It was a completed world in which there could be no fundamental novelty except as God acts in it."[83] There could be change from potentiality to actuality, but this was strictly a movement toward fulfillment of purpose without a true change in structure. There was no thought of organic development or of evolution, where current form and function could change through time to a different form and function. In a divinely predetermined worldview there was no need for fundamental change and development.

Traditional

The need of early society was for security, and security came through conformity and preservation of the status quo.[84] Since the fathers had learned how to survive, then continuing their practices was essential for continued survival. This mind-set rigidified into tradition and authority that could not be travestied.

It was a natural development for certain people to oversee that the traditions were properly kept. In time these persons became authoritative in both the practice of tradition and in the proper method of handing it down to new generations. The rituals which ensured survival became religion, and the process which transmitted knowledge became education. It is easy to see why religion and education in this era were authoritative and traditional. Religious education was an early entrant to the shaping of worldviews!

Summary

The theological worldview was simplistic in approach, divinely ordered in purpose, deductive in thinking, structural in perception, and traditional in guidance. Ian Barbour gave this outline of the theological worldview:

> It was a unified hierarchical order in which each thing played its part, striving to achieve its essential purpose. All nature served man, and man served God. Science, cosmology, history and theology all expressed the same pattern of meaning.[85]

A CLASSICAL SCIENCE WORLDVIEW

There are many ways to approach this worldview. This book employs the term "scientific" to distinguish from "theological." It does not mean to imply that suddenly science sprang full-blown at a certain time or that theology simply died at the start of a move toward scientific method and outlook. The point being made is that science and its thought patterns became dominant and radically transformed the theological way of thinking.

A more personalistic designation used by T. F. Torrance was the "Newtonian" worldview.[86] Isaac Newton (1642-1727) was singled out for his observations and equations that quickly became the standards for science. This is a useful way of referring to the scientific orientation if Newton is understood to be symbolic of the larger movement. The Newtonian worldview was much broader than what Newton himself described. As Torrance noted, in a strict sense it was after Newton's lifetime that the rather rigid and deterministic outlook developed which was to characterize the manner of thought until the twentieth century.[87]

There are many other candidates for symbolic heads of the worldview in question. Nicolaus Copernicus has already been mentioned as a pivotal person in adoption of the heliocentric theory of the universe. Francis Bacon (1561-1626) was an early champion of inductive thought, and discussed four "idols" that contemporary persons used to block the path to clear, logical thinking.[88] John Locke (1632-1704) denied innate principles and understood experience to be the foundation of all learning.[89] Regardless of who is chosen to be the titular leader, the chief point is that science became the dominant influence for intellectual advance.

The qualifier "classical" is added to "science" to denote a particular, historical understanding of science. This adjective has several implications. First, it highlights the fact that a newer conception of science has been developed, necessitating the earlier approach to be termed "classic" in retrospect. Second, "classic" implies that which is foundational. The newer science does not dispose of the older but builds upon it and moves beyond it. Third, the designation of "classic" infers a traditional dimension. Many people (especially nonscientists) tend to identify science as reductionistic and mechanistic, but this is a traditional perspective of a science that is now historical: a "classic" description. Modern science is different from the traditional understanding, and when the older conception is the focus of discussion, it is here referred to as classical science.

Just as the religious worldview was discussed by way of descriptive terms, the scientific worldview is outlined by eight characteristics.

Mechanistic

Humans think in terms of analogy, and since the major force of this era was the machine, it should be no surprise that it was the image of the machine which was used to make sense of the world. The developments made by early scientists, particularly by Isaac Newton, allowed for a new description of the universe. Instead of the hierarchy of the purpose and levels of truth used in the theological worldview, the classical science worldview found structures of mass, force, and energy.[90] As Lewis B. Jennings said, the image which emerged of the universe was that of a "vast and harmonious machine."[91] It is clear that the *universe* did not change; the way that people perceived it was revolutionized. (It could be, of course, that in one sense that universe *did* change—if reality is simply what the observer/participant experiences.)

In a revolution, many things are swept along by the violence of change. The Industrial Revolution left little untouched. Theology did not escape unscathed. If the universe was a machine, then there needed to be a designer. Isaac Newton himself believed in a creator for the newly perceived world machine.[92] One of the most fascinating new machines was the clock. By analogy, if the universe is a clock, then there must be a "cosmic clockmaker" who built the clock, and wound it up.[93] This type of theological accommodation to the classical science worldview came to be called Deism:[94] God may have created the world and "wound it up," but he left it to run on its own. It did not need his intervention. It was self-contained and predetermined.

The mechanistic interpretation of the universe was exemplified in the theorizing of cosmology. Any machine could be fine tuned and perfected, and the universe was no exception. Using many of the same calculations as Claudius Ptolemy, Nicolaus Copernicus found that the answers were expressed more satisfactorily in a heliocentric pattern. Johann Kepler carried this work a step further by refining the theory to make the earth's orbit be elliptical rather than circular.[95] Galileo Galilei improved the equations of Kepler. Isaac Newton, by understanding gravity, was able to make Galileo's equations more elegant. This process of solving more and more problems went on for centuries, at least until Albert Einstein introduced relativity. For many years, there was little doubt that the entire universe would eventually be explained and described mathematically and physically, since it was only a rather complex but comprehensible machine.

The physics of classical science became the key to understanding. As Rupert Sheldrake wrote of this type of thinking: "The mechanistic theory postulates that all phenomena of life, including human behavior, can be explained in terms of physics."[96] The prevailing belief was that it was only a matter of time and research before the "mystery of life" was explained through calculations and natural causes.

Reductionistic

Inseparably linked to mechanistic thinking was reductionistic thinking. Russell Ackoff defined reductionism as "a doctrine that maintains that all objects and events, their properties, and our experience and knowledge of them are made up of ultimate elements, indivisible parts."[97] A natural result of viewing the universe as a machine was to assume that it was made up of parts like any other machine. These parts could be extracted, examined, analyzed, reproduced, and interchanged. Ultimately, there was a logical and experimental explanation to everything in the universe, including the universe itself. By knowing all the parts of the universe (or even some of them), it was believed that the universe was known.

Lawrence LeShan and Henry Margenau defined reductionism as "the practice of attempting to account for all the properties of highly complex systems in terms of their simplest components."[98] Ervin Laszlo called this an "atomistic" view.[99] In a real sense, the process of specialization, individualized research, and ever-increasing minutiae became classical science. To be scientific during this era was to isolate, manipulate, and analyze. The more specific the detail and the more clinical the approach, the more "scientific" the results were.

Reductionism used analytical thinking, which Russell Ackoff defined as "the mental process by which anything to be explained, hence understood, is broken down into its parts."[100] When this kind of process was carried over to problem-solving, then the way to "fix" anything was to work on the individual malfunctioning part.[101] It was not the entire system that needed attention, but the repair or replacement of a part. The broader context or environment was of no consequence. The problem was caused by the part: Change the part, and the problem was solved.

Disciplinary

Mechanistic, reductionistic thinking led to the disciplinary approach. Disciplines such as chemistry, physics, mathematics, and biology were developed to isolate and analyze different parts of the world-machine. Since the universe was made up of parts, then specialists were needed to understand the different kinds of parts. Chemists researched chemical parts, biologists researched the biological parts, and so it went. No cooperation between disciplines was attempted, because the disciplines were just as isolated and specific as the parts themselves were.

John Dillon described disciplinary thinking as it is sometimes still found in an educational setting. He wrote about the "fragmented view of the world" that the disciplines often portray:

> We teach the very young that the world is actually divided up into many parts. *History* is taught for an hour, and the bell rings. Then a new world of *science* is explored for another hour, to be followed by another bell and a completely different discipline. The sounding of that infernal bell signals students that they must pass from one fragment to another with little or no concern for integration. After some years of indoctrination, they begin to believe that the fragmented world is the real thing.[102]

This is the method of the disciplines. Each discipline goes after the parts in isolation, ignorant or uncaring of the larger context. How the disciplines fit together is unimportant, since the whole is a collection of parts. This collection Andras Angyal termed an "aggregate," as opposed to a system which emphasizes arrangement and relationship.[103]

Deterministic

Lawrence LeShan and Henry Margenau rightly said that classical science was built on the concept of cause and effect and that this linear kind of thinking enabled the postulation of a predictable—and deterministic—universe.[104] This was consistent with mechanistic and reductionistic patterns of thought. If the universe was machine-like, and the elements could be analyzed, then the chain of cause and effect could be detected. This was the basis of scientific experimentation: postulate a cause, manipulate the variables, and measure the effect. Fritjof Capra tied it all together this way:

> The mechanistic view of nature is thus closely related to a rigorous determinism, with the giant cosmic machine completely causal and determinate. All that happened had a definite cause and gave rise to a definite effect, and the future of any part of the system would . . . be predictable with absolute certainty if its state at any time was known in all details.[105]

Isaac Newton formulated three laws of motion, the third of which especially illustrated cause and effect: "To every action there is always opposed and equal reaction."[106] The first cause produced an effect, which in turn produced another cause. As Norbert Wiener said: "Newtonian physics . . . described a universe in which everything happened precisely according to law. . . in which the whole future depends strictly upon the whole past."[107] With cause and effect thinking, very little (actually nothing) can happen that is not expected. This kind of closed system has no surprises, no twists, and no miracles. It is no wonder that a deistic theology was devised to explain the cosmos.

Modern scientists have introduced time as a new variable element into equations. Time to Newton was invariant: "Absolute, true and mathematical time, of itself, and from its own nature, flows equably without relation to anything external, and by another name is called duration."[108] Ilya Prigogine said that this kind of time allowed the future to be determined by the present and formed the basis of classical physics.[109] Albert Einstein suggested the relativity of time but still accepted that time could be reversible. He said: "People like us, who believe in physics, know that the distinction between past, present, and future is only a stubbornly persistent illusion."[110] It was not until the work of Ilya Prigogine that time was described as not only variable, but irreversible. For classical physics, then, time was invariant and reversible.

Determinism in classical science, and hence the world, was a limiting but comforting concept. Although humans could do nothing to change things, neither could they do any great harm to the "cosmic clock." This idea was expressed well by Heinz Pagels:

> This rigid determinism implied by Newton's laws promoted a sense of security about the place of humanity in the universe. All that happens—the tragedy and joy of human life—is already predetermined. The objective universe exists independently of human will and purpose. Nothing we do can alter it.[111]

Static

One of the distinct carryovers from the theological worldview to the classical science worldview was the concept of a static universe. "Static" was not understood as lack of activity and movement but as lack of change and development. The Greek idea of the static universe[112] was unchanged by Isaac Newton. As Kenneth Boulding observed: "Newtonian dynamics is essentially the perception of stable patterns in the four-dimensional space-time continuum."[113]

Again it was Ilya Prigogine who injected the concept of time into the discussion. He designated Newtonian thermodynamics[114] as "being" in contrast to nonequilibrium thermodynamics as "becoming."[115] The difference was between the reversibility of Newtonian time and the irreversibility (time's arrow) of Prigoginian time. Prigogine wrote that "everything is given in classical physics: change is nothing but a denial of becoming and time is only a parameter, unaffected by the transformation that it describes."[116]

Entropic

The inclusion of thermodynamics in the preceding paragraph leads naturally to the laws of thermodynamics and the concept of entropy. Rudolf Clausius (1822-1888) restated the first two laws of Newtonian thermodynamics as cosmological formulations:

1. The energy in the universe remains constant, but energy can be transformed from one kind to another.
2. The entropy of the universe ever increases as the energy available for transformation decreases.[117]

The first law (on energy transformation) sets the stage for the second law (on entropy). If the first law is accepted, then the universe must be understood as a closed system, where energy is not gained, created, or discovered, only changed in form. A closed system has no input and no output; by definition, a closed universe has no environment. This is the ultimate "environment-free" system.[118]

The law describing entropy must follow from the law specifying the universe as a closed system. Entropy is the measure of *decrease* in the available energy for transformation.[119] As entropy *increases,* transformable heat energy *decreases.* The final goal of the universe in the classical science worldview was equilibrium: heat-death. In the analogy of the "cosmic clock" the clock must finally wind down and stop. In a truly closed system there is no other possibility but the ultimate dissolution of transformable energy resulting in utter chaos.

Dualistic

Kenneth Boulding said: "There are two kinds of people in the world—those who divide everything in the world into two kinds of things and those who don't."[120] In characteristic tongue-in-cheek style, Boulding was probably correct.

René Descartes (1590-1650) made a valiant attempt to develop a philosophical base that would correlate the traditional teachings of the theologians with the discoveries of the contemporary scientists.[121] Descartes did not desire either to receive the condemnation of the theologians (the fate of such scientists as Copernicus and Galileo) or to ignore the growing conflict he observed between theology and science. Descartes' formulation, called the Cartesian duality, was a philosophical attempt at a resolution to the conflict.

Descartes embraced an ontic dualism of mind and body. The mind was separate from the body, immaterial, inhabiting and controlling the body.[122] The body was made of matter, and followed the physical laws of mechanics.[123] By sharply dividing up the person, theology was given one part and science was given another. Never did the two have to meet, since each was separate and distinct.

Although it is not accurate to say that classical science fully adopted Descartes' formulation, it is fair to say that pragmatically the results were Cartesian. Theology stayed with the "mind": the soul, ethics, and metaphysics. Scientists became agnostic, simply saying that their province was experiential phenomena and that the subject of metaphysics was beyond their boundary. In effect, classical science tended to deny one half of the duality, in the sense of dismissing such concepts as the mind and the supernatural. The classical scientists began to regard as real only that which was within the "touch and see" range of objectivity and experimentation.

Positivistic

While it was Auguste Comte (1798-1857) who gave full expression to positivism, all of the classical science worldview was positivistic. From this perspective, it was science, and science alone, that came to be the sole and final arbiter of truth.[124] To illustrate this point, Paul Abrecht recounted an exchange between Pierre

Simon de LaPlace (an astronomer and mathematician) and Napoleon Bonaparte (emperor of France). LaPlace was in the midst of giving the emperor a "scientific" explanation of the universe when Napoleon stopped him to ask where God fit into the scientific theory. LaPlace supposedly replied: "Sire, I have no need of that hypothesis."[125]

The old attitude of the theological worldview that devalued experience was rejected by the classical science worldview. For example, Isaac Newton formulated four Rules of Reasoning in Philosophy, the fourth of which was:

> In experimental philosophy we are to look upon propositions inferred by general induction from phenomena as accurately or very nearly true, notwithstanding any contrary hypotheses that may be imagined, till such time as other phenomena occur, by which they may either be made more accurate, or liable to exceptions.[126]

Truth was to be measured by experimental evidence and not logical deductions from general principles. The search was on for objectivity.

Vitalists[127] tried to use the Cartesian duality to explain purpose. They postulated a "deus ex machina": the ghost in the machine. Classical science attacked such an idea as "unscientific."[128] It could not be experimentally verified. Such traditional science preferred what it could see and touch. For this reason the classical science worldview became increasingly concerned with materialism as the only reality which could be subjected to testing.

Summary

The classical science worldview was mechanistic in analogy, reductionistic in method, disciplinary in research, deterministic in outlook, static in perception, entropic in direction, dualistic in practice, and positivistic in determination of truth. Fritjof Capra summarized it with the following values:

> Belief in the scientific method as the only valid approach to knowledge; the view of the universe as a mechanical system composed of elementary material building blocks . . . and the belief in unlimited

material progress to be achieved through economic and technological growth.[129]

A SYSTEMIC WORLDVIEW

Worldviews do change, but only slowly, painfully, and extremely infrequently. They are changed through revolution, and violence is always associated in some way with revolutions, whether it is physical, emotional, intellectual, or spiritual. This book suggests that such a revolution and change of worldview is currently underway. The task of this section is to provide evidence of the revolution and to sketch the first outlines of the features of this worldview.

The emerging worldview is labeled "systemic." This term was first invoked in chapter 1, where it was described[130] as dealing with holistic interrelatedness and interdependence. That may be somewhat cryptic, but not intentionally so. The systemic concept, and hence a systemic worldview, is by definition inclusive, dynamic, and emergent. If that is troublesome, it is because the viewer is trying to peer into a new world through the lenses of a "classical science" or possibly a "theological" worldview. The dilemma is readily apparent: How does one describe a new worldview to an older worldview? The old "scientific method" of isolation and analysis contradicts the holistic principle. The result is that the following pages need to be taken as a gestalt. The entire description will reveal what a systemic worldview is; indeed, the remainder of the book is an attempt to articulate some of all that "systemic" implies.

It has surely been noted by now that both the theological and the classical science worldviews were regarded as historical and described in the past tense. That is more a matter of convenience than of reality. The outlook of classical science is still quite prevalent and often assumed to be descriptive of reality (by nonscientists, chiefly). In addition, at least major elements of the theological worldview are still accepted by some. All of this is acknowledged and is fundamental to understanding the systemic worldview. The systemic concept does not ignore or denigrate the approaches of the past, but subsumes and transcends them. The systemic worldview builds upon, yet transforms, the past.

The systemic worldview is still in the formative stage and is by no means completely developed. Lawrence LeShan and Henry Margenau said that the systemic worldview is under development in a number of interrelated disciplines.[131] Fritjof Capra expressed it well when he wrote: "Out of the revolutionary changes in our concepts of reality . . . a consistent worldview is now emerging."[132]

There is no desire to make the systemic worldview an "it"; the point is that the discussion is about an approach, an orientation, a way of viewing the world. Paul Abrecht rightly said that most modern scientists are presently hesitant to subscribe to one view of anything.[133] This reveals one of the basic but confusing elements of the systemic worldview. There really is no such thing. No two people will agree on *the* systemic worldview. That phrase is only a convenience of language for this writing. As Kenneth Boulding wrote: "All images of the universe must be accepted as imperfect and subject to constant revision."[134]

Some may question why a new perspective is needed. In a real sense, there is no other option. The outmoded theological approach and the classical science approach neither address current needs adequately nor assimilate contemporary knowledge about the world situation. The problems facing the world are simply insoluble within the structures of the previous worldviews. This is not to say that the systemic worldview is infallible, but that other attempts have passed their usefulness. It has been said: "Quantification, determinism, the attempt to build mechanical models, all failed in spite of serious and long-continuing effort."[135] Something new must be devised. It is that "something new" which the systemic worldview is trying to create.

The remaining portions of this chapter attempt only to approximate the emerging systemic worldview. The first task is to look at some of the sources and roots of the development of the new worldview.

SOURCES OF A SYSTEMIC WORLDVIEW

An approach so broad and inclusive as a systemic worldview naturally has innumerable contributors. While there is no possibility of giving a comprehensive list, it is descriptive to recall a few major thinkers who have had lasting influence on the effort to find a new way. Five are singled out for recognition here.

Albert Einstein

One of the most fascinating and influential people of this century was Albert Einstein. He was a figure many regard as important to the world as Copernicus, Galileo, and Newton. He was curious, though, because even he had philosophical difficulties with the ramifications of his theories of relativity. A man born into a world of classical science, he was unable (or unwilling) to give up some of his more traditional beliefs.

Einstein is probably best understood as a transitional personage, opening the door from the classical science worldview into the systemic worldview.[136] He himself did not step through, but allowed others to come in. His friend and contemporary Max Born described Einstein's ambivalence to traditional approaches:

> The special theory of relativity of 1905 can be justifiably considered the end of the classical period or the beginning of a new era. For it uses the well-established classical ideas of matter . . . and of deterministic laws of nature. But it introduces revolutionary notions of space and time, resolutely criticizing the traditional concepts as formulated by Newton. Thus it opens a new way of thinking about natural phenomena.[137]

T. F. Torrance preferred to designate the new worldview "Einsteinian" since it was Einstein's theories that provided the change to a new way of thinking.[138] Heinz Pagels disagreed, bluntly saying that Einstein's theories were "the fulfillment of the classical, deterministic worldview."[139] Einstein left the issue unclear. He merely said of his theories of relativity: "This view is not in harmony with the theory of Newton."[140] Anatol Rapoport may have captured it best when he recounted Einstein's pilgrimage by saying: "And finally the story culminates in the ominous equation $E=mc^2$, which shook the world."[141] The world after Einstein was never the same—it never stopped shaking—and one of the first to realize this was Alfred North Whitehead.

Alfred North Whitehead

Alfred North Whitehead was a mathematician, scientist, and philosopher contemporary with Einstein. The story was told of how secure he felt in his Newtonian frame of mind until the work of Einstein. He said: "By the middle of the 1890s there were a few tremors . . . of all not being quite secure, but no one sensed what was coming. By 1900 the Newtonian physics were demolished, done for!"[142] He admitted the profound effect that this had on him and for his own study. He was aware that a whole new way of thinking was needed.

Whitehead formally notified the scientific community of its problems in *Science and the Modern World*.[143] In an astounding sweep of history, he traced the development of science from the Middle Ages to his own days of the mid-1920s. His point was that science and history were at a crucial time of reorganization. He wrote: "The progress of science has now reached a turning point. The stable foundations of physics have broken up. . . . The old foundations of scientific thought are becoming unintelligible."[144]

Whitehead's attempt at solving these problems came in the monumental *Process and Reality*.[145] In this book he developed what he called a "philosophy of organism," which had direct influence on what is now known as systems theory. This relation is explored in more detail elsewhere,[146] but it is important to see that Whitehead understood the implications of Einstein's theories and immediately began an attempt to revise the patterns of thought.

Ludwig von Bertalanffy

Another source of a systemic worldview came through the work of the biologist Ludwig von Bertalanffy. He did his investigations independently of Einstein's physics and Whitehead's philosophy but paralleled their paths. Bertalanffy said that it was in the early 1920s that he found "obvious lacunae in the research and theory of biology."[147] His own research gave evidence that could not be explained by the mechanistic, reductionistic approach to biology. It was Bertalanffy who theorized about "open systems" and who first developed an organismic understanding in biology.[148]

Bertalanffy expanded his biological theory into a general theory. He observed the similarity of his biological findings with other fields, and a "general system theory" began to evolve.[149] As with Whitehead's theory, so much more could and has been said regarding Bertalanffy's development, but the point is that the old mechanistic formulas did not correspond to the data. Bertalanffy was forced to find a more complete and acceptable explanation.

Pierre Teilhard de Chardin

It would seem that there would be virtually no ground common between a Roman Catholic priest and a paleontologist. Pierre Teilhard de Chardin was both. It was his special genius and gift to reconcile and to make productive what otherwise would seem like an extreme tension between the calling of a priest and the vocation of a paleontologist. In order to accomplish this synthesis, Teilhard was forced to develop a new approach to reality. Though essentially unknown during his lifetime because of censorship, Teilhard and his posthumous publications have spawned an explosion of activity in searching for a viable synthesis of religion, science, and philosophy.

Teilhard developed an organismic and holistic vision. In the foreword to his most influential work, *The Phenomenon of Man*, he wrote:

> The time has come to realize that an interpretation of the universe . . . remains unsatisfying unless it covers the interior as well as the exterior of things; mind as well as matter. The true physics is that which will, one day, achieve the inclusion of [humanity] in [its] wholeness in a coherent picture of the world.[150]

The entire scope of Teilhard's thinking is impossible and unnecessary to explain here. The important factor is awareness that here was yet another great personage who saw the need for an organismic understanding of the world and who gave his life to one particular expression of it. The outmoded accounts of a dualistic, mechanistic universe could no longer be used to explain what Teilhard experienced.

Ilya Prigogine

One person who continues to influence and to develop a systemic worldview is Ilya Prigogine. His particular field of investigation is nonequilibrium thermodynamics,[151] with a focus toward the theory of dissipative structures[152] that develop within that environment. His contributions are being recognized, as evidenced by his 1977 Nobel prize in chemistry. *From Being to Becoming*[153] was his effort to show the relationship of his scientific research to the philosophical issues implied by the research. As John Dillon observed, Ilya Prigogine's findings have begun to suggest (demand?) an entirely new and often startling worldview.[154]

Prigogine has focused his investigations on the concept of time.[155] Since he has dealt with thermodynamics, he obviously was aware of the process of change that takes place through time. Time is the only way to measure change. Yet Prigogine's point is not merely the passing of time, but its irreversibility. Time for Newton, and for Einstein, did not need to be directional, so that the ideas of past, present, and future were essentially meaningless.[156] That concept of time Prigogine called "being," to be employed only in the simplest situations.[157] The physics of "becoming" apply to the more complex processes of reality. Irreversibility in time takes over where the work of classical and quantum mechanics must end;[158] or, as Prigogine said: "The concept of time is much more complex than we thought."[159]

This has been quite complicated and revolutionary for contemporary scientists to accept. Not everyone has accepted it: "The jury is still out, and the case will continue to be heard for years to come."[160] The value of Ilya Prigogine's work to this book is in the evidence presented that a static, deterministic, and entropic universe cannot be the whole story. Another explanation—another worldview—must be developed to incorporate his data. This worldview has not yet been created, but it is "becoming."

Conclusion

These five representatives give an indication of the diversity of sources for a new worldview as well as the complexity of the problem. A systemic worldview cannot be developed by one person or by one discipline. The need is a transdisciplinary one, and the creation of the worldview must be done from a transdisciplinary perspective. In full recognition of the difficulties and the ambiguities of what a systemic worldview should include, the following section is an attempt to outline some of the basic characteristics that appear necessary in a systemic worldview.

CHARACTERISTICS OF A SYSTEMIC WORLDVIEW

As there are multitudes of sources for the systemic worldview, so there are multitudes of characteristics describing it. Eight are discussed below. These characteristics are the most fundamental and descriptive. Other divisions and possibilities could be included, but these were selected for their comprehensiveness as well as for their contrast with the classical science worldview. Since each of the characteristics is distinguished from the eight descriptions of the classical science worldview, both the close relationship and the extreme differences of the two worldviews can be easily discerned.

Organismic

The key term for the classical science worldview was "mechanistic," which meant that the main image for interpreting reality was the machine. All of the other characteristics of the classical science worldview make sense when this image is kept to the fore. The same clarity is possible for the systemic worldview: The key term is "organismic," and the image is that of an organism.

It is important to recognize that the concept of organism is an analogy. While it is true that some scientists begin to see the universe not just functioning *like* an organism but that it *is* an organism,[161] the best approach is to keep within the limits of a metaphor. Organismic thinking relies on analogy to simplify and explain certain phenomena,[162] but the simile can be overdrawn and abused to the point of absurdity.

Norbert Wiener, the father of the study of cybernetics, gave a good perspective on the use of the organismic analogy. His explanation was that the organism could be understood as a message, or a pattern, in opposition to chaos, disintegration, and noise.[163] The emphasis remains on relationships and interface in an organism, rather than strictly on the content itself.

Ervin Laszlo carried this thought a step further. He stated that all organisms are actually composed of similar substances: atoms and molecules of carbon, hydrogen, nitrogen, and so on. The difference in organisms is "not primarily a difference in substance but in the relational structuring of the substance."[164] Laszlo has pointed out the ultimate meaninglessness of reductionism when it reduces everything to the basic building components. Meaning is not found in the material, but in the interrelationships.[165]

Fred Hoyle in 1948 was using the metaphor of organism when he made his now-famous statement: "Once a photograph of the earth, taken from outside, is available—once the sheer isolation of the earth becomes plain—a new idea as powerful as any in history will be let loose."[166] His point was that when the earth is seen as an organism a new "worldview" is demanded. Michael Collins (an astronaut on the first manned lunar landing mission) felt the same necessity when he recalled his thoughts at seeing the earth from 100,000 miles. His way of expressing Hoyle's comment also recognized the unity of the earth: "The earth *must* become as it appears: blue and white, not capitalist or communist; blue and white, not rich or poor; blue and white, not envious or envied."[167] Both Hoyle and Collins were saying that the view of the world does make a difference. The systemic worldview uses the image of the organism, then, to emphasize the systemic relationships and operational integration of not only the physical world but of all reality.

The concept of the machine is not entirely discarded but is drastically modified. John Sutherland's choice of terms was "organic machine." In his jargon, an organic machine is an example of "a continuous-state, fully differentiated system, one with the least rigidity, with the fewest structural constraints, and with the widest conceivable repertoire of behavioral states."[168] A more common term for the "organic machine" is "open system." As Ludwig von Bertalanffy said: "The organism is not a closed, but an open system. We term a system 'closed' if no material enters or leaves it; it is called 'open' if there is import and export of material."[169]

To say that an organism is an open system because it imports and exports material, though, is not enough. The same could be said of any functioning machine. The difference, as Bertalanffy went on to say, is the principle of organismic growth.[170] An open system draws from the environment, transforms, and exports to the environment with the additional concept of homeostasis: the organism regulates the flow and is able to grow during the process. An organism, in the midst of transformation of the import, is able to transform *itself*. The basic identity of an organism may remain[171] but with an increase in complexity and permutation of its parts during the process.[172]

Fritjof Capra summed up the difference between machines and organisms by observing that machines are constructed and organisms grow.[173] A machine does not change through its operation, except to deteriorate gradually (as described by the Second Law of Thermodynamics). An organism is able to change, develop, and store up energy for future use. Capra said: "Whereas the activities of a machine are determined by its structure, the relation is reversed in organisms—organic structure is determined by processes."[174]

A more detailed explanation of the dynamic open system and the all-important process of homeostasis was taken up in the previous chapter. The point here is to emphasize that the image of the systemic worldview is not that of a simple machine, but of an organism as an open system. This image allows major modification of the entire classical science worldview, which the remainder of the characteristics are designed to explain more fully.

Relational

The path of the classical science worldview is reductionism and analysis: to find out more and more about less and less. While this approach has given society a lot of good information, it has also provided much information that is essentially meaningless and useless. For example, what value is there in "knowing" every minute detail about (for example) a carburetor separate from its function in the overall design of the automobile? In fact, there is no meaning for such a thing as a carburetor until it is in some way related to an automobile. Parts only have meaning when seen in relation to the whole. The systemic worldview, while appreciating the work of reductionism, is also aware of the limits of analysis. The systemic worldview attempts to see the analyzed part as it relates to the larger context and to give the part meaning in its environment.

The concept of context and relationship was the intention of Gregory Bateson when he discussed the failure of grammarians.[175] Grammar is not just the study of words in isolation but is also about how words relate to one another. Bateson wrote: "It is the context that fixes the meaning."[176] Bateson's interest was not just in grammar. He was addressing the epistemological question of "How do you know?" He said we know through relationship and context.

Kenneth Boulding talked of the "myth" of the environment in his discussion of relationalism. He pointed out that in reality all things are in interaction and that strict divisions (boundaries) are impossible. If in the totality of the universe all things are in interrelation, "everything is the environment of something else."[177] Such a thing as an "environment" then cannot exist if this is to mean a "surrounding system that is independent of what goes on inside it."[178] The universe is a unified system of interactive and interrelated parts. Russell Ackoff made a similar point when he said: "In systems thinking every purposeful system is considered to have an environment and to be a part of one or more larger (supra) systems."[179]

Relationalism has its progenitor in Albert Einstein. His theories of relativity demonstrated the impossibility of excluding the observer from the observation. Jacob Bronowski emphasized this when he wrote:

> If we are to begin at the beginning, we must grasp that we are all part of the world we observe. We cannot divide the world into ourselves on one part of the screen as spectators and everything else as a spectacle on the other side, which we remotely observe.[180]

Ilya Prigogine also noted the role of the observer in current thinking, and believed that "whatever the future developments, this role is essential."[181]

The failure to take into consideration the factor of observer participation was characteristic of the classical science worldview. Anatol Rapoport termed this failure "absolutism."[182] The systemic worldview corrects the problem and is relational. "Facts" are no longer taken as absolutes but are seen as interpretations of data by the observer.

Pluralistic

The classical science approach has held sway for so long that to propose another way appears foolish. Nothing is more heretical than to oppose the disciplines of academia. Systemic thinking does not oppose disciplinary thinking. It only insists that the disciplines be recognized as artificial human constructs: "The universe is really *not* built that way. The physics, chemistry, biology, psychology, sociology, etc., are really all muddled up in the *real world*."[183] Kenneth Boulding observed that the taxonomies of education tell us more about the human brain than about the actual universe they try to describe.[184]

Pluralism is the term employed here to indicate that the disciplines do have value up to a point but that no one description of anything is entirely adequate. John Dillon preferred the term "metadisciplinary" which he defined as those situations where "the parts come together in cooperative and interactive ways so that the total is greater than the sum of the properties of the parts."[185] Russell Ackoff proposed "interdisciplinary." [186] This book has suggested "transdisciplinary." Whatever the term, the effort is to rise above, but not to discard, the ways of classical science, while dissolving its rigidity and exclusivism.

For all of his varied work, Niels Bohr will probably be best remembered for his introduction of the idea of complementarity. As a physicist, he found that what he saw was often determined by what he was looking for. In his study of quantum mechanics he could describe what he had found only in pairs of seeming opposites. He could describe the atomic activity neither as a wave motion nor as a static particle; it had to be understood as *both* at the same time.[187] These complementary pictures, when combined, gave a better and more accurate description. This is but another example of the characteristic of pluralism within the systemic worldview: one description is misleading; two may be inadequate; reality is pluralistic.

There is a temptation to think of pluralism and complementarity as only a Hegelian synthesis. Such is not the case. The goal of systemic thinking is not a synthesis of the thesis and antithesis. The goal is to see all of the aspects at the same time. Erich Jantsch called this activity "process thinking" and spoke of it this way:

> Process thinking does not know any sharp separation between opposite aspects of reality. It also transcends a dialectic synthesis of opposites, that clumsy Western attempt at making a rigid structure of notions move and overcome its dualism. In process thinking there is only *complementarity* in which the opposites include each other.[188]

Pluralism is held together by its pursuit of a common goal. The quest for "truth" by the different disciplines may be quite similar, yet a multitude of different paths is employed. Hans Morgenthau said that such ostensibly unrelated activities as science, philosophy, and religion are only different attempts to find final answers to the same basic questions: "Starting from the same point of departure, they move on different roads toward the same goal."[189] This idea of movement and commonality will be found in various other characteristics. In pluralism, the main point is that there is no one full and final viewpoint; reality comes from a convergence of different starting points and paths.

Stochastic

One of the fundamental aspects of the classical science worldview was determinism. Since determinism means that the future is entirely determined by the past, there was great comfort and security in that way of thinking for humans. There were no true surprises, no sharp corners for history to turn. Heinz Pagels pointed out that classical physics gave support to this characteristic of the classical science worldview and that it was a reflection of the "human need for certainty."[190] While the human need (or at least the desire) for certainty may remain, determinism and classical physics do not. Quantum physics, and its various successors, have closed the door on a logical and closed future.

One of the most exciting—and for some one of the most threatening—aspects of the systemic worldview is the inclusion of randomness. When a random variable is injected into history, the result is that the future is no longer necessarily determined; the future cannot, in any case, be projected and infallibly predicted by events in that past. Ilya Prigogine was prompted to make the following revolutionary statement: "There are no limits to structural stability. Every system may present instabilities when suitable perturbations are introduced. Therefore, there can be no end to history."[191]

The term "stochastic" has been selected to describe the development of a system through time with the possibility (probability) of random components. Gregory Bateson defined the stochastic situation as a sequence of events that combine a random element within a selective process so that only certain of the random outcomes are possible.[192] John Sutherland's definition of the term was "that the relationship between input and outputs will alter in effectively unpredictable (and unallegorizable) ways through some interval."[193] However it is phrased, the key is randomness, which means that there is no absolute method of predicting the next event from the preceding events. The only way to "predict" is to rely on the regularity of probability.[194]

While the detailed work of stochastic process, especially in Ilya Prigogine's work, is beyond the scope of this book, it is essential to see that stochasticity is prominent in the systemic worldview. Prigogine summarized well when he said: "The increased limitation of deterministic laws means that we go from a universe that is closed, in which all is given, to a new one that is open to fluctuations, to innovations."[195]

Dynamic

From the philosophy of the Greeks through the classical science worldview the static concept of the universe remained constant. Movement and change were the exceptions and deviations from the norm. In the systemic worldview, just the opposite is true. Nothing is at rest. Change and dynamism are irresistible, unstoppable, and ubiquitous.

This continual movement and evolution through irreversible time makes systemic thinking difficult. Fritjof Capra was right when he identified systemic thinking with process thinking, saying that "form becomes associated with process, interrelation with interaction, and opposites are unified through oscillation."[196] Process thinking must often deal with the system in terms of structural analysis. This means that for purposes of study the system may be treated as if it were static, or as John Sutherland said, "we take a 'snapshot' of the system at some specific point in time (or space)."[197] Never is this "snapshot" taken as reality or the structure as determined. These are merely devices for analysis and comprehension. There seems to be no better way (presently) for humans to study the components of the dynamic process except to "stop" the process artificially and momentarily.

What appears in the freeze-frame of structural analysis is a pattern. Norbert Wiener wrote: "We are but whirlpools in a river of everflowing water. We are not stuff that abides, but patterns that perpetuate themselves."[198] Gregory Bateson gave music as an example of a dynamic pattern:[199] It "is not" unless it *is* in process. Notes printed on a page are not music. They merely comprise the pattern. The performance of the music produces the reality.

The concept of homeostasis, or of stability through time, is related to dynamism. Without some historical relation of past, present, and future there could only be chaos. The future may be different from the past, but it is always built upon the past.[200] There is a trace of continuity discernible through the process of change.

Another issue of interest is that of boundary. Gerald Weinberg helped significantly in this regard when he identified "boundary" as that which connects, rather than separates. He introduced the term "interface" to emphasize this: " 'Interface' is a more useful word than 'boundary,' for it reminds us to pay attention to the connection, and not just the separation, between system and environment."[201] Systemic (process) thinking focuses less on content and more on the interrelationships of the system. These interfaces can only be present through dynamism.

Again Ilya Prigogine can be cited for a summary statement. The systemic perspective, and hence the systemic worldview, is concerned with process, pattern, and dynamism. The classical science worldview dealt with "being"; the systemic worldview deals with "becoming."[202]

Negentropic

Entropy is the increase of chaos and disintegration. According to the laws of thermodynamics, this is the ultimate fate of the universe—if the universe is a closed system. The classical science worldview assumed the universe to be closed by definition. The systemic worldview suggests another possibility.

Negentropy is increase in order and complexity.[203] On at least a localized scale, an open system demonstrates importation from the environment, transformation, exportation back into the environment, with the *result* of complexity of structure and/or function.[204] Every human baby born is an example of this (at least temporary) denial of the laws of thermodynamics. Eventually entropy overtakes negentropy, and death (or at least some form of transformation) results, but the important point is that negentropy does occur. This simple fact illustrates that the universe is not necessarily the closed system that the classical science of earlier days assumed it to be.

The concept of negentropy is a centerpiece to systems theory and to a systemic worldview. The point at this juncture is realization that the systemic worldview need not accept death as the inevitable fate of the universe. If the universe is not closed, then (to whatever degree) it must be open. In an open universe, only the past is fixed. The future has yet to be developed; or as Ilya Prigogine said, there may not be an "end" to history.[205]

Holistic

The classical science worldview was dualistic, ontically separating body and soul, mind and nature, science and theology. There were different ways of relating these two polarities, but they remained separate (but not necessarily equal). The systemic approach is holistic. To say that it is monistic would be misleading, since that is actually a reflection of a dualistic, categorical type of thinking. Systemic thinking transcends the categories of monism and dualism.

Fritjof Capra was a student of Gregory Bateson, and Capra attacked the problem of dualism in a manner reminiscent of Bateson: by rejecting an absolute and ontic Cartesian division between mind and matter. The attempt to approach reality holistically was expressed by Capra this way:

From the systems point of view, life is not a substance or a force, and mind is not an entity interacting with matter. Both life and mind are manifestations of the same set of systemic properties, a set of processes that represent the dynamics of self-organization. ... Mind and matter no longer appear to belong to two fundamentally separate categories, as Descartes believed, but can be seen to represent merely different aspects of the same universal process.[206]

Systemic perception is an effort to see indivisible, functional wholes whose properties are intact only when seen in context and relationship.[207]

Classical science tended to investigate problems from an isolationistic approach. Ilya Prigogine, representing the new science, said: "The answer can only be that we start at a macroscopic level, and all the results of our measurements, even those of the microscopic world, at some point refer back to the macroscopic level."[208] His reference to the microscopic level is representative of the attitude of systemic thinkers to classical science. The work of classical science is not regarded as totally useless or misguided but as needing a context for the fuller revelation of meaning. The systemic worldview seeks a perspective that makes the results of analysis and reductionism come together. As Ervin Laszlo wrote: "Instead of looking at one thing at a time, and noting its behavior when exposed to one other thing, science now looks at a number of different and interacting things and notes their behavior *as a whole* under diverse influences."[209]

Holism is movement toward integration. The search for differentiation alone has gone far enough. It is time to search for what Gregory Bateson called "the sacred unity of the biosphere."[210]

Cybernetic

The classical science worldview was positivistic: The future was determined by the laws of nature and, since nature was the sole province of science, science was the final arbiter of truth. The systemic worldview, though greatly influenced by science, is not positivistic. The future is not determined by "laws" of nature; nature is not the sole province of science; and truth is much larger than science can contain.

The systemic worldview turns to cybernetics for help in teleology and purpose. The term "cybernetics" was developed by Norbert Wiener from the Greek word for "helmsman," or "steersman,"[211] so that "cybernetics" is the study of guidance and control from *within* the system. As Fritjof Capra wrote: "A living organism is a self-organizing system, which means that its order in structure and function is not imposed by the environment but is established by the system itself."[212]

Cybernetic teleology, then, is a process of feedback and movement that is determined by the monitoring of the system itself. Teleology that was described by the vitalists or by the determinists of past worldviews is redefined in terms of internal guidance and cybernetics. Ervin Laszlo expressed the concept in relation to overall evolution this way:

> We cannot see how evolution could fail to push toward order and integration, complexity and individuation, whatever forms it may choose for realization. Thus there is a plan, but it is not a preestablished one. It sets forth the guidelines and lets chance play the role of selector of alternative pathways for its realization. There is purpose without slavery and freedom without anarchy.[213]

Teleology is a large part of the systemic worldview but in a completely different formulation from previous understandings.

A self-determined future means that absolute prediction is impossible, and classical science was built on prediction. The whole scientific method of hypothesis and experimentation was developed for prediction. As science came closer and closer to accurate prediction, it appeared that science was getting closer and closer to absolute truth. With the introduction of randomness, self-organization, and cybernetics, the old paths toward certainty became hopeless wanderings.

Can there be no guide then? Certainly there must be. The study of heuristics is the way the systemic worldview deals with movement and progress. The future is seen in terms of opportunities to explore and problems to solve. Russell Ackoff said: "The future depends greatly on what problems we decide to work on and how well we use Systems Age technology to solve them."[214] The heuristic process is neither simple nor infallible, but it does provide some options for survival. Russell Ackoff continued by showing the importance of the proper approach when he said:

"The problems we select for solution and the way we formulate them depends more on our philosophy and worldview than on our science and technology."[215]

The future is open, and while that allows freedom it also includes threat. History may continue, as Ilya Prigogine said, but humans do not have to be a part of it. The systemic worldview is more than a way of thinking; it is a quest for survival. Norbert Wiener put the entire situation in clear perspective:

> Thus the new industrial revolution is a two-edged sword. It may be used for the benefit of humanity but only if humanity survives long enough to enter a period in which such a benefit is possible. It may also be used to destroy humanity, and if it is not used intelligently, it can go very far in that direction.[216]

Summary

The systemic worldview is emerging as organismic in image, relational in approach, pluralistic in understanding, stochastic in progress, dynamic in relationship, negentropic in development, holistic in nature, and cybernetic in direction. Whether this worldview continues to develop or not depends upon the seriousness that the present generation gives to the solution of the world's problems.

CONTRASTS TO A SYSTEMIC WORLDVIEW

It seems most useful to give a brief accounting of what a systemic worldview is *not*. Such a review of contrasts is neither comprehensive nor exhaustive but illustrative of the aims of a systemic worldview. While each of the following is in some way related to the systemic perspective, none of them is the totality or even the preeminent consideration.

General Systems Theory

Probably the easiest point of confusion, and the most common, is the identification of General Systems Theory with the systemic worldview. There is an intimate correlation, but they are not identical.

General Systems Theory has provided the paradigm to which the systemic worldview is related. General Systems Theory is developing a set of theoretical principles, with specialties and methodologies peculiar to that work. A systemic worldview is a perspective, a gestalt, an approach to reality. The "theory" is a window to the broader orientation.

Chapter 2 was devoted to an explanation of open systems and to the development of a systemic paradigm. Suffice it to say here that the issue is not an easy one and all are not in agreement. Ludwig von Bertalanffy himself, in a preface to his masterpiece, talked of systems theory as a paradigm, a "new science," a discipline, and as a new way of thinking.[217] If the founder of General Systems Theory was so ambiguous, it is obvious that the issue is problematic. One of the functions of this book is to help clear up some of the confusion that clouds the paradigm and the worldview.

Scientific Imperialism

A most serious accusation put to the systemic worldview, and to systems theory in particular (the confusion compounds), is that of scientific imperialism. The leader of this charge is Robert Lilienfeld, who said that the systemic perspective is merely an extension of Plato's concept of "philosopher-kings" who rule society, with the difference that systems researchers are becoming "scientist-kings."[218] Lilienfeld's evaluation of the approach was not complimentary, describing systems theory as idealistic, utopian, impractical, and more magical than serious research.[219] His evaluation of the researchers was just as condemnatory, saying that "they suffer the relatively innocent delusions of [persons] who do not know their limits, but who have as yet been unable to escape the limits that are part of their historical and empirical situation."[220]

Lilienfeld and his colleagues have simply misunderstood the systemic approach and systems theory. The entire movement is an attempt to shed the positivistic trappings of classical science and to find a complementarity of science with other disciplines. What Lilienfeld has accused the systemic perspective of perpetrating is precisely what it is trying to solve.

Theological Imperialism

Scientific imperialism was the threat of the classical science worldview. Theological imperialism was the threat of the theological worldview. To allow either approach to be dominant is to repeat the mistakes of the past.

The systemic perspective is unashamedly pluralistic. In the global village of the modern day, there is no viable alternative. Science in past generations has tended to exclude theology in particular and religion in general as intangible and as less than real. The new science, while not wishing to retreat to the mystification of the Dark Ages, recognizes that reality need not be only that which can be tested in a laboratory.

This opening door to the religious orientations must not be abused by any party. Some modesty and humility must come from all sides. T. F. Torrance said: "It is now possible for theology to engage in constructive dialogue with natural science, not only for its own good, but for the good of science also."[221]

The permeable boundaries of modern science must find interface with permeable boundaries in theology and religion. Many theologians of the past (and present) have been so unconscionably authoritarian, dogmatic, and rigid (threatened?) that any light shining outside their disciplines was more often blinding than illuminating. If theologians expect to have any positive impact on their environment, they must be prepared for reciprocal change. Authentic interaction and interchange leave no element untouched and unaffected. The alternative is to become a closed system, with its inevitable result of irrelevance, impotence, and extinction.

Summary

The systemic worldview is not to be identified with systems theory, classical science, or rigid theology. Some of these are related, but certainly no one of them is the entire reality. In true systemic fashion, the systemic worldview beginning to take shape forms a composite of many different contributions, creating an emergent and developmental image of reality.

NEED FOR A SYSTEMIC WORLDVIEW

At the close of this chapter on the "dynamics of change," it seems appropriate to address one last, lingering question: Why bother? So there are a variety of opinions that differ; so there are data that do not fit classical formulas; so theology and science often clash. Does it *really* matter, or is all of this just an academic exercise in the construction of cognitive fantasy?

It matters if the future matters. One who struggled with this issue was Pierre Teilhard de Chardin. His maturation in concern for the future was described by Bernard Towers:

> He became increasingly conscious that the patterns displayed throughout the course of evolutionary history are of the greatest insignificance if we are to appreciate what paths might be open to [humankind] in the future. The future of [humanity] is a popular subject these days. . . . For some it represents a nice academic exercise. For Teilhard it was more than this.[222]

For Teilhard, the future course of humanity was a matter to which he devoted his life. He represents at least one individual who believed the future was worth a valuable investment.

The truth is that a vision of the future *must* become the concern of more than a few individuals. It must become a global concern—truly a systemic challenge. The reductionistic approach, dominant for so long, has brought the possibility if not the inevitability of the destruction of the biosphere. The systemic worldview is an effort to regain (or create) a sense of holism and interdependence. Jonathan Schell expressed the need for commitment this way:

> With the generation that has never known a world unmenaced by nuclear weapons, a new order of the generations begins. In it, each person alive is called on to assume his [or her] share of the responsibility for guaranteeing the existence of all future generations.[223]

The need for a systemic worldview may have been a long time in developing, but never was that need made more apparent and obligatory than on August 6, 1945. There the reductionistic approach of splitting to an ever smaller element reached its ultimate end and created a "worldview" that humans had never before experienced: that of a world literally coming apart at the seams.[224] In a real sense, compliments of the charred ruins of Hiroshima, a "ruined" worldview dawned on the consciousness of humanity.[225]

The need is no longer how to be more reductionistic: This can now be done with incomprehensible effect. The present need is not how to take things apart but rather how to put it all back together again. The attempt to find a way to bind the world together is not just a desirable option; it is a question of the survival of the planet.[226]

If there is to be an emergent and transformational worldview, what can be done to actualize it? One of the ways to bring about a systemic worldview is to construct systemic models that interactively develop from the worldview and influence the development of the worldview. These systemic models can be created from the paradigm of open systems. Although there are multitudes of possibilities for systemic models, three are sketched in the following chapters that provide some movement toward operational integration: systemic models of religion, education, and religious education.

NOTES

1. Henry Wadsworth Longfellow, "The Tide Rises, The Tide Falls," *The Complete Poetical Works of Henry Wadsworth Longfellow* (Boston: Houghton, Mifflin, 1902), p. 453.
2. Alvin Toffler, *The Third Wave* (New York: William Morrow, 1980), p. 25.
3. Lawrence LeShan and Henry Margenau, *Einstein's Space and Van Gogh's Sky: Physical Reality and Beyond* (New York: Macmillan, 1980), pp. xii-xiii.
4. Ilya Prigogine, *From Being to Becoming: Time and Complexity in the Physical Sciences* (San Francisco: W. H. Freeman, 1980), pp. xii-xiii.
5. Heinz R. Pagels, *The Cosmic Code: Quantum Physics as the Language of Nature* (New York: Bantam Books, 1983), p. 310.
6. Thomas S. Kuhn, *The Structure of Scientific Revolutions,* 2nd. ed. (Chicago: The University of Chicago Press, 1970).
7. Ibid., p. 92.
8. Ibid., p. 111.
9. Ibid.
10. Ibid., especially all of Chapter 10.
11. Ibid., p. 204.
12. Milton Rokeach, *Beliefs, Attitudes, and Values: A Theory of Organization and Change* (San Francisco: Jossey-Bass, 1968), pp. 6-11.
13. Ibid., p. 6.
14. Louis B. Jennings, *The Function of Religion: An Introduction* (Washington, D.C.: University Press of America, 1979), p. 285. This is a key point that underscores the value of theory. It demonstrates that factual data are not enough by themselves. The data are ultimately useless in the practical sense unless they are situated within a sufficient or appropriate theoretical framework.
15. This was the way Max Born described Ptolemy's work. See Max Born, *Einstein's Theory of Relativity,* rev. ed. (New York: Dover Publications, 1962), p. 10.

16. Claudius Ptolemy, "The Almagest," in *Theories of the Universe from Babylonian Myth to Modern Science,* ed. Milton K. Munitz (Glencoe, Ill.: The Free Press, 1957), p. 109.

17. Ibid., p. 111.

18. J. L. E. Dreyer, "Medieval Cosmology," in *Theories of the Universe from Babylonian Myth to Modern Science,* ed. Milton K. Munitz, p. 116.

19. Milton K. Munitz, "Introduction," in *Theories of the Universe from Babylonian Myth to Modern Science,* ed. Milton K. Munitz, p. 141.

20. Fritjof Capra, *The Turning Point: Science, Society and the Rising Culture* (New York: Simon and Schuster, 1982), p. 54.

21. Nicolaus Copernicus, "On the Revolutions of the Heavenly Spheres," in *Theories of the Universe from Babylonian Myth to Modern Science,* ed. Milton K. Munitz, p. 168.

22. One of the best and clearest explanations of the theories can be found in Albert Einstein, *Relativity: The Special and the General Theory,* trans. Robert W. Lawson (New York: Bonanza Books, 1961).

23. John A. Dillon, Jr., *Foundations of General Systems Theory* (Louisville, Ky.: University of Louisville, 1982), p. 162.

24. Ibid., p. 107.

25. Pagels, *The Cosmic Code,* p. 310.

26. Kenneth E. Boulding, *The Image: Knowledge in Life and Society* (Ann Arbor, Mich.: University of Michigan Press, 1956).

27. Ibid., p. 42.

28. Ibid., p. 17.

29. Ibid.

30. Ibid., p. 175.

31. Ibid., p. 54.

32. Ibid., pp. 5-6.

33. Ibid., p. 14.

34. Ibid., p. 64.

35. Ibid., p. 77.

36. Ninian Smart, *Worldviews: Crosscultural Explorations of Human Belief* (New York: Charles Scribner and Sons, 1983), pp. 1-2.

37. Ibid., pp. 3-4.

38. LeShan and Margenau, *Einstein's Space and Van Gogh's Sky,* p. 1.

39. Ibid., p. 18.

40. Gregory Bateson, *Mind and Nature: A Necessary Unity* (New York: Bantam Books, 1980), p. 5.

41. Ibid., p. 8.

42. Ibid., p. 12.

43. Ibid., p. 13.

44. Pagels, *The Cosmic Code,* p. 84.

45. Toffler, *The Third Wave,* p. 20.

46. Ibid.

47. A. Graham Ikin, *Wholeness Is Living: Scientific Thinking and Religious Experience* (London: Geoffrey Bles, 1970), p. 133.

48. Ibid.

49. To get Toffler's earlier viewpoint, see Alvin Toffler, *Future Shock* (New York: Random House, 1970).

50. Toffler, *The Third Wave,* p. 30.

51. Ibid.
52. Russell L. Ackoff, *Redesigning the Future: A Systems Approach to Societal Problems* (New York: John Wiley & Sons, 1974), pp. 3-18.
53. Ibid., p. 8.
54. Ibid., p. 11.
55. Ibid., p. 17.
56. Ibid., p. 18.
57. Capra, *The Turning Point*, p. 33.
58. Ibid., especially the historical review on pp. 26-35.
59. This is the subject of Chapter One in Ervin Laszlo, *The Systems View of the World: The Natural Philosophy of the New Developments in the Sciences* (New York: George Braziller, 1972), pp. 1-15.
60. Ibid., p. 4.
61. Ibid., p. 15.
62. I am not suggesting a Comtean development of worldviews that would move toward a positivistic imperialism. Such an accusation would stem from a worldview other than a systemic one: possibly a classical science worldview, or more likely a theological worldview.
63. Cha'im Perelman, *A Historical Introduction to Philosophical Thinking*, trans. Kenneth A. Brown (New York: Random House, 1965), p. 7 ff. Also see Reginald E. Allen, ed., *Greek Philosophy: Thales to Aristotle* (New York: The Free Press, 1966).
64. Perelman, *An Historical Introduction to Philosophical Thinking*, pp. 8-9.
65. Ibid., p. 9.
66. Ibid.
67. The allegory of the cave is one of the better known illustrations of Plato's teachings. See Plato, *The Republic*, Book VII, T. E. Page, ed., The Loeb Classical Library, Vol. 6, trans. Paul Shorey (Cambridge, Mass.: Harvard University Press, 1934), pp. 119-233.
68. See, for example, the discussion in Aristotle, *Metaphysics*, Book Beta, trans. Richard Hope (Ann Arbor, Mich.: University of Michigan Press, 1952), pp. 40-60.
69. See Aristotle, *Metaphysics*, Book Alpha, pp. 3-34.
70. This is simply a version of the seemingly ubiquitous but totally meaningless "god of the gaps" type of argument. Such "logic" allowed to go to its final conclusions negates the possibility of any true value to be found in philosophy, science, or research of any kind.
71. Alfred North Whitehead, *Science and the Modern World* (New York: Macmillan, 1925; reprint edition, New York: The Free Press, 1967), pp. 8 ff.
72. Theory deals with "why," whereas laws which lead to theory deal with "how."
73. This story is adopted from Jennings, *The Function of Religion*, p. 295.
74. See Thomas Aquinas, *Summa Theologica*, Vol. One, trans. Fathers of the English Dominican Province (New York: Benziger Brothers, 1947), especially pp. 1-9.
75. Ibid., pp. 4-6.
76. Refer to Claudius Ptolemy, "The Almagest," in *Theories of the Universe from Babylonian Myth to Modern Science*, ed. Milton K. Munitz, pp. 104-114.
77. See Ian G. Barbour, *Issues in Science and Religion* (New York: Harper & Row, 1966), p. 22.

78. This is the Judaic-Christian terminology, but of course other cultures and religious traditions would use another explanation or at least different terminology.

79. See Genesis 1:26, 31.

80. This is translated variously as soul, life, or breath. The reference comes from Genesis 2:7.

81. See Psalm 8:5 for one example of the Judaic-Christian tradition of this order. Other religious traditions would express the human relationship to transcendence/immanence in a radically different way.

82. In a geocentric universe, terms such as "above" and "below" did have meaning. See the discussion in Born, *Einstein's Theory of Relativity,* p. 9.

83. Barbour, *Issues in Science and Religion,* p. 19.

84. Elmer H. Wilds and Kenneth V. Lottich, *The Foundations of Modern Education,* 4th ed. (New York: Holt, Rinehart & Winston, 1970), pp. 6-8.

85. Barbour, *Issues in Science and Religion,* p. 23. The exclusive language in this quote is instructive.

86. T. F. Torrance, "Divine and Contingent Order," in *The Sciences and Theology in the Twentieth Century,* ed. A. R. Peacocke (Stockfield, Eng.: Oriel Press, 1981), p. 89.

87. Ibid.

88. Francis Bacon, "Novum Organum," in *Philosophic Classics,* Vol. II, ed. Walter Kaufman, 2nd ed. (Englewood Cliffs, N.J.: Prentice-Hall, 1968), pp. 8-9. Also see the note in Wilds and Lottich, *The Foundations of Modern Education,* p. 272.

89. John Locke, "Essay Concerning Human Understanding," in *Philosophic Classics,* Vol. II, pp. 164 ff.

90. Barbour, *Issues in Science and Religion,* p. 35.

91. Jennings, *The Function of Religion,* p. 297.

92. Barbour, *Issues in Science and Religion,* p. 36.

93. Ian G. Barbour, *Myth, Models, and Paradigms: A Comparative Study in Science and Religion* (New York: Harper & Row, 1974), p. 2.

94. For a good discussion of the relationship between Deism and the Machine Age, see Ackoff, *Redesigning the Future,* pp. 10-11. Also see E. Graham Waring, ed., *Deism and Natural Religion* (New York: Fred Ungar, 1967).

95. Jennings, *The Function of Religion,* p. 292.

96. Rupert Sheldrake, *A New Science of Life: The Hypothesis of Causative Formation* (Los Angeles: J. P. Tarcher, 1981), p. 25.

97. Ackoff, *Redesigning the Future,* p. 8.

98. LeShan and Margenau, *Einstein's Space and Van Gogh's Sky,* p. 35.

99. Laszlo, *The Systems View of the World,* p. 4.

100. Ackoff, *Redesigning the Future,* p. 9.

101. Ibid., p. 10.

102. John A. Dillon, Jr., "Bells, Books, and Barriers" (an unpublished paper presented at Louisville, Kentucky: The University of Louisville, 1983), p. 5.

103. Andras Angyal, "The Logic of Systems," in *Systems Thinking,* ed. Fred E. Emery (New York: Penguin Books, 1969), p. 25.

104. LeShan and Margenau, *Einstein's Space and Van Gogh's Sky,* p. 5.

105. Capra, *The Turning Point,* p. 66.

106. Isaac Newton, *Mathematical Principles of Natural Science and the System of the World,* ed. Florian Cajori (Berkeley, Calif.: University of California Press, 1934), p. 13.

107. Norbert Wiener, *The Human Use of Human Beings: Cybernetics and Society* (New York: Avon Books, 1967), p. 13.

108. Newton, *Mathematical Principles of Natural Science and the System of the World,* p. 6.

109. Prigogine, *From Being to Becoming,* p. 214.

110. Pagels, *The Cosmic Code,* p. 45.

111. Ibid., pp. 4-5.

112. Ludwig von Bertalanffy, *General System Theory: Foundations, Development, Applications,* rev. ed. (New York: George Braziller, 1968), p. 88.

113. Kenneth E. Boulding, *Ecodynamics: A New Theory of Societal Evolution* (Beverly Hills, Calif.: Sage Publications, 1978), p. 39.

114. Thermodynamics is a branch of physics which deals with the transformation of heat into other forms of energy.

115. Prigogine, *From Being to Becoming,* p. 13.

116. Ibid., p. 3.

117. Dillon, *Foundations of General Systems Theory,* p. 91. Also see Ilya Prigogine and Isabel Stengers, *Order Out of Chaos: Man's New Dialogue with Nature* (New York: Bantam Books, 1984), pp. 117-122.

118. Ackoff, *Redesigning the Future,* p. 10.

119. Dillon, *Foundations of General Systems Theory,* p. 91.

120. As quoted in Gerald M. Weinberg, *An Introduction to General Systems Thinking* (New York: John Wiley & Sons, 1975), p. 150.

121. Perelman, *A Historical Introduction to Philosophical Thinking,* p. 128.

122. Barbour, *Issues in Science and Religion,* p. 6.

123. Ibid., p. 310.

124. Paul Abrecht, ed., *Faith, Science and the Future* (Philadelphia: Fortress Press, 1978), p. 13. The point being made here is that while the classical science worldview was dualistic, it was positivistic in that science became the judge of truth in place of theology.

125. Ibid.

126. Newton, *Mathematical Principles of Natural Science and the System of the World,* p. 400.

127. Vitalists believed that a life-source (or a soul) animated the physical body. Such an ontic division kept body and soul completely separate.

128. Weinberg, *A Introduction to General Systems Thinking,* p. 30.

129. Capra, *The Turning Point,* p. 31.

130. See an introductory treatment in chapter 1 and a more extensive development throughout chapter 2.

131. LeShan and Margenau, *Einstein's Space and Van Gogh's Sky,* p. xiii.

132. Capra, *The Turning Point,* p. 77.

133. Abrecht, *Faith, Science and the Future,* p. 13.

134. Boulding, *Ecodynamics,* p. 9.

135. LeShan and Margenau, *Einstein's Space and Van Gogh's Sky,* p. 9.

136. Refer to the discussions in Born, *Einstein's Theory of Relativity,* p. 11; Pagels, *The Cosmic Code,* p. 5; and Torrance, "Divine and Contingent Order," in *The Sciences and Theology in the Twentieth Century,* p. 92.

137. Born, *Einstein's Theory of Relativity,* pp. 1-2.

138. Torrance, "Divine and Contingent Order," in *The Sciences and Theology in the Twentieth Century,* pp. 90-91.

139. Pagels, *The Cosmic Code,* p. 39.

140. Einstein, *Relativity,* p. 105.

141. Anatol Rapoport, *Science and the Goals of Man: A Study in Semantic Orientation* (New York: Harper & Brothers, 1950), p. xvi.

142. Lucien Price, *Dialogues of Alfred North Whitehead* (Boston: Little, Brown, 1954), p. 345. This is purported to be a verbatim statement by Whitehead to Price.

143. This book of Whitehead's has come to be understood as one of the precedents and creators of systems theory. Whitehead was prior to the systems movement but is a forefather, and without him it probably would not have developed into the paradigm for a worldview.

144. Whitehead, *Science and the Modern World,* p. 16.

145. Alfred North Whitehead, *Process and Reality: An Essay in Cosmology,* ed. David Ray Griffin and Donald W. Sherburne (corrected edition; New York: The Free Press, 1978). This is an expansion of the Gifford Lectures of 1927-28, recognized as the fountainhead for modern process philosophy and process theology.

146. Chapter Two dealt briefly with the historical development of General Systems Theory. Also see James Grier Miller, *Living Systems* (New York: McGraw-Hill, 1978), pp. xiii-xxi.

147. Bertalanffy, *General System Theory,* p. 12.

148. Ibid.

149. Ibid., p. 13.

150. Pierre Teilhard de Chardin, *The Phenomenon of Man,* trans. Bernard Wall (New York: Harper & Row, 1959), pp. 35-36.

151. Nonequilibrium thermodynamics is the study of energy transformation in conditions far from equilibrium, where chaos gives birth to order. See Prigogine, *From Being to Becoming,* pp. 103-128.

152. Dissipative structures are "new dynamic states of matter" which originate in far-from-equilibrium conditions. See Prigogine and Stengers, *Order Out of Chaos,* p. 12.

153. *From Being to Becoming,* by Ilya Prigogine, dealt primarily with research data. For a fuller exploration of the philosophical implications of Prigogine's research, see Prigogine and Stengers, *Order Out of Chaos,* and Erich Jantsch, *The Self-Organizing Universe: Scientific and Human Implications of the Emerging Paradigm of Evolution* (Oxford: Pergamum Press, 1980).

154. Dillon, *Foundations of General Systems Theory,* p. 153.

155. Prigogine began one of his books with: "This book is about time." See Prigogine, *From Being to Becoming,* p. xi.

156. Dillon, *Foundations of General Systems Theory,* p. 163.

157. Prigogine, *From Being to Becoming,* p.xviii.

158. Ibid.

159. Ibid., p. xvi.

160. Dillon, *Foundations of General Systems Theory,* p. 164.

161. Capra, *The Turning Point,* p. 285. The Deists experienced a similar difficulty with their "world machine."

162. Weinberg, *An Introduction to General Systems Thinking,* p. 31.

163. Wiener, *The Human Use of Human Beings,* p. 129.

164. Laszlo, *The Systems View of the World,* pp. 31-32.

165. Even atoms are not "things," but are best viewed as relationships and processes, according to current estimates of science. See Capra, *The Turning Point,* p. 80.

166. Hoyle is referring to a quote he made in 1948. See Fred Hoyle, *The New Face of Science* (New York: World Publishing Company, 1971), p. 129.

167. Michael Collins, *Carrying the Fire: An Astronaut's Journeys* (New York: Farrar, Straus & Giroux, 1974), p. 470. Collins was one of the first humans to see our planet from a truly holistic perspective, irrespective of photographs.

168. John W. Sutherland, *Systems: Analysis, Administration, and Architecture* (New York: Van Nostrand Reinhold, 1975), p. 72.

169. Bertalanffy, *General System Theory,* p. 121.

170. Ibid., p. 136.

171. Ilya Prigogine's research on dissipative structures has shown that even this is not necessarily so.

172. Laszlo, *The Systems View of the World,* pp. 40-41.

173. Capra, *The Turning Point,* p. 268.

174. Ibid.

175. Bateson, *Mind and Nature,* p. 16ff.

176. Ibid., p. 17.

177. Boulding, *Ecodynamics,* p. 31.

178. Ibid.

179. Ackoff, *Redesigning the Future,* p. 55.

180. Jacob Bronowski, *The Common Sense of Science* (New York: Random House, 1951), p. 102.

181. Prigogine, *From Being to Becoming,* p. 215.

182. Rapoport, *Science and the Goals of Men,* p. 141.

183. Dillon, "Bells, Books, and Barriers," p. 3.

184. Boulding, *Ecodynamics,* p. 12.

185. Dillon, "Bells, Books, and Barriers," p. 4.

186. Ackoff, *Redesigning the Future,* p. 15.

187. Capra, *The Turning Point,* p. 79.

188. Jantsch, *The Self-Organizing Universe,* p. 274.

189. Hans J. Morgenthau, *Science: Servant or Master?* (New York: World Publishing Company, 1972), p. 61.

190. Pagels, *The Cosmic Code,* p. 68.

191. Prigogine, *From Being to Becoming,* pp. 127-128.

192. Bateson, *Mind and Nature,* p. 253.

193. Sutherland, *Systems,* p. 81.

194. Bateson, *Mind and Nature,* p. 252.

195. Prigogine, *From Being to Becoming,* p. 215.

196. Capra, *The Turning Point,* p. 267.

197. Sutherland, *Systems,* p. 24.

198. Wiener, *The Human Use of Human Beings,* p. 130.

199. See Bateson, *Mind and Nature,* pp. 13-14.

200. This issue is easily understood by seeing the present as a "bifurcation point." A bifurcation point is a place in time when solutions to various problems may offer multiple possibilities. The option chosen at this critical point determines the following set of options. Such bifurcations can only happen in irreversible time. See Dillon, *Foundations of General Systems Theory,* pp. 163 ff.

201. Weinberg, *An Introduction to General Systems Thinking,* p. 147.

202. Prigogine, *From Being to Becoming,* p. 13.

203. Dillon, *Foundations of General Systems Theory,* p. 149.

204. Laszlo, *The Systems View of the World,* pp. 58-59.

205. Prigogine, *From Being to Becoming,* p. 128.

206. Capra, *The Turning Point,* p. 290.

207. Ackoff, *Redesigning the Future,* p. 14.

208. Prigogine, *From Being to Becoming,* p. xv.

209. Laszlo, *The Systems View of the World,* p. 6.

210. Bateson, *Mind and Nature,* p. 21.

211. Stafford Beer, *Cybernetics and Management* (New York: John Wiley & Sons, 1959), p. 30.

212. Capra, *The Turning Point,* p. 269.

213. Laszlo, *The Systems View of the World,* p. 52.

214. Ackoff, *Redesigning the Future,* p. 18.

215. Ibid., p. 8.

216. Wiener, *The Human Use of Human Beings,* p. 220.

217. Bertalanffy, *General System Theory,* pp.xvii-xviii. This reference is to the preface in the revised edition.

218. Robert Lilienfeld, *The Rise of Systems Theory: An Ideological Analysis* (New York: John Wiley & Sons, 1978), p. 279.

219. Ibid.

220. Ibid., p. 280.

221. Torrance, "Divine and Contingent Order," in *The Sciences and Theology in the Twentieth Century,* pp. 96-97.

222. Bernard Towers, "Teilhard de Chardin," in *Science and Faith in the 21st Century,* ed. Donald Brophy (New York: Paulist Press, 1968), p. 80.

223. Jonathan Schell, *The Fate of the Universe* (New York: Alfred A. Knopf, 1982), p. 173.

224. August 6, 1945, was the day the world at large first knew of the atomic potentials. The first successful test of a nuclear device took place on July 15, 1945, ironically code-named the "Trinity" test. It is reported that at the moment of the firing, Robert Oppenheimer recalled a line from the Bhagavad Gita: "I am become death, the shatterer of worlds." See Peter Wyden, *Day One: Before Hiroshima and After* (New York: Warner Books, 1985), p. 212.

225. Tragically, President Truman declared August 6, 1945 "the greatest day in history." Recorded in Wyden, *Day One: Before Hiroshima and After,* p. 16.

226. If science must bear some guilt for these instruments for mass annihilation, theology must also accept its share in their proliferation. Countless warmongers masquerading as ministers (the root word for minister is servant!) have described a possible nuclear exchange in such abhorrent ways as the fulfillment of biblical prophecy and as a part of their god's plan all along to destroy the earth by fire (citing biblical passages such as Revelation 8). Imagine laying the hands of human guilt on a divine scapegoat! Also consider the negative (almost a gleeful) vision of the apocalypse in popular religious books. For an example of this kind of suicidal literature, examine Hal Lindsey, *The Late Great Planet Earth* (Grand Rapids, Mich.: Zondervan Books, 1970).

Chapter 4

Religion

O welche Lust! O welche Lust!
in freir Luft den Atem leicht zu heben;
Nur hier, nur hier ist Leben,
Der Kerker eine Gruft.[1]

from *Fidelio*

Is religion a vital element of the systemic perspective?

That question is a key to the remainder of this book and indeed to the validity of the entire book. The ultimate purpose is to develop, or at least to demonstrate the possibility of developing, a systemic model of religious education. For that model to be formulated, the task of addressing the larger and more basic question of the viability of religion in a systemic perspective must be addressed. Only after the establishment of a systemic model of religion will the subjects of systemic education and systemic religious education be taken up. It is this first step that is the focus of this chapter.

Recall that the systemic perspective is an "umbrella" term for the theoretical constructs of paradigm, worldview, model, and simulation. Since chapter 2 described the paradigm of open systems and chapter 3 the systemic worldview, it is now time for the discussion of models. Systemic models are constructed from the open systems paradigm with the view of relating to and interacting with a systemic worldview. The entirety of the systemic perspective should be comprehensible with the formulation of the various models.

127

The present chapter addresses only the development of a model for religion, while models of education and religious education follow in the subsequent chapters. Chapter 4 has six main divisions. First is a brief overview of what models are and an explanation of the role they play in the systemic perspective. Second, there is acknowledgment of the modern discomfiture with religion, and some of the challenges that have been put to it. Third is an outline of one possible way to develop a systemic definition of religion. Fourth is a description of systemic religion based on the characteristics of open systems. Fifth is a discussion of how systemic religion fits into the larger systemic worldview. Finally, consideration is given to the interface of systemic religion with related but differentiated areas of study.

MODELS

The art and science of building models is a never-ending activity. Nearly all of the work done in any field is the work of building models. Only rarely does someone come up with a new paradigm, or pattern, for the models. Even more rarely do worldviews come under scrutiny. It is the models that are constantly being developed, tried, modified, and adapted.

This frenetic activity of constructing models was what Thomas Kuhn called "normal science." He saw the work of model building as a "mopping-up" operation that is necessary after any revolution.[2] Kuhn said: "By focusing attention upon a small range of relatively esoteric problems, the paradigm forces the scientists to investigate some part of nature in a detail and depth that would otherwise be unimaginable."[3] He was correct in stating that model building moves toward the specific and the concrete, while the paradigm is general and abstract. The danger for a systems scientist is to become so involved in "detail and depth" that the systemic ideal of integration is lost. Indeed, the challenge of systemic modeling is providing detail and depth while attending to relationships and interface.

This section on models has two foci. First are definitions for the terms employed here. Second is a statement of the design appropriate for systemic models, including a mention of the limits that any model (even a systemic model!) must encounter.

Definitions

The term "model" is an imprecise word in the public vocabulary. Just as "paradigm" and "worldview" have technical meanings in this book, so does the term "model." A variety of terms and definitions is provided here to give clarity and distinction to the particular usage of the term "model" in this book.

Analogy. Ludwig von Bertalanffy defined analogies as "superficial similarities of phenomena which correspond neither in their causal factors nor in their relevant laws."[4] An analogy gives only an implied resemblance: a seeming likeness that is scientifically unverifiable. It is the least useful but the most employed in contemporary language.

Homomorphism. James Grier Miller's definition of homomorphism was "formal identity between two concrete systems."[5] A homomorphism is more applicable to physical sciences, where similarities in characteristics can be demonstrated in actual scientific experiments. Homomorphy is not as useful in discussing such concepts as paradigms and worldviews.

Isomorphism. This is defined as "formal identity between two conceptual systems."[6] Literally meaning "having the same shape," the term does not necessarily mean physical shape. Two abstractions that are similar and parallel are isomorphic, such as the concepts *paradigm* and *worldview.* These two are isomorphic.

Model. A model refers to "formal identity between a conceptual system and a concrete (or an abstracted) system."[7] Calling it a "simplified approximation," James Grier Miller explained a model as "a verbal theory which not only describes observations accurately but also presents an explicit account of how a system is believed to work."[8] The method employed in the following pages is that of modeling. A conceptual system (paradigm) is used to develop an approximation and a verbal theory of abstracted systems (religion, education, religious education).

Simulation. A simulation is a special subsystem of the category of models. A simulation is a working model that can be used and tested after the initial construction of verbal theory is completed.

Simulations are not attempted in this book, but they are the next step in testing and applying the models.

Design

The reason for constructing these "verbal theories" of religion, education, and religious education is to integrate both the paradigm of open systems and the systemic worldview. The models are to be *systemic* models. In order to be systemic, they must be constructed according to systemic design: an interactive and interconnective development of purpose, function, and structure.[9]

The uniqueness and originality of the following models are a result of this kind of systemic design. Most often the design process is corrupted, and models are built to be static entities. Structure is the normative factor in most models of religion, education, and religious education. In the systemic models constructed in this book, the dimensions of purpose and function are considered as well as structure. Rather than being determinative in systemic models, structure is to be the most flexible, the most adaptive, and the most diversified of all the design elements. Structure and content are by no means unimportant but simply need less attention during the design stage of planning and more focus in the implementation stage. The ideal is to create adaptive structures that evolve interactively along with the purpose and function of the model.

The models designed in this book are not intended to be representations of absolute truth or of ultimate reality. As Paul Abrecht said, models are "effective ways of thinking about reality for certain designated human purposes."[10] Frankly, models are susceptible to manipulations and prejudices. They are human constructs. Gloria Durka and Joanmarie Smith pointed to this evolutionary nature of models when they wrote that "perhaps these models are the only access we have to reality, and that perhaps the best we can do is to construct less and less inappropriate models."[11] It is for this reason that the dynamic and interactive design of purpose, function, and structure is so valuable. It allows the creation of systemic models that become more appropriate and useful as they evolve through time, responsive to the needs of the system and of the environment.

No model (or book) can say or do it all. Models can never

represent a system completely or precisely.[12] Models are developed for particular purposes and for highlighting certain aspects of the perceived reality. They are not meant to be exhaustive, perfect, or monopolistic.[13] A "full and final" model of an open system can never be constructed, because an open system itself is never in full and final form. The actual system is always beyond the model's ability or purpose to demonstrate a one-to-one correspondence. The model is not the reality.

RELIGION?

It may seem odd that a book purporting to be a serious and scholarly discussion of an emergent and revolutionary perspective would choose the seemingly anachronistic subject of religion for its first attempt at model construction. Gordon Allport remarked that "the persistence of religion in the modern world appears as an embarrassment to the scholars of today."[14] Such a questionable place to start as religion needs a few words of justification. This can be done under three topics: the problems confronting modern religion; the need for the study of religion; and a sampling of some of the challenges to religion. These discussions prepare the way for a systemic definition of religion.

Some Problems with Religion

A complete catalog of the problems regarding religion and its relation to the modern world would be a study in itself. A look at three areas will suffice to describe the task at hand.

Confusion. One author has given this evaluation of the situation: "Perhaps in no area of human experience now undergoing change is there more confusion than there is in religion."[15] In the present matrix of such competitive viewpoints as Marxism, Hinduism, Americanism, and Christianity, it is not an easy job even to say what religion is. When the worldview changes, so much changes that even so stalwart and tradition-bound a subject as religion undergoes revision. There is simply no choice but to acknowledge the changes demanded by a systemic worldview.

There is no illusion that this book can completely disentangle the confusion. There is hope that the effort here is a movement toward order rather than toward an increase in the noise. Whatever the suggestion, it will probably not meet with universal appeal. Gordon Allport summed up the matter well: "Religion, aiming to deal with the most inclusive of relationships—aiming to bind fact, value, and ultimate reality—is the most controversial, the most doubt-ridden, the most elusive of all the fields of mental activity."[16]

Irrelevance. The code word of the 1960s was relevance, and though that voice is now more muted, the need is still present. Rather than "gimme that old-time religion, it's good enough for me," the present is more likely to cry "throw out the old-time religion, what meaning does that have for me?" Eulalio Baltazar made this point even clearer when he wrote: "It is with the presently evolving world that we have to do and no other; if religion is to be relevant, its role must be shown in it."[17]

The rejection of handed-down laws is becoming commonplace for persons of today. Erich Fromm spoke for many when he rephrased the issue by saying: "The problem of religion is not the problem of God but the problem of [persons]; religious formulations and religious symbols are attempts to give expression to certain kinds of human experience."[18] One of the most respected authorities on religions of the twentieth century, Wilfred Cantwell Smith of Harvard, suggested that the locus of truth is to be found in persons and not in statements or propositions.[19]

If religion is to be relevant, then it must address the needs of these demands. Hiding behind the formulations of the past will not work. Alfred North Whitehead had this observation: "This [relevance] is a question which in some new form challenges each generation. It is the peculiarity of religion that humanity is always shifting its attitude towards it."[20] Harvey Cox made the humorous but accurate remark about theology: "The failure of modern theology is that it continues to supply plausible answers to questions that fewer and fewer people are asking."[21]

Moral failure. The track record of religion is not very good. With disasters too numerous to recount, two will serve to remind. Germany, home of some of the greatest theologians of the twentieth century, has the blood of six million Jews on its hands. America, the "Christian nation," remains the first and only nation to detonate nuclear weapons for purposes of war. This shame forced Maurice Friedman to ask:

For the real question—the question that lies at the inmost core of our very existence—is not Why? but How? How can we live in a world in which Auschwitz and Hiroshima happen? How can we find the resources once more to go out to a meeting with the new moment?[22]

With such past results religion may not deserve another chance. Modern religion must face up to its heritage of failure.

Summary
Confusion, irrelevance, and moral failure are only examples of the problems religion must face and correct if it is to be a viable element in the new worldview. Yet even with this poor performance, the effort goes on. Wilfred Cantwell Smith framed the situation this way, allowing this discussion to move to the deep need for better religion: "The two most fundamental questions confronting twentieth-century [persons] . . . both involve religion: how to turn our nascent world society into a world community; and . . . how to find meaning in modern life."[23]

Need for Religion
As the problems of religion are as the sands of the sea, so the needs for religion are as the stars in the sky. They are innumerable, yet some mention of the necessity for religion helps to explicate the reason for an attempt to rehabilitate religion. In the present section, three needs are cited.

Salvation. Even such a critic of religion as Emile Durkheim realized that humans need hope, and that salvation is a part of any religion.[24] This need is expressed in different forms: Judaism tends toward understanding salvation in terms of a national or racial immortality while Christianity emphasizes personal redemption. The need for "salvation," though, is universal.

Such a need was the focus of Wilfred Cantwell Smith's questions, in the search for a "world community" and personal meaning. Corporate and individual salvation are no longer (if they ever were) separate issues. Carrying Marshall McLuhan's "global village"[25] concept to further depth, Ninian Smart said: "The fact that human civilization is now so tightly knit that its every crisis sends ripples around the globe is one reason why the modern study of religion . . . is so important."²⁶ Systemic religion must see the organic connection of individual and society and seek the salvation of both.

Depth. Religion and its needs are not measured in church attendance, denominational budgets, or any other institutional guideline. The famous (and infamous) James Pike had this in mind when he commented years ago that "the growing disenchantment with the Church does not mean diffidence toward questions about ultimate meaning."²⁷ Lloyd Geering expressed the same thought this way: "No matter who a person is, what his [or her] particular beliefs are, or what cultured tradition he [or she] stems from, his [or her] religion is that in which he [or she] expresses his [or her] ultimate, or most basic concern for life."²⁸ Whatever religion is, and however it is expressed, there is evidence that it needs to be addressed by the systemic worldview.

Incurability. Sidney Jourard had the insight to perceive that humans are "incurably religious."²⁹ He saw that humans have no choice about whether or not to be religious. The true choice concerns only "what one will be religious about, and the ways in which one will be religious."³⁰

The spokesman of a past generation, Harry Emerson Fosdick, foreshadowed Jourard when he wrote:

> No [person] can really become an unbeliever; he [or she] is psychologically shut up to the necessity of believing—in God, for example, or else in no God, or else in the impossibility of deciding. One way or another, in every realm, [a person] is inherently a believer in something or other, positive or negative, good, bad, or indifferent.³¹

Summary

Humans need salvation, search for depth of meaning and understanding, and possess an incurability for belief. Historically, religion has occasioned both enormous damage and great help. Religion surely possesses fundamental importance for it to be tolerated and advanced for so long. That is not to say that everyone has accepted the fact that religion is good and only needs periodic updating. Serious efforts to root out religion, and its "incurable" manifestations, have been mounted. Before a systemic religion is addressed, these challenges need to be considered.

These challenges have something to say to the construction of a systemic model.

Challenges to Religion

It should be obvious that the theoretical design for developing a model of religion started with paradigms and worldviews. The reason for this insistence can now be given clear illustration. The reason is that this is the way it *does* happen in reality, whether the model developer is conscious of it or not. An illustration is provided by the way religion was handled through the paradigm of the machine and the classical science worldview.

For the sake of brevity and clarity, one characteristic of the scientific worldview is selected to show its dominance of "modern" (actually presystemic) Western religious thinking: dualism. From Friedrich Schleiermacher to Karl Barth the answers given to religious issues were how to cope with dualism. The construct of dualism itself was never questioned but assumed as a part of reality.

Friedrich Schleiermacher. It is generally agreed that Friedrich Schleiermacher (1768-1834) was the "father" of modern Christian theology[32] as he tried to "interpret the Christian faith in relation to the 'modern' worldview."[33] His solution to the riddle of understanding religion was to go past the external manifestations and to seek the internal phenomena. His intention was clear when he said: "At all times but few have discerned religion itself, while millions, in various ways, have been satisfied to juggle with its trappings."[34]

What Schleiermacher found beneath the trappings was emotion, not ceremony or dogma or institutions. His interpretation of the basis for true religion, or faith, was "feeling": "The sum total of religion is to feel that, in its highest unity, all that moves us in feeling is one."[35] Richard R. Niebuhr wrote that Schleiermacher's "greatest achievement" was "his articulation of the self-consciousness and God-consciousness that relate to feeling."[36]

One can only applaud the effort to describe "true" religion, and by this effort Schleiermacher joined himself to an ancient tradition harkening back to Augustine. But the point here is that in so doing Schleiermacher divided reality into two parts: feeling and thinking; body and soul; by extension, God and the world, and so on. By identifying feeling as separate and apart from the rest of reality, he blazed a trail taken by disciples and critics alike.

Ludwig Feuerbach. One of the most effective and harshest critics of religion was Ludwig Feuerbach (1804-1872). He gained his success precisely through the exploitation of dualism. He argued that the supposed dualism is only a reflection in the mirror and that the "other half" of the duality is not really there. His argument had four steps.

He began by stating that the uniqueness of humans, that which distinguishes them from the animal world, is self-consciousness.[37] A human realizes he or she is an individual with senses, perception, and judgment, while an animal is only an operator in the environment.

Next Feuerbach defined religion: "Religion being identical with the distinctive characteristic of [a human], is then identical with self-consciousness—with the consciousness which [a human] has of his [or her] nature."[38]

The third step was obvious. If humanity's uniqueness is self-consciousness, and this self-consciousness is what is called religion, then: "In religion [a human] contemplates his [or her] own latent nature."[39]

The final step was to acknowledge that the duality is false: The "God half" is simply a figment of projection. Feuerbach phrased it this way: "We have reduced the supermundane, supernatural, and superhuman nature of God to the elements of human nature as its fundamental elements. . . . The beginning, middle, and end of religion is [HUMANITY]."[40]

Feuerbach regarded religion as a negative because it had the effect of disuniting persons.[41] It split the unity of persons into the natural and the supernatural (calling the supernatural an unattainable ideal). Patrick Masterson summarized the issue this way: "Since the religious projection is essentially a transference of human properties to an illusory God, the richer the notion of God elaborated, the more [humanity] is impoverished and reduced to a miserable and servile condition."[42]

Karl Marx. Karl Marx (1818-1883) closely followed the line of reasoning put forth by Feuerbach, but with a refinement. His agreement is observed in the statement: "[A human] makes religion, religion does not make [a human]. Religion is indeed the self-consciousness and self-awareness of [a human] who either has not yet attained to himself [or herself] or has already lost himself [or herself] again."[43]

Marx's contribution to the critique of religion was not that religion only disunited humans but that it was a tool used by the ruling class to keep the status quo.[44] Religion had to be eradicated because the working class needed to see their true condition as slaves, rather than to be tranquilized by religion. This occasioned the famous quote: "Religion is the sigh of the oppressed creature, the feeling of a heartless world, and the soul of soulless circumstances. It is the opium of the people."[45]

Sigmund Freud. The mirror-like nature of religious dualism had another advocate: Sigmund Freud (1856-1939). Freud was one of the staunchest believers in the methods of classical science the world has ever seen. He rejected religion because of its dangerous dualism and felt religion could be rooted out by the rigors of then-current scientific explanation. Calling religious doctrines "illusions and insusceptible of proof,"[46] Freud had his own method of finding truth:

> The riddles of the universe reveal themselves only slowly to our investigations; there are many questions to which science today can give no answer. But scientific work is the only road which can lead us to a knowledge or reality outside ourselves.[47]

Freud's problem with religion was not that it was only an illusion, as when a person looks in a mirror. Freud said religion was pathological: a universal obsessional neurosis.[48] Religion was not just a feeling, or self-consciousness, or even a tranquilizer. Religion was an illness that needed to be cured through classical science.

Emile Durkheim. Emile Durkheim (1858-1917) had a close affinity to Freud in understanding religion. He did not pick up the idea of neurosis but instead chose to deal with the mass effect of religion. Durkheim began his analysis with the now-standard dualism: the classification of the sacred and the profane.[49] The "profane" was that which related to the regular human concerns; the "sacred" was that which related to the transcendent order beyond individual human awareness. Religion then became the expression of the relations between the profane and the sacred.[50] Durkheim's contribution to the discussion was his identification of religion with the forces of society. What humans were calling sacred, Durkheim called society.[51] He said: "If religion has given birth to all that is essential to society, it is because the idea of society is the soul of religion."[52] Durkheim was able to turn religion into a new science. Religion viewed this way need not be exorcised but be made more precise. He changed Ludwig Feuerbach's individualistic anthropology into the broader study of sociology.

Rudolf Otto. Maybe the most influential theological discussion in this period of classical science came from the pen of Rudolf Otto (1869-1937). Otto claimed his heritage from Schleiermacher but felt he needed to correct and focus the master's teachings.[53] Otto identified "the holy" as the "category of interpretation and valuation peculiar to the sphere of religion."[54]

Otto devised a new term for this category: the "numinous," from the Latin word for supernatural, "numen."[55] Its presence was essential: "There is no religion in which it does not live as the real innermost core, and without it no religion would be worthy of the name."[56] Although the "numinous" cannot be strictly defined, said Otto,[57] it could be described: "The numinous is thus felt as objective and outside the self."[58]

Otto gave the issue of dualism such an attractive exposition that many subsequent theologians followed suit. Whereas the challengers had said that the half of reality called "religious" was either an illusion or a human manifestation, Otto turned the argument around. He said the ultimate reality was in the *sacred* half of the duality. This became the basis for the entire neo-orthodox movement of theology, led by Karl Barth.

Karl Barth. One of the dominant Protestant theologians of the twentieth century was Karl Barth (1886-1968).[59] Interestingly enough, Barth is probably best understood as the refuter of Ludwig Feuerbach.[60] Barth accepted the old dualisms of Schleiermacher, Feuerbach, and Otto and pushed them to their logical extremes. Barth was the ultimate dualistic, classical science theologian.

Barth's rather shocking solution was, in effect, to agree with

Feuerbach: Religion is the creation of humans. Barth said: "Religion is unbelief. It is a concern, indeed, we must say that is the one great concern, of godless [humanity]."[61] Elsewhere Barth wrote: "Religion is not the Kingdom of God. . . . Religion is human work."[62]

Barth then said that Christianity is not a religion and not the work of humans. It is the revelation of God.[63] Barth had craftily caught Feuerbach in his own game and used Otto's category of the numinous, especially as revealed in Christianity, to separate himself from the critics. Of course, the problem was not solved: Barth was simply using the other side of the dualism. Rather than being creative, he was merely refighting the same old battle; hence the term "neo-orthodoxy."

Dietrich Bonhoeffer. The prescient martyr Dietrich Bonhoeffer (1906-1945) clearly saw the problem that Karl Barth created. His term for the dilemma was "religionless Christianity."[64] His plaintive question, written in 1944, was not fully heard and understood until years later: "If religion is only a garment of Christianity—and even if this garment has looked very different at different times—then what is religionless Christianity?"[65] What is it indeed? War and death blocked a full response by Bonhoeffer. What he actually signaled was the dead-end that had been reached with the old dualisms. Theologians have been searching for a way out ever since.

Summary

This section on challenges was in no way meant to be a comprehensive examination of either religion or theology but to be an illustration of the way religion is an outgrowth of paradigms and worldviews. One example drawn from the characteristic of dualism was given. Others abound.

The attempt in the rest of this chapter is to propose a way out of the old categories and barriers of past worldviews and to design another model. Admittedly it too will have defects and imperfections, but it is an effort to transcend and redefine the issues. It is now appropriate to explore the possibilities of a systemic model of religion, beginning with a systemic definition of religion.

A SYSTEMIC DEFINITION OF RELIGION

In order to construct a systemic model of religion, it is first necessary to decide exactly what is to be described. That is no easy task. Definitions of religion have a nearly infinite variety. What follows is a survey of several useful contributions to the definition of religion and then a statement of what this book proposes as a definition of systemic religion.

Contributory Elements

Sifting through the myriad definitions of religion has produced five representative approaches used by various authors that contribute to a systemic understanding of religion. These elements provide the context for a fresh look at how religion can be redefined.

Replacement. The leading proponent for a complete replacement of the term "religion" was Wilfred Cantwell Smith, especially as explained in the book *The Meaning and End of Religion.*[66] After summarizing at least four uses that the term "religion" has had, he made the surprising suggestion that the word, and its concepts, should be dropped from the vocabulary.[67] His point was that since the term was so overburdened and overused, it had become meaningless.

Smith's suggestion was to substitute two other terms: faith and cumulative tradition. His explanation was:

> By "faith" I mean personal faith . . . an inner religious experience or involvement of a particular person; the impingement on him [or her] of the transcendent, putative or real. By "cumulative tradition" I mean the entire mass of overt objective data that constitute the historical deposit, as it were, of the past religious life of the community in question.[68]

Process theologian John Cobb joined Smith in rejecting the old terminology. He proposed several different terms at different times. Among his suggestions were: the category of structures of existence;[69] "vision of reality;"[70] and simply "the Ways."[71]

Regardless of these and other arguments, society still uses the term "religion."[72] The points are well taken, however. This book rejects the change in terminology but accepts the idea that the term does need significant redefinition.

Meaning. The brilliant and courageous Viktor Frankl endured years in a Nazi concentration camp and emerged with the conviction that finding meaning in life is of primary importance. He wrote: "[A person's] search for meaning is a primary force in his [or her] life and not a 'secondary rationalization' of instinctual drives."[73] Frankl believed the "will to meaning" to be more descriptive and valid than Sigmund Freud's "pleasure principle" and Alfred Adler's "will to power."[74]

Frankl did not equate meaning with religion, but his intention seems clear. The important thing in life is how and why one spends the time allowed on earth. This type of value has had some influence on attempts to restructure religion. Ninian Smart employed this line of thinking when he defined religion as "ultimate value questions related to the meaning of human life."[75] Lloyd Geering also agreed, saying that religion is "the response of faith to the ultimate issues of human existence."[76]

Ultimate concern. Similar to Viktor Frankl's formulation was Paul Tillich's approach to religion. Typifying his philosophical tendency, Tillich postulated religion as ultimate concern.[77] One expression of this definition was:

> Religion is more than a system of special symbols, rites, and emotions, directed toward a highest being; religion is ultimate concern; it is the state of being grasped by something unconditional, holy, absolute.[78]

Tillich and his followers[79] in many ways paralleled Frankl's search for meaning, but gave it an even sharper distinction. Tillich pushed not just for individual or existential meaning, but for *ultimate* meaning. In a sense, Tillich sounded a chord that called religion to contemplate teleology and its actualization.

Gestalt. To borrow a term from Sophia Lyon Fahs, religion is a "gestalt," or gathering together, of an individual's life. She said:

> One's religious "belief" or one's "religion" is the "gestalt" of all his [or her] smaller specific beliefs. One's faith is the philosophy of life that gathers up into one emotional whole—and sometimes, al-

though rarely, into a reasoned whole—all the specific beliefs one holds about many kinds of things in many areas of life.[80]

This conception of religion, although somewhat vague, has great potential for helping develop a systemic definition of religion. Fahs has introduced such related topics as holism and integration into the discussion.

Pragmatic. To use the term "pragmatic" is not to suggest that the best way to approach religion is through simply "what works." The plan here is to emphasize that religion *does* work: It is action, movement, result-oriented. William James defined religion as "the feelings, acts, and experiences of individual [persons] in their solitude, so far as they apprehend themselves to stand in relation to whatever they may consider the divine."[81] The interest for this book is that James focused on action, rather than symbols, rites, or concepts.

Closely related to James' definition is the oft-quoted maxim of Alfred North Whitehead: "Religion is what one does with his [or her] own solitariness."[82] Again, the emphasis here is on the "what ones does with" his or her individuality. The value of a pragmatic approach is that religion is something real, active, and productive.

Abraham Maslow introduced the term "peak-experience"[83] to illustrate the experiential and dynamic nature of religion. Maslow pointed out that there can be no substitute for a personal involvement. He said: "Each 'peaker' discovers, develops, and retains his [or her] own religion."[84] In fact, Maslow characterized organized, institutional religion as "an effort to communicate peak-experience to non-peakers."[85] There is no doubt that real religion, for Maslow, had to be "pragmatic."

Summary

Some of the contributory elements useful to a systemic definition of religion are: a need for redefinition; a search for meaning; an establishment of ultimate concern; the creation of a gestalt; and a realization that religion must do something to become real. This background has now prepared the context for a discussion of a systemic definition of religion.

Etymological Overview

The systemic definition of religion presented here begins by examining the etymology of the word "religion." This tack was taken by Lloyd Geering as well, as his justification was: "In moving in this direction we are, in one sense, simply returning to the original sense of the word religion before it became identified with particular forms such as belief in God [or] in a supernatural world."[86] Although the final definition here will depart from Geering, the method of returning to the root is used. There are three key words which are of great influence to a systemic understanding of religion. These three terms are traced to their original sources, which gives a foundation for their usage in the systemic model.

Religion. The term "religion" is derived from the Latin compound verb "religio."[87] The root is one of three possibilities: "ligo," to bind, tie, join together; "lego," to gather or collect; or "lig," to pay attention or give care.[88] The prefix "re" means turning backward, restoration to original condition, or transition into the opposite state. "Religio," then, is to bind back, fasten up, or join together two or more things. Religion is that which binds together.

Whole. The term "whole" is from the Old English "hale," meaning healthy, unhurt, entire.[89] The derivation is actually through "entire" from integrate—the Latin being the compound "integrare." The root is "tangare": to touch. The prefix "in" means "not," or "un." "Integrate" means literally untouched, or whole. That which is untouched, healthy, and entire is whole.

Nexus. "Nexus" is simply a Latin word appropriated directly into English. It has two sources. Its main derivation is from the verb "necto":[90] to twine together, interweave, attach by binding or tying into a single mass. "Necto" is kindred to the same root as religio ("lig"). "Nexus" is a participial form of "necto." A secondary source is from the Latin word for knot, or bunch: "nodus."[91] Nexus, then, is that which is an interconnection, a link, an interlacing.

Definition

Systemic religion is holistic (health-full) nexus: the existential "binding together" of the heritage of the past with a guiding vision of the idealized future.

There are at least two authors who have defined religion similarly and then went on to talk of God. One was Gordon Allport. He said: "A [person's] religion is the audacious bid he [or she] makes to bind himself [or herself] to creation and to the Creator."[92] Allport moved to make religion a binding force and tried to overcome dualism through this interface.

Alfred North Whitehead gave an early definition of religion in his *Science and the Modern World.* He by-passed reference to God as he said:

> Religion is the vision of something which stands beyond, behind, and within the passing flux of immediate things; something which is real and yet waiting to be realized; something which is a remote possibility and yet the greatest of present facts; something that gives meaning to all that passes and yet eludes apprehension; something whose possession is the final good and yet is beyond all reach; something which is the ultimate ideal and the hopeless quest.[93]

He made a more definite statement in *Religion in the Making.* It was there that he identified God as the "binding element in the world."[94] The ultimate statement on the "divine milieu" (to use Teilhard's phrase) may be this sentence by Whitehead:

> The religious insight is the grasp of this truth: That the order of the world, the depth of reality of the world, the value of the world in its whole and in its parts, the beauty of the world, the zest of life, the peace of life, and the mastery of evil are all bound together—not accidentally, but by reason of this truth: that the universe exhibits a creativity with infinite freedom and a realm of forms with infinite possibilities; but that this creativity and these forms are together important to achieve actuality apart from the completed ideal harmony, which is God.[95]

Explanation

Among the multitude of discussion points and areas of explanations for the definition of systemic religion, three are essential. These are the concepts of nexus, time, and health.

Nexus. The heart of religion is nexus: interconnection, interface, intersection. Religion is the process of linking together. This can be institutionalized, nationalized, or personified, but the root concept is still the binding activity.

Erich Jantsch used the term "religio," as distinguished from "religion," to express symmetry, unification, and healing.[96] He defined "religio" as "linking backward to origin," or even more clearly as the "pulling the origin into the present."[97] Jantsch introduced the concept of time, then, along with the linking idea.

Time. It will be recalled that Ilya Prigogine had a preoccupation with time, feeling that a better understanding of it would revolutionize thinking.[98] The systemic definition proposed here agrees with Prigogine.

The systemic definition of religion employs the standard concepts of past, present, and future, but hopefully in a more creative way. The term "existential" is used to denote the "making present" of the past and the future in a dynamic process. Just as Erich Jantsch had spoken of "pulling the origin into the present," so the systemic definition speaks of using the heritage of the past to come to grips with the reality of the present. Ilya Prigogine had pointed out that the past is fixed since the "time's arrow" leads (looking from the present) deterministically to the present.[99] It is the *future* that is undetermined and unending.

While the existential present is the only reality, and it is a product of the past, motivation comes from anticipation of the future. Ervin Laszlo expressed this well:

> The orientation of the religions toward the past needs to be combined with greater emphasis on an orientation toward the future. In place of reliance on received dogma, on revelation to chosen individuals, religions need to look to the needs and desires both of those living today and those to be born tomorrow.[100]

Health. The systemic definition used "holistic" with the qualifier "health-full." It is this dimension that sets systemic religion apart. The point is that while there is an endless variety to religion, the most important determination is whether the religion in question is healthy or unhealthy.

At once it will be noted that the formulation of the categories of healthy and unhealthy religion is the reflection of values. That cannot be denied or avoided. As was discussed, and will continue to be discussed, values and worldviews are impossible to dismiss; they are to be raised to consciousness, however, and made explicit. What will become apparent is that the characteristics of the open system and the properties of a systemic worldview, as they relate to religion, become the *values* that guide, direct, and determine. That is both necessary and desirable.

The understanding of religion only as nexus, without the qualifier, is so vague as to be useless. A prime example is fascism. According to the definition, without the holistic value, fascism could be called religion. A particularly revolting version was created earlier in this century by Nazi Germany. As voiced by Adolf Hitler, this "Third Reich" was the intersection of world history.[101] By continuing and purifying the heritage of the Aryan race, the dream of a "thousand year rule" by superhumans was moving toward actualization. Without some context of values, this "religion" was just as valid as Christianity. Systemic religion can determine that fascism was (and is) unhealthy because of its values concerning health and wholeness.

This approach does not debate the question of truth or error. The systemic approach to religion is to search for or to create religion that contributes to the health of the overall system and to exclude that which is "un-health-full."

This point is no small matter. Julian Huxley recognized that the power of religion must be appreciated. He said: "It can be a potent and violent force for evil as much as for good."[102] As is often the case, Alfred North Whitehead had a good summary:

> The uncritical association of religion with goodness is directly negatived by plain facts. Religion can be, and has been, the main instrument for progress. But if we survey the whole race, we must pronounce that generally it has not been so.[103]

The discussion now turns to see if religion as an "instrument for progress" can be described. The model of systemic religion is developed according to the "healthy" values of open systems and a systemic worldview.

DESIGN OF THE MODEL

A systemic model must address the three design criteria: purpose, function, and structure. As has been stated numerous times throughout this book, these three design elements are not to be separate considerations but interactive and interdependent components. They evolve through time, each element influencing and shaping the others. One is not more important than the others, and one cannot be fully understood without consideration of the others. They are teased apart here for purposes of clarity and identification, but these are only "snapshot" images that are not representative of a truly systemic process.

Purpose

Health and integration mark the purpose of systemic religion. These are processive and developmental characteristics, never to be understood as completed and finalized, and never to be totally achieved. Health, maturity, and growth are examples of qualities that are realized as they are being pursued.

Religion experienced as holistic nexus includes a plurality of religious expression. Since health and maturity are corporate matters as well as individual, various cultures and environments fulfill these in a multitude of ways. The criteria for evaluation are derived from the purpose (holistic nexus), meaning that decisions about quality are made by the measure of increase in the improvement of the health and integration of the open system.

Function

The definition of systemic religion is a functional definition. It describes the dynamic nature of experiential religion. Systemic religion is not a thing, a substance, or a content but is process and activity. Religion is nexus: interconnection, interface, and interchange.

James Michael Lee has provided a functional definition of religion that is complementary to the definition developed in this book:

Religion is that form of lifestyle which expresses and enfleshes the lived relationship a person enjoys with a transpersonal being as a

consequence of the actualized fusion in his [or her] self-esteem of
that knowledge, belief, feeling, experience, and practice that are in
one way or another connected with that which the individual perceives to be divine.[104]

Lee's definition is a holistic one, focusing not only on knowledge
and belief but including other processive elements in the flow of
experience.

Other definitions of religion also give emphasis to function.
Louis Jennings said "Religion emerges as a functional vehicle to
interpret the manifold diversities of life."[105] William Bailey had
an operational understanding of religion, calling it a specific type
of behavior.[106]

Structure

Systemic religion is modeled so that the structures are flexible,
adaptable, and responsive to environmental and systemic needs.
The structures are not set beliefs, rigid traditions, lifeless ceremonies, or repetitious observances, all of which must be performed
to *be* religious. Though healthy religion certainly may involve
beliefs, traditions, ceremonies, and observations, they are not the
determinative and identifying elements. Systemic religion is modeled on the living, self-organizing system which Fritjof Capra
described: "Its order in structure and function is not imposed by
the environment but is established by the system itself."[107] The
structures of systemic religion evolve as they carry out the dynamic function and purpose.

To focus solely on structure in modeling is to spell certain death
to processive and adaptive behavior. An exclusive interest in
structure creates a religious system that is rigid, deterministic,
and closed. Structural religion was characterized by Lucien Saumur as a "system of beliefs" and a "subordinate system of practices which are derived from these beliefs."[108] Erich Fromm
called this type of religion "authoritarian."[109] Sophia Lyon Fahs
said it became reduced simply to a "body of 'affirmations' presented as 'truths' to be understood, appreciated, and accepted."[110]

Synthesis

Purpose flows to function which creates adaptive structures in systemic religion. Each of these elements interact continually and interdependently in the quest for holistic nexus.

RELIGION AND THE PARADIGM OF OPEN SYSTEMS

The definition of systemic religion is now expanded into an outline of a systemic model. The model is patterned from the systemic paradigm so that the eight characteristics of open systems described in chapter 2 are used to portray systemic religion.

Holism

Holism is the unifying and integrating dimension of an open system that is created by the interactive and interdependent relationships between the various elements of the open system. Since systemic religion has been defined in this chapter as holistic nexus, it is clear that holism is an essential ingredient in any discussion of systemic religion. The implications of holism need focused attention.

Alfred North Whitehead described religion as what one does with his or her solitariness.[111] Such a description can be interpreted as a polar opposite to the quest for holism. Martin Marty expressed this when he wrote:

> Yet many have found this pithy definition [of Whitehead's] attractive as a substantiation of the individualist note. It has been easy for some of them to go one step further and to suggest that the religious phenomenon can be understood sui generis in virtually complete separation from environmental and societal factors.[112]

Marty went on to say that these "individualists" (which he termed as mystics, existentialists, and fundamentalists) perceive that the "act of believing is in the end highly personal."[113]

If Whitehead's definition has an emphasis on the actual solitariness of each individual and on the isolation from the environment, then it has very little to add to systemic religion. Yet, if the emphasis is placed on what one *does with* his or her solitariness, then there are very real implications for systemic religion. Certainly no one would deny what Martin Marty pointed out: that "just as each [person] must die for himself [or herself], so he [or she] must believe for himself [or herself]";[114] but many can take issue with the concept that each person is left totally alone to find his or her own way through the maze of belief and doubt. To miss the value, indeed the responsibility, of humans to help each other deal with solitariness and isolation is to miss the entire concept of corporate worship and development. The solitude of a person can be moved into interrelationship, interdependence, and interaction with others. A recognition of individualism is healthy; an insistence on continual isolation is destructive. A better interpretation of Whitehead's intent is facilitated by this further word from him:

> In its solitariness the spirit asks, What, in the way of value, is the attainment of life? And it can find no such values till it has merged its individual claim with that of the objective universe. Religion is world-loyalty.[115]

Peter Berger approached the discussion from the opposite pole of solitariness: "The alienating aspect of modernity has, from the very beginning, brought forth nostalgias for a restored world of order, meaning, and solidarity."[116] His point was that religion, in its "nostalgic," symbolic way, provides humans a way to be

> banded together in the face of death. The power of religion depends, in the last resort, upon the credibility of the banners it puts in the hands of [persons] as they stand before death, or more accurately, as they walk, inevitably, toward it.[117]

There are at least two reactions to be made to Berger's comments as they relate to systemic religion. One is that Berger assumes that religion (or any search for order) is primarily a cognitive or mental activity. Religion that relates only to the mind is not systemic religion. Holistic nexus is inclusive of symbolic and intellectual processes but is not limited to them. Systemic religion is concerned with finding integration in emotional and physical areas as well as in the rational process.

Another point that Berger raises for reaction is the possibility of achieving this "solidarity" through a totalitarian state, whose "central goal is the restoration of a premodern order of stable meanings and firm collective solidarity."[118] Certainly the totalitarian state is one way of achieving uniformity, but systemic religion is not seeking unformity; it is seeking unity. Enforced agreement and rigid forms of thought and behavior violate every principle of the systemic perspective. While Berger does raise a valid fear of totalitarianism, such is not a result of systemic religion, which insists on holism—a harmony composed of variety and differentiation.

The holism of systemic religion is at neither the pole of isolated solitariness nor at the pole of rigid totalitarianism. It is rather a quest for what Gregory Bateson termed the "sacred unity of the biosphere."[119] This kind of holism goes beyond the rational processes and seeks to meet the needs of the whole person, inclusive of emotional needs, physical needs, and spiritual needs. The "sacred unity" also implies more than an anthropocentric interest. Peter Berger said that "religion is the audacious attempt to conceive of the entire universe as being humanly significant."[120] This is not descriptive of systemic religion, which does understand humans as significant but also seeks to find the place of humans within the larger environment. Humans are not the most important element in the universe but are one element in the interactive whole. Systemic religion is an effort to attend to the needs of humans while also attending to the needs of the environment.

Differentiation

The flip side of holism is differentiation. Differentiation is variety and diversity among the elements that make up the system, while holism is the integration of these elements. If there is no variety, there is no true integration. A lack of variety produces sameness and uniformity, but not integration. So long as there is coherence and relationship between the elements, systemic religion encourages (requires) specialization, complexity, and creativity.

Differentiation in religion was the issue when Gordon Allport surmised that "no threads may be rejected" in weaving the tapestry of religion, but he also added that the result must have an integrative and homogenous pattern.[121] Julian Huxley supported the notion of differentiation when he said: "If our religion is a true religion, a religion of fuller life, it must both tolerate and reverence variety."[122]

An analogy of the need for differentiation in systemic religion can be found in music. It is difficult to imagine an aesthetically pleasing and emotionally stirring tune composed of one note produced by one instrument. Normally, ears of the Western world expect a bit more variety than one note and one instrument. The variety that comes through different notes, different patterns, and different instruments and voices combine to create a unity and a harmony that make music an art form. Music is a result of the integration from the variety of sounds. By extension, systemic religion is the result of an integration of the variety of structures and functions.

The music analogy can serve to illustrate another point: that of "right" and "wrong" in both music and religion. What is the "proper" type of music for people to experience? Is there a "right kind" of music? If so, it is typified by the music of Johannes Brahms, Scott Joplin, or the Beatles? Music is notoriously hard to define and even more difficult to judge. Usually, beauty of music is left to the ear of the listener, with the recognition that "music" is the variety of sound that meets the needs of the listener and is satisfying to the listener. Systemic religion has a similar problem in declaring exactly what religion is and which form is "proper." Holistic nexus is a celebration of variety and diversity, with the insistence on health and integration for the sake of the system.

Systemic religion cannot dictate the *means* of holistic nexus. Think of the variety of individuals, denominations, faiths, and cultures that exist. Can one particular form of religion be the best for everyone? An affirmative answer is as absurd as the question. The means of holistic nexus are multitudinous. It is the focus of the variety toward unity and integration that provides the possibility of a discussion on systemic religion.

Boundaries

Boundaries of a system are a matter of life and death, because boundaries determine to what degree this system is closed or open. Ludwig von Bertalanffy gave clarity to the issue by saying that "a system is 'closed' if no material enters or leaves it; it is called 'open' if there is import and export of material."[123] A closed system, then, has rigid boundaries; an open system has flexible, permeable boundaries.

A permeable boundary, which allows both input and output to flow through the system, provides the differentiation between the system and its environment. Admittedly, this type of boundary is usually difficult to ascertain because it is a matter of interface: how the system joins and interconnects *with* the environment, more than how the system separates itself *from* the environment.[124] If systemic religion is to be authentic in its quest for holistic nexus, then the key issue is how interface is effected *within* the environment rather than how religion is distinguished *from* the environment.

Gerald Weinberg pointed out that "open systems baffle us, and we prefer to think of our systems—or create our systems—to be as closed as possible."[125] Weinberg was emphasizing the risk that is involved in creating an open system. Open systems are characterized by constant change because of their interaction with the environment. Closed systems "tend to be self-contained or only minimally responsive to outside influences."[126] Religion can become a closed system: safe, secure, unchanging, nonrisking, ineffectual, and doomed to oblivion. Religion can become an open system: creative, risky, evolutionary, revolutionary, transformative, and capable of health and maturity.

If religion becomes systemic, there is a two-edged sword to be encountered. Systemic religion *will* change the environment because of the flow-through and the transformation process. Systemic religion will also *be* changed by the environment. In order to be open, systemic religion must be willing to take the risk of change, adaptation, and accommodation. Wilfred Cantwell Smith recognized the interactive change that happens when religion is subjected to the environment when he wrote that "in one fashion or another, for good or for ill, wittingly or unwittingly, little or much, Muslims, Hindus, and Buddhists may be seen as participating in the future evolution of the Western religious tradition."[127]

It may be that religion needs to be less afraid of change and more interested in health. What is so threatening in the environment that thick, rigid boundaries should be reinforced to protect the system? A whimsical word from Robert Frost speaks to this issue of boundary:

> Before I built a wall I'd ask to know
> What I was walling in or walling out,
> And to whom I was like to give offence.
> Something there is that doesn't love a wall,
> That wants it down.[128]

Dynamism

The systemic perspective enjoys full appreciation for the processive character of life. Ludwig von Bertalanffy stated that "dynamic interaction appears to be the central problem in all fields of reality."[129] Norbert Wiener made the issue more personal when he wrote: "We are but whirlpools in a river of ever-flowing water. We are not stuff that abides, but patterns that perpetuate themselves."[130]

There is no doubt that dynamism makes systemic religion a complex process. Alfred North Whitehead said: "It is the peculiarity of religion that humanity is always shifting its attitude toward it."[131] In truth, not only is the attitude toward religion perpetually changing, but the entire religious process is perpetually in flux. As a nexus of values, goals, and ideals, systemic religion evolves through time just as society does. Systemic religion *is* process and not a static entity. Wilfred Cantwell Smith described this by saying: "To be Christian or Muslim or Buddhist, to be religious, is a creative act of participation in a community in motion."[132]

An open system is dynamic because of the constant flow through it. The flow is from the environment, into the system where it is transformed, and back into the environment again. It is inevitable for this kind of dynamism to force change. Systemic religion is changed because of the transformation process. The environment is changed because of the presence of religion and because of the outputs that are injected back into the environment. The dynamism of an open system changes both the system and the environment.

Louis Jennings referred to processive religion as authentic religion. He said:

> Religion, moreover, must be abreast of the times in which it exists. It must move courageously forward. . . . It cannot stand on the sidelines and refuse to become involved in the daily happenings. To the contrary, it must be able to interrelate with every facet of personal concerns and interests.[133]

It is a contradiction in terms to think of systemic religion as some "thing," separate and apart from the flux of life. Systemic religion is found only amid the flow of human activity.

Equifinality

Equifinality is movement toward an ultimate desired state from a variety of initial conditions and through a diversity of paths. For an open system this means that an emergent teleology can be developed by the system as it dynamically and interactively moves through time by any number of means, structures, and functions. For systemic religion this means that holistic nexus is the processive ideal and that the ways for this equifinal goal to emerge are unprescribed, unlimited, and uncensored.

Wilfred Cantwell Smith discussed the variety of initial conditions and paths that exist throughout the various forms of religious faith. He talked of God in terms of equifinality:

> Through Islamic patterns God across the centuries has been participating in the life of Muslims; through Buddhist patterns in the life of Buddhists; through Hindu modes in the life of India; through Jewish forms . . . in the life, individual and social, of Jews; and some of us know, through Christian forms in our lives. It is through His participation in the religious history of the world . . . that He has chiefly entered human lives to act in human history. Right now, He is calling us to let Him act through new forms, continuous with the old, as we human beings across the globe enter our strange new age.[134]

Smith was saying that teleology could emerge through the ceaseless dynamism of function and structure.

Ervin Laszlo (with companion writers) noted the influence

religion can have to "promote the growth of world solidarity" and its ability to "increase ethnic and cultural disharmony," depending on its orientation and intentions.[135] He pleaded for the various religions to "overcome the divisiveness, exclusiveness, and intolerance that have marked much of religious history" and to find a way to "include the right to freedom of belief without diminution of esteem or weakening the bonds of solidarity."[136] He described the effect of achieving an equifinal harmony this way:

> The coming together of the great religious movements in today's world is a sign of greater unity within their diversity, not of syncretism and uniformity. A single world religion is as unlikely, and as undesirable, as a single philosophy, a single social order, and a single set of values. But unity within current diversity is possible, and it is necessary if some of the deepest thoughts and experiences of [humankind] are not to give rise to the exclusiveness and intolerance that breeds inhumanity and violence. Such unity is beginning to arise today. Promoting it is one of the major tasks and responsibilities of all people who cherish their religious heritage and believe that it has a constructive role to play in overcoming the inner limits which currently constrain [humankind's] options for a better future.[137]

Pierre Teilhard de Chardin envisioned the convergence of reality toward what he called the "Omega Point," the focus of all nature and history. Doran McCarty described this Omega Point as the end result of such things as "economic interdependence, communion among political groups, communications network . . . the coalescence of science and religion, and even the ecumenics of the moving together of the religious world."[138] Teilhard himself phrased it this way:

> By its structure Omega, in its ultimate principle, can only be a distinct Centre [sic] radiating at the core of a system of centres; a grouping in which personalisation of the All and personalisations of the elements reach their maximum, simultaneously and without merging, under the influence of a supremely autonomous focus of union.[139]

Alfred North Whitehead is a final example of one who described the process of equifinality, and he used the term "God" to express his understanding:

> God's role is not the combat of productive force with productive force, of destructive force with destructive force; it lies in the patient operation of the overpowering rationality of his conceptual harmonization. He does not create the world, he saves it; or, more accurately, he is the poet of the world, with tender patience leading it by his vision of truth, beauty, and goodness.[140]

Feedback

The focus of systemic religion is holistic nexus. It cannot be assumed that systemic religion (or any open system) is always true to its purpose, but, as Kenneth Boulding gave reminder, it is through failure that learning often results.[141] Failure provides feedback, and the most valuable feedback is negative (corrective) feedback. Through the monitoring of the progress, or lack of progress, systemic religion can be evaluated. Corrective feedback reveals when the system is off-target.

The goal of systemic religion (holistic nexus) is a dynamic and evolutionary goal. The feedback from that goal must also be dynamic and evolutionary while providing information on precisely what kind of "holistic nexus" is being achieved. Ervin Laszlo recognized that feedback is actually a reflection of basic values. He wrote: "Values are goals which behavior strives to realize. Any activity which is oriented toward the accomplishment of some end is value-oriented activity."[142] Systemic religion with its feedback process is overtly a value-oriented activity. The goal is movement toward health, maturity, and development, and when those values are not being reflected in systemic religion, the feedback allows the problem to be detected and corrected.

Systemic religion needs its checks and balances, because as Alfred North Whitehead remarked: "Religion is by no means necessarily good. It may be evil."[143] Sidney Jourard gave a description of personal health and maturity that speaks clearly to the value orientation of systemic religion:

> A religious orientation is healthy if it enhances life and fosters growth of one's powers as a human being, including the power to

love, to be productive and creative. Thus, no matter whether a person be Christian, Jew, Moslem, Hindu, or Buddhist, the criterion of whether his [or her] religion is healthy is provided not by the piety and scrupulosity of ritual observations, but by its effect on life. Is he [or she] a loving, strong, growing person who does not diminish others? Or is his [or her] piety accompanied by prudery, inability to love others, and lack of joy in living?[144]

Homeostasis

An open system must have a certain degree of "steady-state" (homeostasis) to be viable. This is to be distinguished from equilibrium, which is the final result of entropy: chaos and dissolution. Homeostasis is dynamic stability and continuity in the midst of change and movement.

The extended definition of systemic religion spoke of binding together the heritage of the past with a guiding vision of the future. This refers to the continuity with what has led to the present and to the changes that are needed for the future. Lloyd Geering addressed the need for homeostasis when he said: "We need a definition of religion therefore that will do justice both to the variety of past religious forms and to the possibility that in the modern world there may be quite new forms of religion coming to birth."[145] Harvey Cox also raised the possibility of new designs of religion in what he called the "postmodern world."[146]

Certainly no one would deny the instability of the current world order. At times it appears that humanity will literally "blow itself apart." At the same time, no one could deny the great need to synthesize stability, continuity, and change. Systemic religion holds the possibility. As Ilya Prigogine insisted, it is especially in times of turbulence and dissipation that new forms of order and coherence are forced into existence.[147]

While systemic religion insists on homeostasis, this emphasis should not be regarded as an interest in mere maintenance of the status quo. The kind of process descriptive of systemic religion is an adaptive and dynamic process that is "consciously and intelligently opportunistic."[148] John Sutherland explained this kind of process as "one that constantly seeks to exploit new opportunities as they emerge, seeking always to maximize its efficiency rather than to maintain its historical structure or preserve tradition."[149]

This is a good understanding of how a homeostatic open system need not simply "hold its own," if indeed such is even a true possibility. The challenge is in creativity, development, and growth. It is this kind of homeostatic process that is descriptive of systemic religion.

Growth

A living system either takes in fresh inputs and grows, or it closes itself off from the environment and dies. This is the same choice presented to religion. Systemic religion seeks the option of growth, development, and transformation.

Alfred North Whitehead provided a strong argument for the element of growth in religion. In the 1925 Lowell Lectures, published as *Science and the Modern World*, Whitehead proposed that religion accept the same attitude toward change that science (ideally) does. Rather than to see the breakthroughs of Charles Darwin or Albert Einstein as defeats for old ways, they are treated as triumphs for the progress of science.[150] Whitehead then gave this advice: "Religion will not regain its old power until it can face change in the same spirit as does science. Its principles may be eternal, but the expression of those principles requires continual development."[151] Systemic religion is merely another step in the evolutionary development of religion and of humanity. Its growth is essential to the continuing need for integration, health, and survival.

The issue of growth was given even more emphasis by Julian Huxley. He combined the ideas of change, progress, and evolutionary development in this way:

> In all spiritual activities we should expect steady change and improvement as [humankind] accumulates experience and perfects his [or her] mental tools. In art it is a triumph if a Beethoven or a Titian finds new ways of building beauty; in science it is acclaimed a triumph if an old universally accepted theory is dethroned to make way for one more comprehensive, as when Newton's mechanics gave place to Einstein's, or the assumed indivisibility of the atom was exploded in favor of the compound atom, organized out of subatomic particles; but in the religious sphere . . . the reverse is the case, and change, even progressive change, is . . . looked upon as defeat; whereas once it is realized that religious truth is . . . as

incomplete as scientific truth, as partial as artistic expression, the proof or even suggestion of inadequacy would be welcomed as a means to arriving at a fuller truth and an expression more complete.[152]

Systemic religion, while keeping the heritage, experience, and learning of the past, looks to the future and to the possibilities of creative expression and development that can be created.

Summary
Systemic religion is modeled on the paradigm of the open system, with the eight essential properties of an open system serving as the outline of the model. The properties become the guides and values for the construction of holistic nexus. Even more clarity is gained about systemic religion as it is related to the systemic worldview.

RELIGION AND THE SYSTEMIC WORLDVIEW

It is logical to assume that a systemic model would fit into a systemic worldview. A brief review of the characteristics of a systemic worldview will serve to illustrate the relationships of the worldview and systemic religion.

Organismic
A systemic worldview uses the open system as its chief pattern of cognition. Systemic religion can be viewed as a subsystem within that worldview, operating as an open system, with the flow-through and transformation of inputs into outputs. Religion is changed by the process, but so is the overall system. Such interchange is both natural and desirable.

A worldview without religion could not be called "systemic." As this chapter has argued, religion is an essential part of the systemic perspective. The exclusion of religion from the approach would destroy the analogy of organismic functioning, where each element is essential to the ongoing life of the whole.

Relational
The systemic model of religion is able to function only as an integral part of the overall system. Systemic religion does not deal

with a subject or a reality that is somehow separate from everything else; it is that which integrates and binds together. There
can be no "binding together" in isolation.

Time has been a dimension of great importance since Albert
Einstein's formulas were introduced. In that regard, systemic religion was defined in existential terminology, making past and
future real in the present. Systemic religion takes the dimension
of time seriously, accepting the heritage of the past in the present
to actualize an ideal future.

Relationalism also serves to remind that religion cannot be
analyzed and described in a detached manner. To do so is to lose
the reality. Harvey Cox recognized this when he said: "No one
can study religion merely descriptively. This in turn makes the
modern myths of neutrality and objectivity increasingly implausi-
ble."[153] Isolated religion is no religion.

Pluralistic

No one characteristic will reveal the entirety of the systemic
worldview; the same is true of systemic religion. An infinite
variety of models of religion are possible, but the "full and final
model" is unattainable. As Alfred North Whitehead said: "Progress in truth . . . is mainly a process in the framing of concepts,
in disregarding artificial abstractions or partial metaphors, and in
evolving notions which strike more deeply into the root of reality."[154]

The acknowledgment of incompleteness does not devalue specific models. To the contrary, it demands them. John Hick stated
this clearly: "The concrete particularities forming a spiritual
home in which people can live . . . must continue in their separate
streams of living tradition: for in losing their particularity they
would lose their life and their power to nourish."[155] Ultimately
religion must be expressed concretely and individualistically. The
systemic approach simply recognizes that each expression is always incomplete and refinable.

One of the features of the systemic worldview is the freedom
that can exist within it. As a functioning element in the systemic
worldview, systemic religion is not in a position to determine (by
virtue of its emphasis and value on pluralism) what is the right or
the best form of religion. It does not judge whether one expres-

sion of religion is the most proper. Insistence on a particular type of religious tradition or on a hierarchy that decides what is "right" or "wrong" is totally contrary to the values and ideals of systemic religion. Systemic religion is evaluated on the progress toward holistic nexus: how the system is evolving toward health, integration, and maturity. This is not an issue of right or wrong, but one of progressive transformation.

Systemic religion is *not* a new "world religion." It is only an approach to, and an understanding of, religion. Wilfred Cantwell Smith rightly said: "The religious life of [humankind] from now on, if it is to be lived at all, will be lived in a context of religious pluralism."[156] This pluralism is to be encouraged, along with interface and cooperation among the expressions of systemic religion.

Stochastic

The past is determined; the future is open. Such is true of the systemic worldview and of a systemic model of religion. The existential present carries the heritage of the past but dreams into reality what the future will be. The bifurcations of the future are unknowable except as they are conceived in the minds of the present.

The future forms and structures of systemic religion will surely be different from those now known, because the needs and circumstances of life will change. There may be historical continuity, but the future structures are indeterminate. They simply have not yet emerged and evolved. The direction these future structures take will depend on the needs encountered and the adaptive responses systemic religion makes to those needs.

Dynamic

The systemic worldview takes process as reality. Systemic religion accepts that reality. Snapshots in a moving-picture world are deceiving at best. Wilfred Cantwell Smith gave an appropriate warning:

> If we go about trying to understand the flux of change in terms of notions that postulate or require static religious entities, or trying to understand global interconnections in terms that postulate or

require discrete religious entities, independent of each other, then clearly we shall be in trouble.[157]

Models of systemic religion must be flexible and adaptable to reflect and relate to the dynamic nature of reality. Rigidity and inflexibility are destructive to the flow-through necessary for an open system to experience continued health and development.

Negentropic

An open system must have the ability to create order and transformation of inputs to survive. If death is entropy (equilibrium), then life is negentropy (homeostasis). Order and complexity are natural by-products of life.

If life is the overcoming of chaos, then certainly systemic religion is a critical element. Systemic religion is the effort to bind together, to integrate, to make whole. Systemic religion contributes to the life of the organism by creating holistic nexus.[158]

Holistic

Wholeness and health are the quest of the systemic worldview and systemic religion. This is not an idle hope, but a need that Gregory Bateson said was crucial to the "survival of the whole biosphere."[159] He proposed that a "sacred unity" be sought "which would bind and reassure us all."[160] If this need is crucial, it is not automatic. It will not just "come together." Wilfred Cantwell Smith was most accurate when he cited the responsibility for this issue: "As we all know, human development has reached a point where we must construct some kind of world order, or we perish."[161]

Cybernetic

The future is not uncontrollable: It *is* unpredictable in any absolute sense. There is a means of guidance for open systems through cybernetic feedback. The systemic worldview has a "built-in" monitoring capability through systemic religion. The search for holistic nexus is a search guided by values. In a real sense this entire section on a systemic model of religion has been a discussion of systemic values. Not just *any* kind of nexus is being sought, but a nexus of health. Health is determined by the progress toward the properties and characteristics within the systemic perspective.

Summary

The systemic worldview and systemic religion are compatible. In fact, they are interdependent upon one another: neither can function systemically without the other. Without systemic religion there can be no truly systemic worldview. Systemic religion divorced from a systemic worldview is vacuous and meaningless.

SYSTEMIC RELIGION IN ENVIRONMENTAL PERSPECTIVE

It would seem that such a grandiose project as redefining and restructuring religion would be sufficient challenge for one chapter of a book. There is little need to stir up more trouble by redefining and restructuring various other fields of study. Such an attempt would prove both vapid and short-sighted, as Auguste Comte brilliantly illustrated.[162]

In place of an in-depth exploration of all the systemic relationships that exist between religion and other fields, a brief overview of some of the areas of interface is given. Systemic religion, as holistic nexus, has interconnection with a great variety of fields, disciplines, and approaches. Some of the ones mentioned in this section are obvious and traditional, while others are not so often associated with religion. The intention here is to be catalytic in the search for interface rather than to attempt any comprehensive listing.

Religions

Systemic religion has been defined as holistic nexus: that quest for health and integration which is done in the present with the influence of past heritage and the guidance of a future vision. Such an understanding of religion does not necessarily require the frameworks of particular, organized religions, such as Christianity, but some structured expression is often a way religion is actualized. Holistic nexus is more than organized, corporate traditions but can be inclusive of them if these traditions do lead to health and integration.

Religions represent some of the ways different cultures and societies have worked for holistic nexus, The principle of equifinality describes a variety of starting points and a diversity of paths for the pursuit of a desired end. Religions are expressions of equifinality: there is no *one* way to experience and create health and integration and no *best* structure common to every culture, society, and individual. The number of religions (and the incredible variety that exists within the religions) is startling evidence of the diversity of expressions but also is confirmation of the universal need for the expressions.

The multiple expressions of religion are not only expected but encouraged from the systemic perspective. In an age of pluralism, the approaches can be understood to perform like facets of a diamond: Each reveals a unique perspective of beauty. Hand in hand with this differentiation, though, is the need for integration and interface. Ervin Laszlo addressed the future of religions this way:

> It is not likely, nor is it desirable, that differences of religions and philosophical views will disappear from the world scene. But the different religions and philosophies must learn to live and work together on this small and interdependent planet.[163]

It could be argued that there is no need for the concept of "religion" and that the discussion should simply focus on religions. Ninian Smart recognized this point of view:

> Of course we should at the outset be clear as to whether we are talking about religion or religions. Perhaps there is no such thing as religion in general—all that we meet are particular religions . . . [yet] we should not too easily dismiss the concept of religion in general.[164]

The difficulty with dismissing "religion in general" in favor of particular religions is that such an approach would say that the whole of religion can be found within the various frameworks of organized religions. If religion is understood as holistic nexus, this is just not so. Health and integration are much broader processes than can be forced into the structures of organized religions. Religions may contribute to holistic nexus, but they are by no means the totality. A few examples refuting the imperialism of organized religion (if understood as the totality of systemic religion) are found throughout the remainder of this chapter.

Theology

The translation of the term "theology" is literally "god-talk," but such a designation has its dangers. Certainly theology may be involved in "god-talk," but theology is neither the exclusive possessor of this activity nor necessarily the best equipped to conduct it. John Macquarrie defined theology as "a study that seeks to express the content of . . . faith in the clearest and most coherent language available."[165] Paul Tillich defined theology similarly as "the methodological interpretation of the contents of faith."[166] Theology is by definition and by nature a cognitive, reflective, and verbal activity. Theology is different than, but not necessarily opposed to, systemic religion. James Michael Lee said that theology is best understood as "a cognitive interpretation of religion,"[167] a comment which points to the distinction between theology and religion. Theology and religion are interactive systems that interrelate and contribute to each other but do not subsume or control each other.

The differentiation between theology and religion allows religion to interface with persons who do not hold to a theistic interpretation of reality. If theology is synonymous with religion, then (for example) an atheist is excluded from a discussion of the quest for holistic nexus, which would be both illogical and unwarranted. The same applies to religions that do not include theistic language, such as Mahayana Buddhism.[168] The issue for religion is holistic nexus, and theistic formulations may or may not be a part of the process.

Though often criticized as rigid and dogmatic, theology is not necessarily so described. Theology can be adaptive and transformational; indeed, it must be in order to function as an element in the systemic perspective. John Cobb, a Christian theologian, is an example of one who is open to environmental influence. He described how Christianity would profit (and change) if it were to be involved in authentic dialogue with Eastern religions:

My conviction is that the Christianity which would emerge from those several appropriations of aspects of truth which other traditions have developed would be a different Christianity from what the West now knows. I do not, however, believe it would be less Christian. On the contrary, my argument is that in faithfulness to Christ we are to expose ourselves to those multiple transformations.[169]

In truly systemic fashion, the only way for Christianity (or any open system) to have impact and influence on its environment is to be open and willing to be impacted and influenced—transformed—by the environment. The alternative to being an open system is to be a closed system: deterministic, impotent, and doomed to isolation and extinction.

Religion is experiential, holistic, integrative, and dynamic and can be aided by the cognitive, verbal, reflective, and adaptive structures of theology. Theology is not the sole resource of systemic religion, however. As James Michael Lee said: "If religion is to be vital, it must broaden itself to include at its deepest foundation not only theology, but the other sciences as well."[170]

Philosophy

A literal translation of the term "philosophy" is rendered "love of wisdom and knowledge." Eric Rust defined philosophy as "the attempt, by rational reflection upon human experience in its totality, to arrive at some integrative insight in which the nature of [persons], the nature of the universe, and the relation of the two may become intelligible."[171] Philosophy has great value to systemic religion by virtue of its integrative search. The difference is the emphasis on cognition and intellect.

Philosophy has much the same relationship to systemic religion that theology has to systemic religion. Philosophy is also a cognitive activity that provides opportunity for reflection, critical analysis and feedback, and verbal expression. At times it may be difficult to distinguish philosophy and theology, especially as they participate and contribute to systemic religion. The chief difference is that while theology seeks the theistic and theological interpretations, philosophy may or may not need theism in its "ra-

tional reflection." Karl Rahner expressed the difference in traditional dualistic language: "Theology is based on the grace of
revealed faith and regards the revealed mysteries of God, while
philosophy proceeds from natural reason."[172] While neither theology nor philosophy need accept the dualistic points of origin
for exploration, the distinction of theistic interpretations is a
proper way to distinguish between theology and philosophy.

Philosophy isolated in its own cognitive wonderland is of little
use to a systemic perspective. It must be linked to the entire
transformation process. This was the point of Karl Marx when he
wrote: "The philosophers have only interpreted the world in various ways; the point is to change it."[173] Philosophy can have a
great influence for change, but it must become more than a
thinking process. It must proceed into action. Gordon Allport
expressed this as he described the relationship of philosophy and
religion:

> A philosopher may achieve what for him [or her] is a satisfying
> conception of truth without finding therein a way of life. His [or
> her] knowledge need not lead to action, nor affect the remainder of
> his [or her] life. It is only when philosophy becomes practical as
> well as theoretical, when it acquires the power of integrating the
> individual's life without remainder—intellectual, emotional, or
> aspirational—that it turns into religion.[174]

Social Science

Social science represents a tremendous area of interface with
systemic religion. Evidence of the potential in social science for
systemic religion rests in the fact that the systemic perspective
developed in this book can be considered one mode of social
science. This attempt is by no means the first. Others, such as
James Michael Lee, have pursued a similar approach. Indeed, the
disciplines of sociology of religion and of psychology of religion
bear further evidence of the interconnection of religion and the
social sciences. Since this aspect of the systemic perspective receives repeated attention throughout this book, two examples
suffice to make the interrelationship plain.

Carl Rogers, a psychotherapist, has been one person who has
relentlessly and courageously championed the cause of "client-

centered therapy" over against a rigid, deterministic, and manipulative style of therapy. He has refused to accept the idea that a person is only known through a rational process, or through the observation of a narrow range of behaviors. Rogers has not hesitated to interject himself into personal relationship with clients to effect a mutual interchange of growth and development. He summarized his guiding hypothesis this way: "If I can produce a certain type of relationship, the other person will discover within himself [or herself] the capacity to use that relationship for growth, and change and personal development will occur."[175] Rogers trusted the natural ability of the human personality to emerge and develop in the nurturing atmosphere of deep, interpersonal relationship. He described his reasons for taking the time and the risk of interface with other human beings:

> It is because I find value and reward in human relationships that I enter into a relationship known as therapeutic, where feelings and cognition merge into one unitary experience which is lived rather than examined, in which awareness is nonreflective, and where I am participant rather than observer.[176]

Such a health-giving nexus between two persons is a beautiful example of authentic systemic religion.

Gregory Bateson was influential in a number of social sciences, including anthropology, psychiatry, sociology, and cybernetics. At the close of his long and fruitful life, he lamented what he saw as the loss of "the sense of unity of biosphere and humanity that would bind and reassure us all with an affirmation of beauty."[177] He went on to detail the loss:

> We have lost the core of Christianity. We have lost Shiva, the dancer of Hinduism whose dance at the trivial level is both creation and destruction but in whole is beauty. We have lost Abraxas, the terrible and beautiful god of both day and night in Gnosticism. We have lost totemism, the sense of parallelism between [humanity's] organization and that of the animals and plants. We have lost even the Dying God.
>
> We are beginning to play with ideas of ecology, and although we immediately trivialize these ideas into commerce or politics, there is at least an impulse still in the human breast to unify and thereby sanctify the total natural world, of which we are.[178]

Bateson articulated a harmonized understanding of mind and nature that is no longer a dualism but is rather an interactive, dynamic, and necessary unity. He summarized all of this by saying that "mental function is immanent in the interaction of differentiated 'parts.' 'Wholes' are constituted by such combined interaction."[179] This same search for unity, interaction, and interdependence is reflective of the quest for systemic religion.

Natural Science

Since the systemic perspective—inclusive of systemic religion—is predicated on the paradigm of open systems, it is no surprise that natural science provides another permeable boundary of systemic religion. From a truly systemic perspective, the "conflict" of science and religion is inexplicable and anachronistic. Contemporary science and systemic religion work together to understand and interpret reality.

One of the better-known persons who synthesized science and religion was Pierre Teilhard de Chardin. As priest and paleontologist, he combined vocation and faith in a unique way that left both science and religion radically affected. The preface to *The Phenomenon of Man* opened with these revealing words:

> If this book is to be properly understood, it must be read not as a work on metaphysics, still less as a sort of theological essay, but purely and simply as a scientific treatise. This book deals with [humanity] *solely* as a phenomenon: but it also deals with the *whole* phenomenon of [humanity].[180]

Teilhard was dealing with science but not with a classical, dualistic, and reductionistic kind of science. He explored the systemic perceptions of science, which he helped to make clearer and more acceptable.

A somewhat less successful attempt to link science and religion was made by Paul Davies in a book with the intriguing title *God and the New Physics*.[181] Davies, a physicist, found "religion" unable to accommodate his new scientific understandings. His problem was that he was referring to a rigid, deterministic, and dualistic kind of religion, which he described as being "founded on dogma and received wisdom, which purports to represent immutable truth."[182] Such a conception of religion led him to say that "the idea of religion's fundamental dogma being abandoned in favor of a more accurate 'model' of reality is unthinkable."[183] With these pathetic and tragic presuppositions, it is no wonder he felt forced to admit: "It may seem bizarre, but in my opinion science offers a surer path to God than religion."[184] If religion is as he described it, he was correct in choosing science. The truth is, of course, that Davies was simply as uninformed on the progress of religion as many theologians and "religious experts" are on the developments in science. Davies' "new physics" is most acceptable in a systemic worldview and complementary to the development of systemic religion.[185]

Medical science is becoming more responsive to the holistic needs of the person. Hans Selye studied the effects of stress and found that the effect of stress on the person is actually a reflection of the way a person encounters all of life. Selye produced evidence of the change in the organs of living bodies as a result of stress, and although he dealt with the problem "purely as a biologist in the light of laboratory experience,"[186] Selye phrased his interpretation in holistic terms:

> It seems to me that [a person's] ultimate aim in life is to express himself [or herself] as fully as possible, according to his [or her] own lights, and to achieve a sense of security. To accomplish this you must first find your optimal stress level and then use your adaptation energy at a rate and in a direction adjusted to your innate qualifications and preferences.[187]

In others words, Selye was suggesting that stress should be managed by each individual in such a way as to produce health and integration.

In related research, Meyer Friedman and Diane Ulmer described a study designed to explain the cause of heart attacks among humans. The research was pursued by "scrutinizing each patient as a *total* human being, not just a mobile exemplar of medical statistics such as blood pressure, pulse rate, electrocardiographic squiggles, and . . . sugar levels."[188] When the patients were perceived as individuals who possessed other organs besides their ailing hearts and also personalities, it became obvious that it was not simply their hearts that had gone awry. Something in the way they felt, thought, and acted was also in alarming disarray.[189]

Friedman and Ulmer portrayed a growing awareness that health and integration are not just cognitive ideals, but are essential ingredients in the lives of human beings.

Ilya Prigogine is another example of a scientist who has provided for interaction between science and religion. Though a chemist by vocation, Prigogine has produced theories and data that have had influence far beyond the field of chemistry. The discovery of what he has called "dissipative structures" where order arises out of the most chaotic of environments may prove to allow an entirely new vision of evolution, life, and the future. Just as Prigogine demonstrated that classical understandings of thermodynamics relate only to closed systems and that open systems need a radically different interpretation, so do the classical formulations of religion speak more to a static worldview than to one where there is authentic growth, transformation, and emergence of order from chaos. Modern science must learn what to do with such shocking data, and so must systemic religion. Modern science and systemic religion have the opportunity and the responsibility to work interactively and interdependently (with other fields) in the creation of a truly systemic worldview.

The Arts

One of the most fertile and yet one of the most unrecognized areas of interface with religion is that of the arts. Certainly many have heard a minister give the "three points and a poem" that often comprise a sermon, but surely there is a deeper role for the arts to play than as an ornamental appendage. The arts (especially when they are "fine" arts!) exhibit the full range of human potential: cognition, affect, psychomotor activity, creativity, and expression. The possibilities of cooperation between religion and the arts are limitless, and humanity has yet to realize the full depth of this resource.

The power of the arts to express the depth of religion sometimes comes as a shock and as a revelation. John Westerhoff related the story of how this truth came home to him:

> One night a small group of us were recounting the struggles of our souls in the presence of Paul Tillich. Instead of an intellectual response he turned on Bach's *B Minor Mass*. I will always remember that the only answer this great theologian had for his students' doubt was the church singing its faith, singing *credo*. . . . Ever since those days I have been convinced that the arts and liturgy, better than the sciences and theology, express and illumine the spiritual dimensions of life.[190]

Whether or not one agrees that one dimension is "better" at expression, the point is well made that there are varieties of ways to experience, learn, and integrate.

John Westerhoff's encounter with Bach brings to mind the variety of ways music (as one example of the arts) reaches different individuals. Where so-called "classical" music may leave one person ecstatic, it may leave another unmoved. The latter decades of the twentieth century have had ample illustration of the diversity of music that can excite, motivate, and interpret. What power and influence the folksong had in the 1960s! Society continues to feel the breeze of Bob Dylan's answers "blowin' in the wind." Rock music in the 1970s searched for new answers, or at least asked different questions, in works like "Jesus Christ Superstar" ("Jesus Christ, Jesus Christ, who are you? What have you sacrificed?"[191]). Persons in the 1980s were called upon to "feed the world," showing that the message of global responsibility for famine can be delivered through a simple but haunting melody. While none of these examples threaten to replace "Amazing Grace" as a favorite church hymn, surely the power and communicability of the music is unquestionable. Times, needs, and tastes change, but music and the arts also continue to change, giving each generation the means to address the quest for holistic nexus.

The arts can also point to the lack of holistic nexus. Who can sit through a performance of "Death of a Salesman" and not stare at themselves through the tired eyes and vapid values of Willy Loman? Who can gaze at Pablo Picasso's "Guernica" and not only relive the horror of that battle but also consider the insanity of *any* war? Who can stand in the presence of Michelangelo's "Pieta" and not share the grief, shock, doubt, and wonder of Mary as she holds the lifeless corpse of her son?

The arts have a way of articulating holistic nexus that traditional "religious" forms and structures cannot. Arguments about the interpretation and the historicity of the biblical accounts of creation have gone on for decades, but John Steinbeck was able to cut through all of that and make the message clear in *East of Eden*. Brotherly love may be discussed in Sunday School, but it does not match the learning one experiences by singing "We Will Overcome" on a ghetto sidewalk, white arms linked with black. Imagine trying to explain death and resurrection to a child (or an adult) more effectively than Steven Spielberg did in the movie "E.T."!

Examples of the arts and systemic religion combining to create health and integration flood the mind, but by now the issue should be clearly delineated. Holistic nexus can be pursued with infinite variety through interface with the arts. Systemic religion celebrates, learns, and develops through the permeable boundary that exists with the fertile environment of artistic expression.

CONCLUSION

This chapter opened with a simple but crucial question: Is religion a vital element of the systemic perspective? The answer is a resounding yes—as long as religion is healthy, maturational, and systemic. Holistic nexus is that which binds the entire approach into a systemic whole. Without systemic religion, there is no systemic perspective. The model of systemic religion certainly must develop and adapt to the changing environment, but the need for systemic religion remains.

NOTES

1. Ludwig van Beethoven, *Fidelio* (London: Boosey and Company, 1948). My own free translation is:
O what pleasure! O what delight!
To take a light breath in the free air,
Only here, solely here is life,
The dungeon is a tomb.

2. Thomas S. Kuhn, *The Structure of Scientific Revolutions,* 2nd ed. (Chicago: University of Chicago Press, 1970), p. 24.

3. Ibid.

4. Ludwig von Bertalanffy, *General System Theory: Foundations, Development, Applications,* rev. ed. (New York: George Braziller, 1968), p. 84.

5. James Grier Miller, *Living Systems* (New York: McGraw-Hill, 1978), p. 83.

6. Ibid.

7. Ibid.

8. Ibid., p. 84.

9. See the discussion of the design of open systems in chapter 2 of this book. Closely related is chapter 2, "Structure, Function, and Purpose," in Russell L. Ackoff and Fred E. Emery, *On Purposeful Systems* (Chicago: Aldine-Atherton, 1972), pp. 13-32.

10. Paul Abrecht, ed., *Faith, Science and the Future* (Philadelphia: Fortress Press, 1978), p. 14.

11. Gloria Durka and Joanmarie Smith, *Modeling God: Religious Education for Tomorrow* (New York: Paulist Press, 1976), p. 5.

12. Miller, *Living Systems,* p. 84.

13. Bertalanffy, *General System Theory,* p. 94.

14. Gordon W. Allport, *An Individual and His Religion: A Psychological Interpretation* (New York: Macmillan, 1950), p. 1.

15. Lloyd Geering, *Faith's New Age: A Perspective on Contemporary Religious Change* (London: William Collins and Sons, 1980), p. 15.

16. Allport, *An Individual and His Religion,* p. 117.

17. Eulalio R. Baltazar, *God Within Process* (New York: Newman Press, 1970), p. 4.

18. Erich Fromm, *Psychoanalysis and Religion* (New Haven, Conn.: Yale University Press, 1950), p. 113.

19. See Wilfred Cantwell Smith, "A Human View of Truth," in *Truth and Dialogue in World Religions: Conflicting Truth-Claims,* ed. John Hick (Philadelphia: Westminster Press, 1974), pp. 20 ff.

20. Alfred North Whitehead, *Religion in the Making* (New York: Macmillan, 1923; reprint edition; New York: The American Library, 1974), p. 13.

21. Harvey Cox, *Religion in the Secular City: Toward a Postmodern Theology* (New York: Simon and Schuster, 1984), p. 159.

22. Maurice Friedman, *The Human Way: A Dialogic Approach to Religion and Human Experience* (Chambersburg, Pa.: Anima Books, 1982), pp. 180-181.

23. Wilfred Cantwell Smith, *The Meaning and End of Religion: A New Approach to the Religious Traditions of Mankind* (New York: Macmillan, 1963), p. 8.

24. Emile Durkheim, *The Elementary Forms of the Religious Life: A Study in Religious Sociology,* trans. Joseph Ward Swain (New York: Macmillan, 1915), p. 416.

25. For example, see Marshall McLuhan, *Understanding Media: The Extensions of Man,* 2nd ed. (New York: New American Library, 1964), p. 20.

26. Ninian Smart, *Worldviews: Crosscultural Explorations of Human Belief* (New York: Charles Scribner's Sons, 1983), p. 3.

27. James A. Pike, *If This Be Heresy* (New York: Harper & Row, 1967), p. 21.

28. Geering, *Faith's New Age,* p. 9.

29. Sidney M. Jourard, *Healthy Personality: An Approach from the Viewpoint of Humanistic Psychology* (New York: Macmillan, 1974), p. 306.

30. Ibid., p. 308.

31. Harry Emerson Fosdick, *On Being a Real Person* (New York: Harper & Brothers, 1943), pp. 240-241.

32. For example, see Richard R. Niebuhr, "Friedrich Schleiermacher," in *A Handbook of Christian Theologians,* ed. Martin E. Marty and Dean G. Peerman (Cleveland: World Publishing Company, 1965), pp. 17 ff; Mason Olds, *Religious Humanism in America: Dietrich, Reese, and Potter* (Washington, D.C.: University Press of America, 1978), p. 12; and Cox, *Religion in the Secular City,* p. 176.

33. Cox, *Religion in the Secular City,* p. 177. This worldview is the "classical science worldview" in the language of the present book.

34. Friedrich Schleiermacher, *On Religion: Speeches to Its Cultured Despisers,* trans. John Oman (London: Kegan Paul, Trench, Trubner and Company, 1893), p. 1.

35. Ibid., pp. 49-50.

36. Niebuhr, "Friedrich Schleiermacher," p. 33.

37. Ludwig Feuerbach, *The Essence of Christianity,* trans. George Eliot (New York: Harper Torchbooks, 1957), p. 1.

38. Ibid., p. 2.

39. Ibid., p. 33.

40. Ibid., p. 184. The emphasis is from Feuerbach.

41. Ibid., p. 33.

42. Patrick Masterson, *Atheism and Alienation: A Study of the Philosophical Sources of Contemporary Atheism* (Notre Dame, Ind.: University of Notre Dame Press, 1971), p. 65.

43. Karl Marx, "Towards a Critique of Hegel's *Philosophy of Right:* Introduction," in *Selected Writings,* ed. David McLellan (Oxford: Oxford University Press, 1977), p. 63.

44. S. Paul Schilling, *God in an Age of Atheism* (Nashville: Abingdon Press, 1969), pp. 51-52.

45. Marx, "Towards a Critique of Hegel's *Philosophy of Right:* Introduction," p. 64.

46. Sigmund Freud, *The Future of an Illusion,* in *The Standard Edition of the Complete Psychological Works of Sigmund Freud,* Vol. XXI, ed. and trans. James Strachey (London: The Hogarth Press, 1961), p. 31.

47. Ibid.

48. Sigmund Freud, "Obsessive Actions and Religious Practices," in *The Standard Edition of the Complete Psychological Works of Sigmund Freud,* Vol. IX, ed. and trans. James Strachey (London: The Hogarth Press, 1959), pp. 126-127.

49. Durkheim, *The Elementary Forms of the Religious Life,* p. 37.

50. Ibid., p. 4.

51. Ibid., p. 418.

52. Ibid., p. 419.

53. Rudolf Otto, *The Idea of the Holy,* trans. John W. Harvey (London: Oxford University Press, 1923: reprint edition, 1973), pp. 9-10.

54. Ibid., p. 5.

55. Ibid., pp. 6-7.
56. Ibid., p. 6.
57. Ibid., p. 7.
58. Ibid., p. 11.
59. For example, see Daniel Jenkins, "Karl Barth," in *A Handbook of Christian Theologians,* ed. Marty and Peerman, p. 396.
60. See H. Richard Niebuhr, "Foreword," in Feuerbach, *The Essence of Christianity,* pp. vii-ix; Karl Barth, "An Introductory Essay," in Feuerbach, *The Essence of Christianity,* pp. x-xxxii, especially xxix; and Masterson, *Atheism and Alienation,* p. 63.
61. Karl Barth, *The Doctrine of the Word of God: Prolegomena to Church Dogmatics,* Vol. 1, Part 2, trans. G. T. Thompson and Harold Knight (New York: Charles Scribner's Sons, 1956), pp. 299-300.
62. Karl Barth, *The Epistle to the Romans,* trans. Edwyn C. Hoskins, 6th ed. (London: Oxford University Press, 1933; reprint edition, 1980), p. 306. For a good discussion of this point, see Martin E. Marty, "Religious Development in Historical, Social, and Cultural Context," in *Research on Religious Development: A Comprehensive Handbook,* ed. Merton P. Strommen (New York: Hawthorne Books, 1971), pp. 61-65.
63. Barth, *The Epistle to the Romans,* p. 306.
64. Examine the two letters to Eberhard Bethage in Dietrich Bonhoeffer, *Letters and Papers from Prison,* ed. Eberhard Bethage (enlarged edition; New York: Macmillan Company, 1971), pp. 278-282.
65. Ibid., p. 280.
66. This book has become a classic in the effort to define religion. Refer to the extensive notes at the end of the book for a comprehensive understanding of the history of the terminology.
67. Smith, *The Meaning and End of Religion,* pp. 48-49. The four uses he described were personal piety, ideal, faith, empirical phenomenon of faith, and generic summation.
68. Ibid., p. 156.
69. John B. Cobb, Jr., *The Structure of Christian Existence* (Philadelphia: Westminster Press, 1967; paperback edition; New York: Seabury Press, 1979), p. 15.
70. John B. Cobb, Jr., *God and the World* (Philadelphia: Westminster Press, 1969), p. 119.
71. John B. Cobb, Jr., "Is Christianity a Religion?" in *What Is Christianity? An Inquiry for Christian Theology,* ed. Mircea Eliade and David Tracy (New York: Seabury Press, 1980), p. 8.
72. Interestingly enough, Wilfred Cantwell Smith continued to use the term out of necessity. This illustrates the difficulty of trying to drop a word from the vocabulary, or radically redefining it.
73. Viktor E. Frankl, *Man's Search for Meaning: An Introduction to Logotherapy* (New York: Washington Square Press, 1963), p. 154.
74. Ibid.
75. Ninian Smart, "What Is Religion?" in *New Movements in Religious Education,* ed. Ninian Smart and Donald Horder (London: Temple Smith, 1975), p. 20.
76. Geering, *Faith's New Age,* p. 19.
77. Tillich expressed this same thought in many ways. For example, see Paul

Tillich, *What Is Religion?* ed. James Luther Adams (New York: Harper & Row, 1969), p. 59; and Paul Tillich, *Systematic Theology,* Vol. 1 (Chicago: University of Chicago Press, 1951), pp. 12-14.

78. Paul Tillich, *The Protestant Era,* trans. James Luther Adams (Chicago: University of Chicago Press, 1948), p. 59.

79. Many authors have picked up Tillich's phrase and adapted it. See, for example, J. Wesley Robb, *The Reverent Skeptic: A Critical Inquiry into the Religion of Secular Humanism* (New York: Philosophical Library, 1979), p. 18; Theodosius Dobzhansky, *The Biology of Ultimate Concern* (New York: World Publishing Company, 1967), p. 5; and Friedman, *The Human Way,* p. 29.

80. Sophia Lyon Fahs, *Today's Children and Yesterday's Heritage: A Philosophy of Creative Religious Development* (Boston: Beacon Press, 1952), p. 8.

81. William James, *The Varieties of Religious Experience: A Study in Human Nature* (New York: Macmillan, 1961), p. 43. The inclusive language is my interjection.

82. Whitehead, *Religion in the Making,* p. 16.

83. For a clear statement of values in these "peak-experiences," see Appendix G in Abraham E. Maslow, *Religions, Values, and Peak-Experiences* (New York: Penguin Books, 1970), pp. 91-96.

84. Ibid., p. 28.

85. Ibid., p. 24.

86. Geering, *Faith's New Age,* p. 18.

87. Charleton T. Lewis and Charles Short, *A New Latin Dictionary,* revised and enlarged edition (New York: American Book Company, 1879), pp. 1556-1557; P. G. W. Glare, *Oxford Latin Dictionary* (Oxford: At the Clarendon Press, 1982), p. 1605.

88. See Smith, *The Meaning and End of Religion,* pp. 19 ff; notes 4-6, pp. 203-205; Martin E. Marty, "Religious Development in Historical, Social, and Cultural Context," in *Research on Religious Development,* pp. 53-56; and James Michael Lee, *The Content of Religious Instruction: A Social Science Approach* (Birmingham, Ala.: Religious Education Press, 1985), p. 718 (note 175).

89. Lewis and Short, *A New Latin Dictionary,* p. 973; p. 1840; Glare, *Oxford Latin Dictionary,* p. 935; pp. 1904-1905.

90. Lewis and Short, *A New Latin Dictionary,* p. 1166; Glare, *Oxford Latin Dictionary,* p. 1198; p. 1205.

91. Glare, *Oxford Latin Dictionary,* p. 1184.

92. Allport, *An Individual and His Religion,* p. 161. The sexist language should be interpreted in a generic way.

93. Alfred North Whitehead, *Science and the Modern World* (New York: Macmillan, 1925; reprint edition; New York: The Free Press, 1967), pp. 191-192.

94. Whitehead, *Religion in the Making,* p. 152.

95. Ibid., p. 115.

96. Erich Jantsch, *The Self-Organizing Universe: Scientific and Human Implications of the Emerging Paradigm of Evolution* (Oxford: Pergamon Press, 1980), pp. 218, 301, and elsewhere.

97. Ibid., p. 301.

98. See especially Ilya Prigogine, "Preface," *From Being to Becoming: Time and Complexity in the Physical Sciences* (San Francisco: W. H. Freeman and Company, 1980), pp. xi-xix; and Ilya Prigogine and Isabelle Stengers, "Rediscov-

ering Time," Chapter Seven in *Order Out of Chaos: Man's New Dialogue with Nature* (New York: Bantam Books, 1984), pp. 213-232.

99. Prigogine, *From Being to Becoming*, pp. 2-3.

100. Ervin Laszlo et. al., *Goals for Mankind: A Report to the Club of Rome on the New Horizons of Global Community*, rev. ed. (New York: New American Library, 1977), p. 330.

101. Adolf Hitler, *Mein Kampf*, trans. E. T. S. Dugdale (Boston: Houghton Mifflin, 1933), pp. 156 ff.

102. Julian Huxley, *Religion Without Revelation*, rev. ed. (New York: Harper & Brothers, 1957), p. 200.

103. Whitehead, *Religion in the Making*, p. 36.

104. Lee, *The Content of Religious Instruction*, p. 3.

105. Louis B. Jennings, *The Function of Religion: An Introduction* (Washington, D.C.: University Press of America, 1979), p. vii.

106. William Bailey, *Man, Religion, and Science: A Functional View* (Santa Barbara, Calif.: William Bailey, 1980), p. 49.

107. Fritjof Capra, *The Turning Point: Science, Society and the Rising Culture* (New York: Simon and Schuster, 1982), p. 269.

108. Lucien Saumur, *The Humanist Evangel* (Buffalo, N.Y.: Prometheus Books, 1982), p. 17.

109. Fromm, *Psychoanalysis and Religion*, p. 35.

110. Fahs, *Today's Children and Yesterday's Heritage*, p. 15.

111. Whitehead, *Religion in the Making*, p. 16.

112. Marty, "Religious Development in Historical, Social, and Cultural Context," p. 43.

113. Ibid., p. 44.

114. Ibid.

115. Whitehead, *Religion in the Making*, p. 59.

116. Peter L. Berger, *The Heretical Imperative: Contemporary Possibilities of Religious Affirmation* (Garden City, N.Y.: Anchor Press, 1979), p. 24.

117. Peter L. Berger, *The Sacred Canopy: Elements of a Sociological Theory of Religion* (Garden City, N.Y.: Anchor Books, 1969), p. 51.

118. Berger, *The Heretical Imperative*, p. 25.

119. Gregory Bateson, *Mind and Nature: A Necessary Unity* (New York: Bantam Books, 1980), p. 21.

120. Berger, *The Sacred Canopy*, p. 28.

121. Allport, *An Individual and His Religion*, p. 79.

122. Huxley, *Religion Without Revelation*, p. 176.

123. Bertalanffy, *General System Theory*, p. 121.

124. See Capra, *The Turning Point*, p. 275; also see Gerald M. Weinberg, *An Introduction to General Systems Thinking* (New York: John Wiley & Sons, 1975), pp. 149 ff.

125. Weinberg, *An Introduction to General Systems Thinking*, p. 209.

126. John W. Sutherland, *Systems: Analysis, Administration, Architecture* (New York: Van Nostrand Reinhold, 1975), p. 38.

127. Wilfred Cantwell Smith, *Towards a World Theology: Faith and the Comparative History of Religion* (Philadelphia: Westminster Press, 1981), p. 41.

128. Robert Frost, "Mending Wall," in *Robert Frost's Poems*, ed. Louis Untermeyer (New York: Washington Square Press, 1971), p. 95.

129. Bertalanffy, *General System Theory*, p. 88.

130. Norbert Wiener, *The Human Use of Human Beings: Cybernetics and Society* (New York: Avon Books, 1967), p. 130.
131. Whitehead, *Religion in the Making,* p. 13.
132. Smith, *Towards a World Theology,* p. 35.
133. Jennings, *The Function of Religion,* p. 12.
134. Smith, *Towards a World Theology,* p. 194.
135. Laszlo et. al., *Goals for Mankind,* p. 328.
136. Ibid., p. 329.
137. Ibid., p. 330.
138. Doran McCarty, *Teilhard de Chardin* (Waco Tex.: Word Books, 1976), p. 98.
139. Pierre Teilhard de Chardin, *The Phenomenon of Man,* trans. Bernard Wall (New York: Harper & Row, 1959), pp. 262-263.
140. Alfred North Whitehead, *Process and Reality: An Essay in Cosmology,* ed. David Ray Griffin and Donald W. Sherburne (corrected edition; New York: The Free Press, 1978), p. 346.
141. Kenneth E. Boulding, *Ecodynamics: A New Theory of Societal Evolution* (Beverly Hills, Calif.: Sage Publications, 1978), p. 42.
142. Ervin Laszlo, *The Systems View of the World: The Natural Philosophy of the New Developments in the Sciences* (New York: George Braziller, 1972), p. 105.
143. Whitehead, *Religion in the Making,* p. 17.
144. Jourard, *Healthy Personality,* p. 309.
145. Geering, *Faith's New Age,* p. 17.
146. Cox, *Religion in the Secular City,* pp. 206-207.
147. Prigogine, *From Being to Becoming,* pp. 127-128.
148. Sutherland, *Systems,* p. 72.
149. Ibid.
150. Whitehead, *Science and the Modern World,* p. 188.
151. Ibid., p. 224.
152. Huxley, *Religion Without Revelation,* p. 17.
153. Cox, *Religion in the Secular City,* p. 224.
154. Whitehead, *Religion in the Making,* p. 127.
155. John Hick, *God Has Many Names* (Philadelphia: Westminster Press, 1980), p. 21.
156. Wilfred Cantwell Smith, *The Faith of Other Men* (New York: Harper & Row, 1962), p. 11.
157. Smith, *Towards a World Theology,* p. 22.
158. Genesis, ch. 1, tells a story of life and order coming from a primordial chaos.
159. Bateson, *Mind and Nature,* p. 8.
160. Ibid., pp. 19-21.
161. Smith, *The Faith of Other Men,* p. 100.
162. Auguste Comte did reorganize the whole of science and, from his perspective, all of society. It did not meet with universal acceptance. For an overview, see the table of contents to Auguste Comte, *A General View of Positivism,* trans. J. H. Bridges, (London: Trubner and Company, 1865; reprint edition; Dubuque, Iowa: Brown Reprints, 1971).
163. Laszlo et al., *Goals for Mankind,* p. 329.
164. Smart, "What Is Religion?" p. 13.

165. John Macquarrie, *Principles of Christian Theology* (New York: Charles Scribner's Sons, 1966), p. 1.

166. Paul Tillich, *Systematic Theology,* Vol. 1 (Chicago: University of Chicago Press, 1951), p. 15.

167. Lee, *The Content of Religious Instruction,* p. 637.

168. See John B. Cobb, Jr., *Beyond Dialogue: Toward a Mutual Transformation of Christianity and Buddhism* (Philadelphia: Fortress Press, 1982).

169. Ibid., p. 149.

170. Lee, *The Content of Religious Instruction,* p. 761.

171. Eric C. Rust, *Evolutionary Philosophies and Contemporary Theology* (Philadelphia: Westminster Press, 1966), p. 16.

172. Karl Rahner, "Theology," in *Encyclopedia of Theology: A Concise Sacramentum, Mundi,* ed. Karl Rahner (London: Burns and Oates, 1975), p. 1692.

173. Marx, "Theses on Feuerbach," p. 158.

174. Allport, *An Individual and His Religion,* p. 150.

175. Carl R. Rogers, *On Becoming a Person: A Therapist's View of Psychotherapy* (Boston: Houghton Mifflin, 1961), p. 33.

176. Ibid., pp. 222-223.

177. Bateson, *Mind and Nature,* p. 19.

178. Ibid.

179. Ibid., p. 104.

180. Teilhard de Chardin, *The Phenomenon of Man,* p. 29. The emphasis is from Teilhard.

181. Paul Davies, *God and the New Physics* (New York: Simon and Schuster, 1983).

182. Ibid., p. 220.

183. Ibid.

184. Ibid., p. ix.

185. For a better understanding of how modern science can interface with systemic religion, see Gary Zukov, *The Dancing Wu Li Masters: An Overview of the New Physics* (New York: Bantam Books, 1979); Fritjof Capra, *The Tao of Physics: An Exploration of the Parallels Between Modern Physics and Eastern Mysticism* (New York: Bantam Books, 1975); and David Arthur Bickimer, *Christ the Placenta: Letters to My Mentor on Religious Education* (Birmingham, Ala.: Religious Education Press, 1983).

186. Hans Selye, *Stress Without Distress* (New York: New American Library, 1974), p. 102.

187. Ibid., p. 110.

188. Meyer Friedman and Diane Ulmer, *Treating Type A Behavior and Your Heart* (New York: Alfred A. Knopf, 1984), p. 5.

189. Ibid.

190. John H. Westerhoff III, "A Journey into Self-Understanding," in *Modern Masters of Religious Education,* ed. Marlene Mayr (Birmingham, Ala.: Religious Education Press, 1983), p. 123.

191. Andrew Lloyd Weber and Tim Rice, "Superstar," in *Jesus Christ Superstar: A Rock Opera* (London: Leeds Music Limited, 1970).

Chapter 5

Education

A child said, What is the grass? fetching it
to me with full hands;
How could I answer the child? I do not know
what it is any more than he.[1]
                              Walt Whitman

One of the great moments of discovery often comes in kindergarten, when a child wants to paint green grass with the new set of watercolors. At first the child faces a dilemma because the paint set has only the three primary colors and no green cake of paint to use. Either by guided experimentation or pure accident, the child soon finds that the blue and yellow paints that are available can be transformed into a wonderful new reality: green!

By extension, this book is guided experimentation (rather than pure accident, ideally) to find a solution to a similar dilemma. Chapter 4 provided the primary "blue" of religion, and now chapter 5 presents the primary "yellow" of education. The following chapter seeks a synthesis of these to create a different entity: the "green" of religious education.

The systemic model of education outlined and constructed in this chapter follows the same general procedure that was developed for the systemic model of religion. Included is a systemic definition of education; a systemic design for education; a discussion of education based on the paradigm of open systems; and a look at education from the perspective of a systemic worldview. Attention is also given to the environmental context of systemic education as a theoretical approach, showing how it relates to various other theoretical approaches.

The previous paragraph is quite important since it is descriptive of the modeling *process* for systemic education as well as for other areas. Systemic education is an attempt at an existential synthesis that is illustrative and illuminative for the future, similar to Alvin Toffler's advice: "Education must shift into the future tense."[2] The focus is on the overriding need for integration and development in systemic education, rather than on particular structures or specific contents. The effort here is to describe a transdisciplinary and holistic approach to education where structure and content are interactive elements of the whole, but not the determinative elements.

Jeremy Rifkin made a sweeping indictment of current educational practice by calling it "little more than a twelve-to-sixteen-year training program for the Newtonian [classical science] worldview."[3] While that is an overstatement, Rifkin did have a point. The normative disciplinary approach to education is essentially reductionistic. He went on to say:

> Our educational process is devoted to specialization. Every time we learn something new and different about the world, a new academic or professional discipline is set up to collect and interpret new data. Learning has become fragmented into tinier and tinier frameworks of study on the Newtonian assumption that the more we know about the individual parts, the more we will be able to make deductions about the whole those parts make up.[4]

The result of this kind of segregated and reductionistic learning is that "an interdisciplinary or general approach to learning is labeled 'not serious.' "[5] It is the argument of this chapter and this book that interdisciplinary and transdisciplinary learning *is* serious learning. Systemic education does not deny the value of disciplinary research, analysis, or specialization *if* there is complementary integration, interdisciplinary networking, and holism. Morris Bigge and Maurice Hunt admitted that the reductionistic and mechanistic approach to education held sway into the 1960s but that it is now on the defensive. Bigge and Hunt said the mechanistic approach "is perhaps in about the same situation physics was in after classical mechanics was confronted with relativity."[6]

The degree of change and the amount of information being generated is increasing and likely will continue increasing at an exponential rate. The task of keeping abreast with all the new information is an inhuman one. Rollo May described the anxiety of the situation this way:

> But what with the "knowledge explosion" these days—what with microfilms, abstracts, endless cross-references, new research, all increasing geometrically every day—the student can never catch up no matter how fast he runs. Indeed, he generally finds himself getting farther and farther behind each day. So the Ph.D. candidate has to work in frantic haste to get his research in, for he never knows which bright morning he will pick up the *New York Times* at his door to find that a new discovery made by Dr. X here or there on the globe makes his whole approach invalid and washes out all his work.[7]

Systemic education is not what May called the "externalized acquisition of data."[8] Systemic education is the facilitating and the equipping of persons (actually any open system) on *how* to learn rather than simply *what* to learn. Alvin Toffler said that education must "increase the individual's 'cope-ability'—the speed and economy with which he [or she] can adapt to continual change."[9] It is this "cope-ability" (referred to in this book as the "learning-adaptive process") that is the ideal of systemic education.

Of all the lessons of history, surely one of the clearest is that one single way is not always the best way. This is certainly true of systemic education. Models of education are at every hand and have been a consuming interest for humans since before the time of written records. With this in mind, the systemic model of education formulated here is in no way designed to be the full and final answer. It is designed to be more complete and more useful than other models. The outline that follows gives suggestions as to the ways it can be conceptualized. The appropriate point of origin is a determination of precisely how systemic education can be defined.

A SYSTEMIC DEFINITION OF EDUCATION

A systemic definition of education is approached in a similar manner as was the systemic definition of religion. There is an etymological study, then the stated definition, and finally a few words of explanation.

Etymological Overview

The derivation of the English word "education" is directly from the Latin compound verb "educo." The stem is "duco": lead, conduct, draw, guide, or direct.[10] The prefix "e" is a form of the preposition "ex," meaning "out of" or "away from."[11] "Educo," then, means to lead forth, to bring out of, to direct away from.[12] Education is that which leads out.

Definition

Systemic education is the existential learning-adaptive process of leading out from past heritage into an idealized future.

Other educational theorists have devised definitions of education that have similarities to the definition of systemic education. One of the more familiar definitions was written by John Dewey: "It is that reconstruction or reorganization of experience which adds to the meaning of experience and which increases ability to direct the course of subsequent experience."[13] The most obvious relationship of Dewey's definition to the systemic definition is that both definitions emphasize the interpretation of the past ("experience" and "heritage") for the purpose of informing the present and the future. Neither Dewey's definition nor the systemic definition put value in the past simply for its historical data but for its ability to enlighten and improve the activity of the present as it creates a more desirable future.

Another similarity is the recognition in both definitions that education is much more than thinking and remembering. Cognition and memory are elements but not the totality. Education must address the holistic needs of persons and of society, and this includes physical, emotional, cognitive, and interpersonal experience.

Marc Belth defined education as

the deliberate effort to enhance the unique capacity of [persons] to bring together the tokens of experience in such a way as to be able to establish a comprehensibility about those experiences, for better experiences to come, for better enjoyment of those already past.[14]

Belth's definition also deals with the meaning and interpretation of the past for the improvement of the future. An added feature of Belth's definition is the interest in the synthesis and integration of experience. Belth pointed to the idea that experiences left unrelated to others and unevaluated do not produce learning. They are simply activities that happened. The worth of the experiences comes from the gleaning of relationship to other experiences and from the "comprehensibility" of those relationships.

Explanations

The systemic definition has at least four important points that should be recognized. First is the close affinity to the systemic definition of religion. This is obviously not by accident, and the systemic definition of religious education will bring these two definitions into even closer relationship. Differences do exist, however. The chief difference is that religion focuses on binding and interface. Education stresses movement out of the past and into the future. One binds together, the other leads out. The two are complementary, neither opposite nor contrary to each other. Systemic education is deeply interested in integration, while also creating paths to the desired future.

Second is the continued emphasis on time and process. The systemic definition of religion introduced the flow of past, present, and future. Systemic education is also understood in these processive terms. The importance of time was given emphasis by Norbert Wiener. He described a system that truly "learns" as one that is able to move "ahead from a known past into an unknown future and this future is not interchangeable with that past."[15] The future is undetermined and uncreated. Understanding the heritage of the past allows the learning-adaptive open system to create a more desirable future.

Third is the use of the phrase "learning-adaptive process." This is drawn from comments by Kenneth Boulding[16] and Russell Ackoff.[17] "Learning" refers to the evaluation, interpretation, and application of the information accumulated and created by the open system as a result of the cybernetic process. "Adaptive" refers to the evolutionary transformation of structures and processes within the system that reflects learning and that leads toward a desired end. Learning and adaptive processes are inseparably linked to be a mutually reactive system that insures progress toward a more desirable future.

Russell Ackoff described the management of the learning-adaptive process by means of four functions. These functions were:

> 1) Identify problems (including threats and opportunities) and relationships between them; 2) make decisions and plans; 3) implement and control the decisions and plans made; 4) provide the information required to perform each of the first three functions.[18]

His point was that the learning-adaptive process responds to situations without predetermined and ready-made solutions. The decisions, plans, and structures that solve problems and exploit opportunities are flexible and responsive. The learning-adaptive process is descriptive of the way systemic education can lead out into the future: through flexible, creative, and responsive structures and processes that address the needs encountered in a variety of circumstances.

The fourth point of explanation is the use of "idealized future." This same phrase was used with systemic religion. It is also a term appropriated from Russell Ackoff.[19] The idealized future is not a Platonic Form, but it is purpose pursued by the learning-adaptive process. Systemic education is a means to the attainment of the purpose. The future can be created and designed from the present. The past is fixed, but its "reconstruction and reorganization" (to use John Dewey's words) allows the emergence of meaning from past experience to inform the work of creating the future.

DESIGN OF THE MODEL

The interactive and interdependent constructs of purpose, function, and structure are again employed to describe the design for the model of systemic education. In a sense the issue of purpose has already been addressed by the definition of systemic education, but further clarification may be helpful. A more specific breakdown of the purpose of systemic education is provided, and then the concepts of function and structure are related to the purpose.

Purpose

The purpose of systemic education is to provide the process which leads out of the past, through the present, and into the future. That is such a broad statement that some way to make it more applicable to the human condition is essential. This is accomplished by recognizing that, in true systemic fashion, systemic education has a framework of subsystems and suprasystems. Three levels are distinguished for present purposes.

The first level is that of the "education" of the brain: the individual level. This was termed "genetic epistemology" by Jean Piaget,[20] one of the pioneers in the effort to understand from a combined empirical and philosophical approach how humans learn and think. Piaget postulated four periods of development that moved from sensory-motor experience to preoperational thought, to concrete operational thought, and finally to formal operational thought.[21] Piaget understood this process to move to interiorization, complexity, and integration. He sought to describe the learning-adaptive process that takes place in the development of mind.

Another source of this type of investigation is physiology, where the effort is to find out how the brain itself works. The complete answers are far in the future, but some interesting hypotheses have been proposed.[22] One of these is an understanding of "right-brain" and "left-brain" functions. Experiments have shown that the halves of the brain process information differently and that complementarity of the halves can be "learned."[23] The facts seem to indicate that, rather than isolated portions of the brain performing particular functions, the entire brain functions as a whole: The human brain is certainly more than a sum of its "parts." Physiology appears to be saying that the brain functions systemically.

A second level is that of the group. This is the usual level of interest among educators, where teachers employ various means that allow groups of people, or "classes," to learn and adapt through schooling. When one studies "education" it is nearly exclusively at the group level, and authors are commensurate in number.

It is important for systemic educators to remember that, while groups of persons can be taught collectively and that work can be done in and by groups quite effectively, individuals make up the groups. The dual foci of group issues and individual concerns must be maintained. Individuals can learn through interaction and interdependence with other individuals, and educators must allow these individuals the freedom to develop their creativity. Educators must also permit the diversity and variety among the individuals to coalesce into integration and synthesis. Systemic education has no desire to mass-produce classes of humanoid automatons but instead seeks to facilitate persons who individually and collectively learn and adapt while experiencing dynamic situations.

Systemic education does not expect any teacher to make a student or a class learn. A systemic educator facilitates the learning-adaptive process by creating opportunities for the transformation of individuals and groups. Systemic education is not something "done to" others. It is *process* which permits change and transformation to take place. These ideas resonate with what Ivan Illich wrote as he described the planning of institutional forms of education: "It must not start with the question 'What should someone learn?' but with the question, 'What kinds of things and people might learners want to be in contact with in order to learn?' "24

The third level of education is societal. This level is the broadest of all education, conventionally called long-range planning. Long-range planning qualifies as systemic education if it is what Russell Ackoff has described as interactive planning.25 Interactive planning envisions a desirable future and creates ways of bringing that future into reality. This kind of planning is the ultimate in systemic education as it leads out existentially from the determined past into an idealized future. This is achieved through a learning-adaptive process, not unlike what Jean Piaget proposed at a different level. Where Piaget found four levels of thinking, interactive planning is a possible fifth level: formal operational

thought that is done interpersonally rather than simply intraper-
sonally.[26] Unified thought and action is spun out into a much
larger scale in interactive planning. There is no deterministic
"plan," but a creative and dynamic learning-adaptive process that
evolves on the way to an idealized future.[27]

Function
    Education that deals with function as its primary focus is best
understood as training. In systemic education, function/training
is important but is by no means primary or normative. Education that emphasizes training is illustrated by B. F. Skinner's
operant conditioning.
    Skinner's approach was to deal only with observable behavior
since he wanted to avoid postulation of unobserved effects to
explain observed events.[28] Skinner observed empirical activity,
which he understood to be the only proper activity of science. He
advocated a strict, inductive approach. His problem with the
more "mental" approaches, such as Gestaltism, was that they
were simply speculation. As he told Richard Evans in an inter-
view, Skinner thought Gestalt research was "nonsense" because
"I don't feel one should answer the most difficult questions in
science first."[29] The proper procedure is from the simple to the
complex: "I feel that scientific progress comes about by a progression from the more easily answered questions to the more difficult."[30]
    It is important to note that systemic education does not totally
reject B. F. Skinner's contributions, nor other efforts at training.
Where systemic education differs is at the point of design. Skinner began (and ended) with function. Systemic education includes purpose, while also including function/training in the
overall model. It should also be recognized, though, that training
is of markedly less importance in systemic education than in
Skinner's.
    Function is performed through a great variety of means, and
these means are determined by the needs of the situation. Systemic education seeks to develop interactive and responsive ways
to learn and adapt. Carl Rogers (often found poles apart from
positions taken by B. F. Skinner) gave an explanation of the
diverse expressions of function: "I see the facilitation of learning

as the function that may hold constructive, tentative, changing, *process* answers to some of the deepest perplexities that beset humankind today."[31] If systemic education is to lead out, it will be through a flexible, transformational, learning-adaptive process.

Structure

Education that begins with structure deals fundamentally with content alone. Systemic education includes content but is neither controlled by it nor dominated by its transmission.

One of the more popular appeals currently is for educators to get "back to basics," which in essence translates into the teaching of elementary facts, principles, and procedures in a no-nonsense, directive, authoritarian manner. The full intent of this diverse movement is still a bit unclear, although it has the appearance of a desire for a nostalgic return to a simpler time when there was (at least in the imagination of some) a fixed body of information that needed to be received, and one could "get an education" by mastering that specific data. Such a reactionary and deterministic understanding of education is not systemic education, but some possibility exists for redirecting this desire for structure. Marilyn Ferguson stated it this way: "Perhaps the back-to-basics movement can be channeled deeper—to bedrock fundamentals, to underlying principles and relationships, real 'universal' education."[32] Ferguson was expressing a hope quite similar to systemic education: to get back to the true "basics" of holism and integration as the way to create a more desirable future.

Jerome Bruner has been one educator that at first blush appears to support a learning-adaptive understanding of education, but such support may not hold up under scrutiny. For all his verbiage about process in education, closer examination reveals a primary interest in structure and content.[33] It seems that Bruner wanted students to learn "subjects," and he devised various theories and processes to get the subject matter to the student.[34] Neil Postman and Charles Weingartner gave this critical comment: "Bruner seems to think of a subject as a closed system of finite, fixed, 'structured' bits of data. The subject is given. It is *there*."[35] This kind of approach rigidifies and concretizes the subject and limits deterministically both function and purpose.

Summary

The systemic design of education does include the interactive elements of purpose, function, and structure. All three are essential; all three are interdependent. The learning-adaptive process requires the evolutionary transformation of all three elements as paths to a desired future are created.

EDUCATION AND THE PARADIGM OF OPEN SYSTEMS

Systemic education is modeled from the paradigm of open systems. The eight properties provide the primary values that outline the educational model, as they did for the religion model and as they will for the religious education model. The properties are the guides to the appropriate conceptualization of the model.

Holism

Systemic education seeks holism as it moves from the past into the future. It does not try to become a subject, an object, or an isolated discipline. It is an effort to find a learning-adaptive process that transcends particular institutions or habits in order to "lead out" in all areas of life.

The hierarchical explanation of education into levels of the individual, group, and society is an effort to address holism. All of these levels work interdependently to create the future, and that activity cannot be limited to any particular institution. This was Theodore Brameld's point when he wrote:

> We are realizing more profoundly than before that education, far from being limited to schools, embraces the whole complex of human dynamics through which every culture seeks both to maintain and to innovate its structures, operations, and purposes.[36]

Systemic education seeks to address the needs of the whole person. Too much education in the past has focused nearly exclusively on the cognitive processes and has ignored the holistic needs and abilities of humans. The narrow, mentalistic view of education was illustrated by Albert Nock when he described who could—and should—be educated: "The educable person, in contrast to the ineducable, is one who gives promise of someday being able to think; and the object of educating him . . . is to put him in the way of right thinking, clear thinking, mature and profound thinking."[37] Systemic education obviously is not opposed to cognitive, conceptual ability, but realizes that there is much more to a person—and to learning—than simply the mind. Perhaps Carl Rogers had a clearer vision of holism in learning:

> Significant learning combines the logical *and* the intuitive, the intellect *and* the feelings, the concept *and* the experience, the idea *and* the meaning. When we learn in that way, we are whole, utilizing all our masculine and feminine capacities.[38]

Differentiation

If there is to be holism, then there must be differentiation. There is no one, eternal, best way to learn and adapt. It must be an integrative process that draws from many disciplines. Certainly systemic education does not seek to destroy the disciplines but does try to bring them together to work toward shared purposes. Systemic education insists on depth while including breadth.

Systemic education promises no certain golden road to the future, no computer printout or chart that reduces the difficulty. It seeks just the opposite: a convergence of variety and innovation that blends into new process. Alfred North Whitehead recognized the frustrations inherent in the activity many years ago: "The education of a human being is a most complex topic which we have hardly begun to understand. The only point of which I feel certain is that there is no widespread, simple solution."[39]

At times education seems to become something that children must endure, and when they finally reach the border of adulthood they have "finished" their education and can get on with real life. This conception of education John Dewey criticized as a "process of preparation," where childhood is merely a training period for becoming an adult, i.e., a "real person."[40] The property of differentiation produces a much broader understanding of education, where education is a continuing, lifelong process that constantly changes and evolves as the needs of the person change and evolve.[41] Fritjof Capra observed that this kind of transformational, emergent education "is not occurring in our academic institutions as much as among the general population, in thousands of spontaneous adult-education efforts."[42] The learning-adaptive process can range across taking tennis lessons from a professional player to being in group therapy with ten other individuals, but it is still a systemic, educational process of leading out into growth. The variety of systemic education is limited only by the needs of the person, the group, or the society.

Boundaries

Boundaries are better understood as interconnection and interface than as barriers or inhibitors. This is especially true regarding systemic education, as the discussion of holism and differentiation has stressed.

The boundaries of systemic education cannot be the walls of a school, the covers of a book, or the certification of a teacher. The boundaries of systemic education link up learning and adapting with the ongoing processes of life. Schools, books, and teachers may be included, but they are not education. They are only some of the obvious and traditional means that society has formalized which illustrate the more diffuse learning-adaptive process.

One of the ways the learning-adaptive process has been described was through the work of Piaget.[43] He introduced such terms as "organization" and "adaptation" to point to the functional invariants of learning, and to "schemes" as the structural variants.[44] Through interaction these evolve to form a dynamic process that seeks equilibration. Taken holistically, the entire process is "a functioning-cognitive system."[45] Clearly this kind of conceptualization goes beyond the barriers of any one institution or discipline.[46] The learning-adaptive process is found at the interconnections of life.

Dynamism

Systemic education is process. There is no such thing as "receiving" an education; instead, one participates in the process. It was Alfred North Whitehead who protested what he called "dead knowledge, that is to say... inert ideas."[47] His argument was that since the "students" are alive, then so should their education be alive: "The purpose of education is to stimulate and guide their self-development."[48] Alvin Toffler had a similar comment: "Students must learn how to discard old ideas, how and when to replace them."[49] The point is that systemic education must be a part of life: learning, adapting, interpreting, integrating, and leading.

Equifinality

The purpose of systemic education is to lead out into the future. The paths to the future are innumerable. The learning-adaptive process is free to develop the means that are needed to create a desirable future. The means are incessantly changing as progress toward this goal is being realized.

Just as the learning-adaptive process is creative and flexible, so is the future. The future can be envisioned, planned, idealized, and actualized, but it is by no means absolutely certain. Only the past is determined. The paths leading to the present are fixed; the paths leading into the desired future are yet to be formed. It is the task of systemic education to create those paths.

Feedback

Feedback is the key to equifinality. Norbert Wiener was able to say that organisms are learning when they can "modify their patterns of behavior on the basis of past experience so as to achieve specific anti-entropic ends."[50] Since systemic education is defined as a process of leading out, it is essential that progress toward an end be monitored. Feedback provides this information. If progress is not being made toward the goal, then the learning-adaptive process corrects its path: hence, the attainment of equifinality.

A rather simple example of how feedback affects the learning-adaptive process is that of a baseball batter standing at the plate. The baseball can be thrown to the batter at various speeds and placements. In the space of about one second, the batter's eyes receive incoming data about the approaching baseball; the batter's brain decides whether or not to swing; if so, the entire body of the batter moves and positions to allow the bat to meet the ball at a precise moment, angle, and place. It is important to realize that the data coming in are constantly changing within that second or so after the ball is released by the pitcher and that the batter is constantly making adjustments and decisions as to the best way to address the baseball.

To carry the example a bit further is to see the value of feedback and memory storage. Suppose the batter misses the baseball when it comes over the plate. The batter steps back for a moment, reflects on the last pitch, recalls other pitches he has seen this pitcher make in similar situations, and glances at the coach who flashes the batter a sign on what to expect. Now, armed with this bank of past experience, interpretation of it, and some expectations of the future, the batter steps up to the plate once more. This time the negative, corrective feedback from the first attempt to hit the ball affects the second swing. The batter learns, adapting the swing of the bat to the pitcher's effort, and makes the desired contact with the ball. The more the batter goes through the batting experience—the more the learning-adaptive process develops—the better the batter becomes in achieving the desired end. Feedback, information which proceeds backwards from the actual performance, is able to change the general method and pattern of performance in future experience.[51] This kind of change is the learning-adaptive process, foundational to the functioning of systemic education.

Homeostasis

Theodore Brameld was quoted earlier as saying that education includes both maintenance and innovation.[52] It is this recognition that systemic education elucidates as it utilizes the resources and heritage of the past existentially to create a way to the future. It would be absurd to cast the knowledge of past generations overboard simply because it was discovered at an earlier time. Yet it would be just as absurd to insist on the same means and processes when the needs and purposes have changed. Systemic education seeks a homeostatic balance of using the wisdom of the past and the needs of the present to produce an idealized future. Alfred North Whitehead suggested this kind of approach when he addressed the concept of institutional education:

> The tragedy of the world is that those who are imaginative have but slight experience, and those who are experienced have feeble imaginations. Fools act on imagination without knowledge; pedants act on knowledge without imagination. The task of a university is to weld together imagination and experience.[53]

One of the functions of education *is* to pass along the heritage and the wisdom of the past. Albert Nock believed, though, that education was directed totally from the past. He said:

> Whole societies may disallow it and set it as nought, as ours has done . . . but in the end they will find, as so many societies have already found, that they must retain and seek the regenerative power of the Great Tradition, or lapse into decay and death.[54]

The problem with Nock's approach is that too often his kind of education becomes simply a look at the past and a reverence for historical heroes. Systemic education recognizes the value of the past in the sense of using that data to inform the learning-adaptive process as it moves into the future. Systemic education has no desire to conserve the traditions of history as buffers against the realities and needs of the present or as nostalgic escapes from the necessities of planning the future.

Growth

John Dewey emphatically stated that "the aim of education is to enable individuals to continue their education—or that the object and reward of learning is continued capacity for growth."[55] Systemic education affirms this emphasis of Dewey's educational approach. Systemic education seeks to equip persons for a lifetime of learning, rather than to teach them what some external authority has decided these persons need to know.

Jean Piaget preferred the term "development" to learning.[56] He was trying to express the concepts of change, of restructuring, and of growth that go on in true education as opposed to mere acquaintance with subject matter. Systemic education must accept new inputs and create new transformations of them. Growth need not imply simply the accumulation of data, but rather a process of assimilation and accommodation[57] of inputs in relation to the developments of the past for the actualization of the future.

Sheldon Kopp gave insight into the continual process of growth. One of the perplexing but essential aspects of the reality of growth is that there is no end to it, short of death. Either an open system grows, develops, evolves, and becomes more complex or it dies. Kopp suggested this when he wrote:

> Ironically, as a man grows and gains new freedom, he becomes aware that at each point at which he must risk himself anew, aided by his new-found freedom, new experiences for which he is unprepared then present themselves. He confronts new aspects of himself, which, though wonderful, may also be terrible (like becoming a grown-up). The growing edge eats away at itself, and . . . to be a man, in the best sense, is to be willing to keep moving.[58]

Systemic education is designed to facilitate growth and maturity for the individual, the group, and the society. There is no promise that the maturing process is easy, but the alternative is stagnation, disintegration, and chaos. The choice cannot be made on the basis of ease or simplicity, but on the provision for health, integration, and life.

Summary
Systemic education can be modeled on the properties of the open systems paradigm. The properties are guides that control and direct the process for leading out into the future. The model of systemic education not only uses the open systems paradigm but also relates to the systemic worldview. This relationship is explored in the next section.

EDUCATION AND THE SYSTEMIC WORLDVIEW

Systemic education and the systemic worldview have a reciprocal need for interrelationship. Because the worldview has been discussed at length in various places throughout this book, only a brief section is needed to show the linkage to education. The eight characteristics are used to describe the connections.

Organismic
Systemic education is an effort to create the means for an organismic worldview. Using the paradigm of the open system, systemic education transcends the barriers of disciplines with the interdependence of the organism. If the universe is understood to

be organismic in conception, then the experience and learning related to that universe should also be organismic. As Ludwig von Bertalanffy was aware, traditional education presents physics, psychology, or mathematics as being "unconnected with the rest."[59] Instead, he proposed that there be movement "toward interdisciplinary synthesis and integrated education."[60] As the world is perceived and encountered, so it becomes.

Relational

Systemic education insists on the utilization of the wisdom of the past, but only as it impacts existentially on creating the future. In other words, the value of the past is found in how it informs the present. A study of history has no inherent worth until it is related to the needs and situations of the present.

At the same time, systemic education emphasizes that the present without context is inexplicable. Context comes from interpretation of the past and from awareness of what is taking place in the contemporary environment. The futility of isolation was pointed out by Alfred North Whitehead: "A [person] who knows only his [or her] own science, as a routine peculiar to that science, does not even know that."[61]

Pluralistic

Systemic education can be of great value to the systemic worldview by insuring that there are multiple ways of understanding and that no one of them gives the entire or "proper" answer. Education is less an explanation of truth than a search for it. The need is for process, not for an achievement. The means are equifinal. This was Kenneth Boulding's intention when he referred to the real weaknesses of human efforts at education: "It seems clear that for the most part genetic limits on learning are quite rarely reached. It is the learning patterns themselves that are self-limiting."[62]

The learning-adaptive process is certainly not limited to institutional education. Schools and universities are places where systemic education may be experienced, but to perceive of education in such restricted categories and structures is to miss the potential inherent in systemic education. The family meeting with a psychotherapist can be learning and adapting just as surely as the college freshman who attends a philosophy lecture (probably more so!). The structure and content are limitless in systemic education, since the learning-adaptive process is flexible and responsive to the needs and interests of the learner.

Stochastic

Since the future is still uncharted, so is the future of education. Plainly, at least some of the education of the past was adequate, since civilization is still functioning. The danger is to assume that the processes of education which served the past will be adequate for the future. Systemic education must be stochastic: using the heritage of the past as a launching pad for new and creative ways of actualizing the future. Since the possibilities of the future are limited only by the dreams of humans, it is the task of systemic education to create ways of bringing that idealized future into reality.

Dynamic

The systemic worldview understands dynamism as the most accurate perception of reality. The poetic language of Alfred North Whitehead expressed it this way: "Time has then lost its character of 'perceptual perishing'; it becomes the 'moving image of eternity.' "[63] In that same way, systemic education is understood as an existential learning-adaptive process. Systemic education cannot be isolated from the total flow of life.

Negentropic

Life is a constant struggle to overcome entropy. In an ever-changing world, there is no assurance that what worked yesterday will work today. Continual effort toward negentropy and the ongoing process of life is central to education. This stark reality was expressed by Neil Postman and Charles Weingartner: "The basic function of all education . . . is to increase the survival prospects of the group. If this function is fulfilled, the group survives. If not, it doesn't."[64]

A systemic approach to education is important because no one person and no one group has all the answers; indeed, at this point even the questions are unclear. Survival of this, and future, generations is at stake: "It is not too much to say that this novel adaptation of education is one of the factors which may save civilization."[65]

Holistic

The systemic worldview is an effort to see the whole, and systemic education participates in the process of facilitating awareness of the whole. Education, while keeping its interest in analysis and specialization, must complement that with setting the particular in the context of the broader picture. Alfred North Whitehead summed it up well: "The problem of education is to make the pupil see the wood by means of the tree."[66]

The concept of holism also intimates that systemic education is involved with much more than cognitive processes. A human is a total integration of such areas as cognition, emotion, physical reactions, and interpersonal relationships. Systemic education has responsibility for facilitating persons (individuals as well as corporate systems) toward maturity, integration, and growth in every area of life.

Cybernetic

Ends are achieved by the system's monitoring its progress, or lack of it, toward its goal. Continual correction of the system is necessary. This cybernetic activity is the occasion for inclusion of the "learning-adaptive process" in the definition of systemic education. Education is not simply a "leading out"; it is a purposeful movement toward an idealized future. Systemic education provides the self-correcting process through the activity of learning and adapting.

Education and society have always been in the process of change, but modern life has significantly increased the rate of that change. Learning and adapting must keep pace, as Russell Ackoff noted: "Society does not yet know how to respond rapidly and effectively. . . and it may not do so in time. Therefore, there is an urgent need to change our society in ways that increase its ability to learn and adapt."[67] It is the task of systemic education to create these ways for the survival of civilization.

Summary

Systemic education and the systemic worldview are intimately related. Systemic education is the means of leading out and achieving the systemic view of reality. Not everyone has conceived of education in these terms, however. The next section sets systemic education in its environmental context with other understandings of education.

SYSTEMIC EDUCATION IN
ENVIRONMENTAL PERSPECTIVE

One final effort is now made to clarify systemic education. Systemic education is placed in the environment of various other theories of education and shown where it fits most comfortably.

It should be no surprise by now that systemic education is rooted firmly in social science with interactive feedback from other fields, such as natural science and philosophy. Systemic education is an attempt to transcend traditional boundaries that have historically hindered education. The mental discipline theories that have had contemporary expression from such theorists as Robert Hutchins[68] and Mortimer Adler[69] have focused on the cultivation of the intellect and on training the "powers of the mind." The mechanistic theory of apperception advanced by Johann Herbart[70] (1776-1841), where the presentation of material and ideas was structured through a hierarchical lesson plan, still has amazing influence today. Behaviorism, referred to in this book as essentially training exercises, has focused on conditioning responses of the organism through the manipulation of stimuli or through careful positive reinforcement. Systemic education seeks a holistic process of education that is more than the training of a "mind" or the training for performance of specific behavioral responses. Systemic education is concerned for the health, maturity, and development of the entire organism.

In order to get some kind of perspective on the context of systemic education, five possible categorizations of educational theory are now considered. The categories used here are taken from the work of Theodore Brameld,[71] but other authors have discussed similar divisions.[72] Systemic education is best understood when it is surveyed from the context of perennialism, essentialism, progressivism, reconstructionism, and eclecticism.

Perennialism

Perennialism looks to the past for the eternal answers. The classics are the best expression of the search for absolute truth and remain the guides for the present.[73] Truth does not change, and intellectually trained persons can find it and lead others to it. This kind of education is "perennial" because it need not change year after year in response to personal or situational differences. The path is clearly marked, and the student need only walk down it as others have done before.

As the definition implied, systemic education has great appreciation for the heritage of the past, but that past is not allowed to determine the future. The past is of value only as it helps create the future. Systemic education recognizes no one, infallible, best way and no final point of "arrival" at truth. Systemic education is relational and pluralistic, not absolutistic and authoritarian.[74]

Essentialism

Essentialism is something of a mixed bag in its philosophical and experiential foundations.[75] It is a "via media" between perennialism and progressivism. George Kneller said essentialism is best understood in four principles.[76] First, learning is hard work and should not be confused with fun. Second, it is the teacher, and not the pupil, who is the authority and the initiator. Third, education is primarily acquisition of subject matter. Fourth, mental discipline is the proper procedure for learning.

Systemic education has these four responses. First, education and learning are inseparable from the flow of life and involve both work and "fun." Second, systemic education rejects the "trickle down"[77] theory of authority and initiation and prefers a joint search by the "teacher" (facilitator and co-learner) and "student" (learner). Third, the purpose of systemic education is not the acquisition of objective subject matter, but is rather the development of a learning-adaptive process for the creation of a more desirable future. Fourth, mentalistic conceptions of learning are more representative of a classical science worldview, and systemic education is an effort to transcend and transform such mechanistic and dualistic formulations.

Progressivism

Theodore Brameld correctly identified progressivism as representative of the genuine "liberal" approach.[78] By "liberal" he meant a "flexible, curious, tolerant, and open-minded attitude."[79] Much of what progressive education has done is compatible with systemic education, especially as articulated by John Dewey. Dewey and his disciples understood the impact and value of the environment regarding the learning process and were open to evolutionary progress. While it would be unfair and inaccurate to equate progressivism with systemic education, it would be appropriate to understand progressivism as a precursor of systemic education. It may even be fair to call John Dewey the forerunner of systemic education, much as his contemporary, Alfred North Whitehead, was the fountainhead of systems theory.

Reconstructionism

The fundamental work of reconstructionism is found in Theodore Brameld's writings. While never especially popular or heeded, Brameld spoke passionately and convincingly. He gave this summary of his vision of the future:

> In short, it should be a world in which the dreams of both ancient Christianity and modern democracy are fused with modern technology and art into a society under the control of the great majority of the people who are rightly the sovereign determiners of their own destiny. Reconstructionism is thus a philosophy of magnetic foresight—a philosophy of ends attainable through the development of powerful means possessed latently by the people. To learn how to exercise that power for these ends is the first priority of education.[80]

Systemic education is quite similar to some of the tenets of reconstructionism.[81] Reconstructionism is purposeful, allows function and structure to follow purpose, and does seek a "way out" of the problems of humankind, but yet there are significant differences from systemic education. The difficulties of Brameld's reconstructionism include an understanding of ends in static terms,[82] a penchant for assuming Christianity and democracy are inherently good, and a rather programatic solution of the world's problems through an institutional approach.[83]

The relationship between systemic education and reconstructionism is best perceived as model and simulation. The model of systemic education under development in this chapter has avoided specific proposals of how the work of education could be carried out. Brameld's reconstructionism is actually a simulation, specifying ages, schools, subjects, and so on. In summary then, reconstructionism is less of an educational theory than a particular manifestation of one. The actual theory is closer to what has been described as a model of systemic education.

Eclecticism

The final category is eclecticism.[84] Theodore Brameld described an eclectic as "one who believes that the most honest approach of philosophy is one refusing to commit itself to any unified or consistent pattern of beliefs."[85] This is the pragmatic "pick-and-choose" style of education, which probably is not a true philosophy at all. Its value for inclusion here is to point out that systemic education is not eclectic. The systemic approach is misunderstood if it is seen as an aggregate of ideas; indeed, it is exactly the opposite of that. The systemic approach is holistic, organic, and integrative: the whole is more than the sum of the parts. Systemic education *does* have a "unified or consistent pattern of beliefs," which was the intention of this articulation of a systemic model of education.

Summary

The systemic model of education is an attempt at a fresh approach to the theory of education. While it is distinct from the other theories, it also has some relationship to all of the theories. It is most closely associated with progressivism and reconstructionism. This section attempted to show that the systemic model is an improvement on the progressive theory and that reconstructionism is best seen as a simulation of a systemic model.

CONCLUSION

The systemic model of education has now been outlined. This was accomplished first by presenting a systemic definition of education. Second was a design for education that emphasized the importance of purpose and how purpose controls construction of function and structure. Third was a discussion of education in relation to the paradigm of open systems and to the systemic worldview. Finally, systemic education was set in its environmental context of other educational approaches.

The "primary colors" are now ready for experimentation. The "blue" of systemic religion and the "yellow" of systemic education are such that the next chapter can mix these primary colors into the desired "green" of a unique creation: systemic religious education.

NOTES

1. Walt Whitman, "Song of Myself," in *Walt Whitman: The Complete Poems,* ed. Francis Murphy (New York: Penguin Books, 1975), p. 68.

2. Alvin Toffler, *Future Shock* (New York: Bantam Books, 1970). p. 427.

3. Jeremy Rifkin with Ted Howard, *Entropy: A New World View* (New York: Bantam Books, 1981), p. 226.

4. Ibid., p. 227.

5. Ibid., p. 224.

6. Morris L. Bigge and Maurice P. Hunt, *Psychological Foundations of Education: An Introduction to Human Motivation, Development, and Learning,* 3rd ed. (New York: Harper & Row, 1980), p. 22. The reference here is specifically about educational psychologists.

7. Rollo May, *Psychology and the Human Dilemma* (Princeton, N.J.: D.van Nostrand Company, 1967), p. 45. The male language can be interpreted generically.

8. Ibid.

9. Toffler, *Future Shock,* p. 403.

10. Charlton T. Lewis and Charles Short, *A New Latin Dictionary,* rev. and enl. ed. (New York: New American Book Company, 1879), p. 615; P. G. W. Glare, *Oxford Latin Dictionary* (Oxford: At the Clarendon Press, 1982), pp. 576-577.

11. Lewis and Short, *A New Latin Dictionary,* p. 622; Glare, *Oxford Latin Dictionary,* pp. 628-629.

12. Lewis and Short, *A New Latin Dictionary,* p. 627; Glare, *Oxford Latin Dictionary,* p. 587.

13. John Dewey, *Democracy and Education: An Introduction to the Philosophy of Education* (New York: Macmillan, 1916), pp. 89-90.

14. Marc Belth, *Education as a Discipline: A Study of the Role of Models in Thinking* (Boston: Allyn and Bacon, 1965), p. 22.

15. Norbert Wiener, *The Human Use of Human Beings: Cybernetics and Society* (New York: Avon Books, 1967), p. 68.

16. See especially Kenneth E. Boulding, *Ecodynamics: A New Theory of Societal Evolution* (Beverly Hills, Calif.: Sage Publications, 1978), pp. 133 ff.

17. The best discussions are found in Russell L. Ackoff, *Redesigning the Future: A Systems Approach to Societal Problems* (New York: John Wiley & Sons, 1974), pp. 5, 32.

18. Ibid., p. 32.

19. Ibid., pp. 27-31; also see Chapter 14, "Ideal Seeking Systems," in Russell L. Ackoff and Fred E. Emery, *On Purposeful Systems* (Chicago: Aldine Atherton, 1972), pp. 237-247.

20. See Jean Piaget, *The Principles of Genetic Epistemology*, trans. Wolfe Mays (London: Routledge and Kegan Paul, 1972).

21. A good summary of these periods of development is found in John H. Flavell, *The Developmental Psychology of Jean Piaget* (Princeton, N.J.: D. van Nostrand Company, 1963), pp. 264-266,

22. For example, see Howard Gardner, *The Quest for Mind: Piaget, Lévi-Strauss, and the Structuralist Movement,* 2nd ed. (Chicago: University of Chicago Press, 1981); Carl Sagan, *The Dragons of Eden: Speculations on the Evolution of Human Intelligence* (New York: Ballatine Books, 1977); Morton Hunt, *The Universe Within: A New Science Explores the Mind* (New York: Simon and Schuster, 1982); and Lawrence LeShan and Henry Margenau, *Einstein's Space and Van Gogh's Sky: Physical Reality and Beyond* (New York: Macmillan, 1982).

23. Robert G. Meyer and Paul Salmon, *Abnormal Psychology* (Boston: Allyn and Bacon, 1984), p. 371.

24. Ivan Illich, *Deschooling Society* (New York: Harper & Row, 1970), p. 111.

25. Ackoff, *Redesigning the Future,* pp. 26 ff.

26. For further development of such a possibility, see Pierre Teilhard de Chardin, *The Phenomenon of Man,* trans. Bernard Wall (New York: Harper & Row, 1959); Gisela Labourie-Vief, "Beyond Formal Operations: Uses and Limits of Pure Logic in Life-Span Development," *Human Development* 23 (1980), pp. 141-161; and John A. Dillon, Jr., Chapter XIV, "Social Systems," *Foundations of General Systems Theory* (Louisville, Ky.: University of Louisville, 1982), pp. 233-254.

27. See Ackoff, *Redesigning the Future,* p. 16. See also the development of this concept found throughout Erich Jantsch, *The Self-Organizing Universe: Scientific and Human Implications of the Emerging Paradigm of Evolution* (Oxford: Pergamon Press, 1980).

28. A good overview of this approach is found in B. F. Skinner, *About Behaviorism* (New York: Vintage Books, 1974).

29. Richard I. Evans, *B. F. Skinner: The Man and His Ideas* (New York: E. P. Dutton, 1968), p. 14.

30. Ibid.

31. Carl R. Rogers, *Freedom To Learn for the 80's* (Columbus, Ohio: Charles E. Merrill, 1983), p. 121.

32. Marilyn Ferguson, *The Aquarian Conspiracy: Personal and Social Transformation in the 1980's* (Los Angeles: J. P. Tarcher, 1980), p. 23.

33. Ironically, one of Jerome Bruner's better known books is *The Process of Education* (New York: Vintage Books, 1960).

34. This was the focus of his theoretical book on teaching. See Jerome S. Bruner, *Toward a Theory of Instruction* (Cambridge, Mass.: Harvard University Press, 1966).

35. Neil Postman and Charles Weingartner, *Teaching as a Subversive Activity* (New York: Delacort Press, 1969), p. 77.

36. Theodore Brameld, *Education for the Emerging Age: Newer Ends and Stronger Means* (New York: Harper & Row, 1965), p. 15.

37. Albert J. Nock, *The Theory of Education in the United States* (Chicago: Henry Regnery, 1932), p. 123. The sexism is inherent in the quote.

38. Rogers, *Freedom To Learn for the 80's*, p. 20.

39. Alfred North Whitehead, "Autobiographical Notes," in *Science and Philosophy* (New York: Philosophical Library, 1948), p. 13.

40. Dewey, *Democracy and Education,* pp. 63-65. This is not only an inadequate understanding of learning but of personhood.

41. See Ackoff, *Redesigning the Future,* p. 79; Rogers, *Freedom To Learn for the 80's,* p. 120.

42. Fritjof Capra, *The Turning Point: Science, Society and the Rising Culture* (New York: Simon and Schuster, 1982), p. 409. Also see "Resources for Change" in Ferguson, *The Aquarian Conspiracy: Personal and Social Transformation in the 80's,* pp. 421-428 for a list of examples.

43. A good introduction to this is found in summary form in Jean Piaget and Bärbel Inhelder, *The Psychology of the Child,* trans. Helen Weaver (New York: Basic Books, 1966).

44. These are clearly outlined in John L. Phillips, Jr., *The Origins of Intellect: Piaget's Theory,* 2nd ed. (San Francisco: W. H. Freeman, 1975), p. 12.

45. Ibid., p. 13.

46. Maybe the best model was the person of Piaget himself, who created a unique blend of science and philosophy. See Terrance A. Brown, "Foreword," in Jean Piaget, *Adaptation and Intelligence: Organic Selection and Phenocopy,* trans. Stewart Eames (Chicago: University of Chicago Press, 1980), pp. 1-6.

47. Alfred North Whitehead, "Preface," in *The Aims of Education and Other Essays* (New York: Macmillan, 1929; reprint edition; New York: The Free Press, 1967), p. v.

48. Ibid.

49. Toffler, *Future Shock,* p. 414.

50. Wiener, *The Human Use of Human Beings,* p. 67.

51. Ibid., p. 84.

52. Brameld, *Education for the Emerging Age,* p. 5.

53. Whitehead, "Universities and Their Function," in *The Aims of Education and Other Essays,* p. 93.

54. Nock, *The Theory of Education in the United States,* p. 151.

55. Dewey, *Democracy and Education,* p. 117.

56. Phillips, *The Origins of Intellect,* p. 6.

57. These are Piaget's technical terms that combine to create adaptation. They are appropriated for similar but less technical uses here.

58. Sheldon B. Kopp, *If You Meet the Buddha on the Road, Kill Him! The Pilgrimage of Psychotherapy Patients* (New York: Bantam Books, 1972), pp. 194-195. This male language can be interpreted generically.

59. Ludwig von Bertalanffy, *General System Theory: Foundations, Develop-*

ment, Applications, rev. ed. (New York: George Braziller, 1968), p. 51.

60. Ibid.

61. Whitehead, "Technical Education and Its Relation to Science and Literature," in *The Aims of Education and Other Essays,* p. 52.

62. Boulding, *Ecodynamics,* p. 123.

63. Alfred North Whitehead, *Process and Reality: An Essay in Cosmology,* ed. Donald Ray Griffin and Donald W. Sherburne, cor. ed. (New York: The Free Press, 1978), p. 238.

64. Postman and Weingartner, *Teaching as a Subversive Activity,* p. 207.

65. Whitehead, "Autobiographical Notes," in *Science and Philosophy,* p. 19.

66. Whitehead, "The Aims of Education," in *The Aims of Education and Other Essays,* p. 6.

67. Ackoff, *Redesigning the Future,* p. 5.

68. See, for example, Robert M. Hutchins, *Education for Freedom* (Baton Rouge, La.: Louisiana State University Press, 1943).

69. Although Adler may be best known for his work with *The Great Books of the Western World,* a good example of perennialism can be found in Mortimer J. Adler and Charles Van Doren, *How to Read a Book,* rev. ed. (New York: Simon and Schuster, 1972).

70. For example, see Johann Friedrich Herbart, *The Science of Education,* trans. Henry M. Felkin and Emmie Felkin (Boston: Health, 1896).

71. These are presented briefly in Brameld, *Education for the Emerging Age,* but are greatly expanded in Theodore Brameld, *Philosophies of Education in Cultural Perspective* (New York: Holt, Rinehart & Winston, 1955).

72. For example, see George R. Knight, *Philosophy and Education: An Introduction in Christian Perspective* (Berrien Springs, Mich.: Andrews University Press, 1980), pp. 90-124; and George F. Kneller, *Introduction to the Philosophy of Education,* 2nd ed. (New York: John Wiley & Sons, 1971), pp. 41-67.

73. Good examples of perennialism are Hutchins, *Education for Freedom,* and Nock, *The Theory of Education in the United States.*

74. For examples of current work that is being done with the concept of tradition and change, see Mary Elizabeth Moore, *Education for Continuity and Change: A New Model for Christian Religious Education* (Nashville: Abingdon Press, 1983); and Padraic O'Hare, ed., *Tradition and Transformation in Religious Education* (Birmingham, Ala.: Religious Education Press, 1979).

75. See, for example, Michael J. Demiashkevich, *An Introduction to the Philosophy of Education* (New York: American Book Company, 1935).

76. Kneller, *Introduction to the Philosophy of Education,* pp. 58-61.

77. Harvey Cox, *Religion in the Secular City: Toward a Postmodern Theology* (New York: Simon and Schuster, 1984), p. 136.

78. Brameld, *Philosophies of Education in Cultural Perspective,* p. 77.

79. Ibid., p. 90.

80. Brameld, *Education for the Emerging Age,* p. 25.

81. A more accurate interpretation of reconstructionism may be to understand it as a somewhat more radical and specific form of progressivism. If so, the similarities between systemic education and reconstructionism are easily explained.

82. For example, see Brameld, *Education for the Emerging Age,* pp. 6-7.

83. Brameld proposed "Schools of the People" and designed a curriculum

especially for secondary education. See Theodore Brameld, *Toward a Reconstructed Philosophy of Education* (New York: The Dryden Press, 1956), especially pp. 211-260.

84. See, for example, John S. Brubacher, ed., *Eclectic Philosophy of Education: A Book of Readings,* 2d. ed. (Englewood Cliffs, N.J.: Prentice-Hall, 1962).

85. Brameld, *Education for the Emerging Age,* p. 22.

Chapter 6

Religious Education

My heart leaps up when I behold
    A rainbow in the sky;
So was it when my life began;
So is it now that I am a man;
So be it when I shall grow old.
    Or let me die!
The Child is Father of the Man;
And I could wish my days to be
Bound each to each by natural piety.[1]
                William Wordsworth

The crucial question of this book was first raised at the beginning of chapter 2: "How can religious education be done better?" From that initial inquiry the progression of chapters has moved through discussions of paradigms, worldviews, and models of religion and education. Only now, it appears, has the focus turned to religious education. Have the previous chapters been only prelude to the true intention of this book? No. The truth is just the opposite. The previous chapters have actually been an exercise in systemic religious education!

Ironically, in one sense there is no need at all for this book to include a separate chapter on systemic religious education. Rather than finally arriving at it, religious education has already "been done" through the preceding chapters. To come to this chapter with the expectation of "getting to" religious education is to miss the point of the entire book. The way for religious education to be "done better" is to work through the paradigms, world-views, and models that comprise the systemic perspective.

While the preceding paragraph is adequate as far as it goes, it is even more accurate to say that there *is* a need for a chapter on systemic religious education. Gregory Bateson recalled that in his experience of teaching one of the recurring questions was: "What is this course about?" Hard-pressed for a good answer, Bateson formulated at least a partial solution: "Gradually I discovered that what made it difficult to tell the class what the course was about was the fact that my way of thinking was different from theirs."[2] A similar situation results from the question: "How can religious education be done better?" It can be done better by thinking differently—but *not only* by thinking differently. Systemic religious education does include cognition but is not limited to mental activity. Systemic religious education looks to find an integration of thinking and doing. This was Leon McKenzie's point when he wrote: "A mutuality exists between thinking and doing: Thinking about doing can improve the doing of something; the doing of something can help in the development of new ways of thinking."[3]

Religious education from a systemic perspective cannot be relegated to one brief chapter, and it is certainly not the purpose of this chapter to give systemic religious education an exhaustive treatment. It is the purpose of the chapter to show how religious education can be understood systemically. "The answers" to all of the problems of religious education are not provided in this chapter. What is developed is an outline of a systemic model of religious education which is but one interdependent part of the entire systemic perspective. A solution to "how religious education can be done better" is provided by the gestalt of the systemic perspective.

A systemic model of religious education is constructed in similar form to the previous models of systemic religion and systemic education. The first task lies in defining religious education from a systemic perspective. Second is the design of the model, starting from a teleological understanding and flowing into function and structure. Next the values of the model are discussed, as religious education is related to both the paradigm of open systems and the systemic worldview. Finally the model is set in its environmental context.

A SYSTEMIC DEFINITION OF RELIGIOUS EDUCATION

Defining religious education is not an easy task. Many definitions have been offered, but none (not surprisingly) has achieved universal acceptance. In fact, there is even disagreement as to what to label the field. In the paragraphs that follow the territory is surveyed to see how a few others have identified the field. The systemic definition of religious education is then given along with some attention to related definitions. Finally, a brief explication of some of the foundational concepts in the systemic definition is provided.

A Struggle for Identity

Biology is the "study of life" (bio=life). Theology is one form of the "study of God" (theo=God). Sociology is the study of society and its interconnected relationships. What is religious education? At the present time there does not seem to be a consensus.

Religious education is something of a perpetual teenager: It can never quite decide who it is.[4] Erik Erikson described adolescents this way:

> In their search for a new sense of continuity and sameness, adolescents have to refight many of the battles of earlier years, even though to do so they must artificially appoint perfectly well-meaning people to play the roles of adversaries; and they are ever ready to install lasting idols and ideals as guardians of a final identity.[5]

This seems an apt description of religious education. It keeps refighting old battles, installing adversaries and idols, but never emerging into full identity and maturity.

Iris Cully viewed religious education as a corpse rather than as a teenager. She delivered its eulogy in an article entitled: "What Killed Religious Education?"[6] Even a quick survey of work since the article shows that if religious education was a corpse in 1971, it has somehow revived. In avataristic fashion it has reappeared in at least four different forms.

James Michael Lee has chosen to focus on the term "religious instruction." Religious instruction is in no way antipodal to religious education but instead is one part of the entirety of religious education. As Lee wrote: "Instruction is not a pejorative term to be used in disparaging contradistinction to the more fulsome term education; rather, it is a technical term used in pedagogical parlance to indicate a specific type of educational activity."[7] Other parts, such as religious counseling and the administration of religious education activities, combine with religious instruction to make up the whole of religious education.[8] Lee concentrated on the "teaching-learning dimension of religious education" as the primary concern of his writings and research.

John Westerhoff resurrected the old Roman Catholic term "catechesis" to substitute[9] for religious education. While he acknowledged the "unfortunate history" associated with the term,[10] Westerhoff still supported catechesis as the method of understanding the relationship between theory and practice.[11] Catechesis was defined as "a pastoral ministry which aims to help the faithful, individually and corporately, meet the twofold responsibilities which faith asks of them; community with God and community with one's fellow human beings."[12] Westerhoff employed the term to point to the enculturation and socialization process within a community of faith,[13] rather than the rote memorization and programed question-and-answer method often associated with the word.[14] From Westerhoff's understanding, the central question of catechesis is: "What is it to be Christian together in community and the world?"[15]

Lois LeBar insisted on the term "Christian education." She saw a very real difference between secular education and Christian education. Her question was: "Why should Christians borrow a system of education from the secular world?"[16] Although LeBar did allow for "correlation between the secular and the sacred," she went on to say that "the foundations and the orientation of Christian education are distinctive if they are truly Christian."[17] To give her division of sacred and secular even more clarity, LeBar said Christian education is fundamentally an imitation of the methods of the "Master Teacher": "Though our local situations differ from those of His day, our basic problems and principles are the same."[18] For LeBar, the proper (correct) approach for Christian education is a return to the basics laid out in the authoritative Word since "the answers to all our problems, or at least the principles, are to be found in God's written Revelation of Himself rather than in any human source."[19] LeBar's type of approach is one of recovery and rediscovery of the answers provided in the past as opposed to one of creativity and transformation.

Thomas Groome tried to be inclusive and suggested "Christian religious education." He agreed that there could be such a thing as religious education,[20] but "when religious education is done by and from within a Christian community, the most descriptive term to name it is Christian religious education."[21] Groome included under this aegis catechesis, religious instruction, and other current educational terms.[22]

Marvin Taylor has used both the terms "Christian education" and "religious education" in the works he has edited over the years. For example, his 1976 book was entitled *Foundations for Christian Education in an Era of Change,* but Taylor said in the book's introduction that the term "religious education" was more generic and more frequently utilized.[23] In 1984 Taylor edited a book with the title *Changing Patterns of Religious Education.* In that book's introduction, Taylor wrote that while the earlier shift to "Christian education" language was a reflection of theological influence, reverting to the use of "religious education" should not be attributed to theology but to custom.[24] Taylor's point in all of that seems to have been that the least particularistic term for the field is religious education.

Many other terms and preferences for labels could be cited,[25] but the confusion about identity is surely well-illustrated. This book supports the use of the term "religious education," a term which has the capacity to make the field nonparticularistic, inclusive, and unified. The qualifier "systemic" is added to give further emphasis to the effort toward integration, interdependence, and holism. Systemic religious education is an offering designed to be helpful in the resolution of the "identity crisis" for a fragmented and confused field and to facilitate its maturity and growth.

Definition

Systemic religious education is the search for, attempt at, and creation of holistic nexus through the existential learning-adaptive process of transforming the heritage of the past into an actualized vision of the ideal future.

Others have approached religious education from a similar perspective. One from a past generation was Ernest Chave. Chave, in his functional approach to religion and religious education, said that since religion is pervasive in all of life,[26] then religious education is "a systematic, planned procedure for making religion meaningful and operative in individual and collective living."[27] Although it would be inexcusably anachronistic to call Chave a systemic religious educator, it would be proper to recognize Chave as a forerunner of systemic religious education by virtue of his emphasis on making religion "meaningful and operative" through functional religious education. Systemic religious education also seeks to make religion (as holistic nexus) meaningful in its transformation of the past for present use and to make religion operational as a growing, evolving process of integration, interconnection, and interrelationship.

Mary Cove and Mary Louise Mueller expected religious education to be "personal, integrative, informative, and yet experiential rather than transmissive. It requires an atmosphere which is warm, open, and respectful of both teachers and product-content."[28] This type of approach to religious education keeps the focus on process, encounter, and experience. As Cove and Mueller pointed out, religious education can include information, but the mere transmission of data is by no means the entirety of religious education. Religious education from a systemic perspective is not so much what is received as that which is experienced; not so much what is accepted as that which is explored; not so much what is memorized as that which is interpreted.

Explanations

There are at least four distinctive points that should be observed in the definition of systemic religious education. The first is the incorporation of the elements from the definitions for systemic religion and systemic education. The various repetitive phrases show how inseparably religion and education are linked together into the reality called religious education. One focuses on binding and integration; the other on leading out. Systemic religious education is the existential fusion of both.

Second is the fact that although elements of the other definitions are used, the definition of systemic religious education still has a uniqueness beyond the simple aggregation of the definitions for systemic religion and systemic education. In systemic fashion, the total is more than the sum of the parts. Religion and education are fused into a new and different entity. This same concept was discussed by James Michael Lee in slightly different language. He described the "mediation stage" of religious instruction this way: "As mediator religious instruction does not stand between theology and practiced life; instead, it fuses them together, empowering both to actively share in a new ontological form toward the making of a genuine and authentic religious experience for the learner."[29] Lee went on to explain how the interdependent and interactive elements integrate into a "radically new ontic entity":

> Mediatorship means that substantive and structural content are so united in religious instruction that religion no longer exists as religion *in se* but now exists under the form of religious instruction, and that instruction does not exist as instruction *in se* but now exists under the form of religious instruction.[30]

Such an example illustrates the interactive and synergistic way that systemic religion and systemic education unite to create systemic religious education.

Third is the reemphasis on time. The familiar recognitions of past, present, and future are important elements of the definition. Systemic religious education is an existential reality dealing with both the past and the future. Shirley Heckman had a parallel understanding of religious education when she wrote that the goal of religious education "is to help people of all ages 1) to develop and maintain a linkage with the past, 2) to anticipate the future, and 3) to participate responsibly in decision-making about their lives in the present."[31] Systemic religious education is *process,* dynamically, interactively, and holistically creating a more desirable future. The past is consulted, used, evaluated, and interpreted. Systemic religious education is not simply a repository for the content of the past. It is an integrative and transforming process, rather than a static body of literature, doctrines, or moralisms.

Fourth is the focus on the various verb forms: search, attempt, create, and transform. Systemic religious education brings about holistic nexus through the learning-adaptive process. If religion and education are to become real, there must be systemic religious education. In venturing toward a systemic understanding of religious education, religious education then becomes the actualizing process for the entire systemic perspective.

DESIGN OF THE MODEL

An appropriate design for a systemic model of religious education includes the interactive elements of purpose, function, and structure. Each of these three has dynamic influence on each other, and each is interdependent with each other. As has been stated repeatedly throughout this book, these three design elements are teased apart here only for clarity and explanation but in reality are inseparable. This has been shown to be true through the various other models and is particularly true of the systemic model of religious education since it is a complement to the models of systemic religion and systemic education.

Purpose

The purpose of systemic religious education was described in the definition as the establishment of holistic nexus through the learning-adaptive process. While the purpose of systemic religious education is intimately related to systemic religion and systemic education, it is yet distinct from them. Religion has the purpose of binding together; education of leading out. Religious education is the search for, attempt at, and creation of ways for binding together and leading out. The purpose of religious education is to actualize and integrate religion and education through transforming experience.

James Michael Lee expressed a related teleology when he identified "Christian living" as the dynamic, integrative, and experiential purpose of religious education. He wrote:

Christian living is at once the means toward and the goal of religious instruction and indeed of all of religious education. The term "Christian living" means that the sum total of an individual's personality structure is integrated into and acts in accord with behavior we can call Christian. In the concrete, Christian living is the confluence of the thoughts, emotions, desires, and overt actions of a person to form an integrated behavioral pattern and lifestyle.[32]

This element of purpose is crucial to a clear understanding of systemic religious education. Some may misunderstand and assume that purpose is an external imposition from outside the system, but this is not systemic teleology. Purpose, as understood from a systemic perspective, is emergent from within the system through its internal and external interactions. Systemic teleology is dynamic, evolutionary, and transformational.

Function
Systemic religious education is processive and dynamic. James Michael Lee reflected this emphasis when he described Christian living as "at once the means and the goal of . . . religious education."[33] Lee not only demonstrated the processive dimension but also the integrative and interactive nature of systemic purpose and function. A religious educator of another time, Ernest Chave, also had a like notion of the functional aspects of religious education:

> Religious education that is to help growing persons live spiritually in their real world of daily experience must speak in terms which honor the natural processes and which integrate the learnings from all of life. It must be specific and concrete, normative and directional, motivating and energizing, and always developmental and adapted to particular needs and situations.[34]

Leon McKenzie, a representative of the administration of religious education activity, understood the functional dimension of religious education and took the "content and structure specialists" to task for presupposing their expertise upon religious education. McKenzie expressed well the difficulty that arises when content (and content specialists) are allowed to determine and inhibit the flow of religious education:

One must wonder, then, about the credibility of content specialists in theology who do not hesitate to express, authoritatively, views about education. Frequently such views are utterly simplistic. But the authority of the specialist in theology is often assumed to relate to the field of education. The fallacy of misplaced authority is rampant in the field of religious education.

One must also wonder about the relevance of using the bible or ecclesiastical documentation to develop education theories or norms for the conduct of education. The bible is no more a textbook for the study of education than it is a book for astronomy. Its value lies in other directions.[35]

McKenzie's point was that content or capability in content information does not necessarily equip a person for the task of religious education.

From counseling, Carl Rogers represents a functional perception. His particular expertise was in psychotherapy, and he described the growth of health in clients this way: "It means that a person is a fluid process, not a static entity; a flowing river of change, not a block of solid material; a continually changing constellation of potentialities, not a fixed quantity of traits."[36] Taking Rogers' human example and applying it to the field of religious education reveals that religious education needs sufficient "therapy" to release its preoccupation with specified content and rigid structure and allow itself to evolve through a process of becoming. The content and structure can develop as the needs arise. Systemic religious education seeks maturity and health by becoming (in Rogers' words) a fluid process, a flowing river of change, and a continually changing constellation of potentialities that searches for, attempts at, and creates holistic nexus.

Structure

Structure and content have long been the primary consideration of religious education. Randolph Crump Miller said theology is the "clue" to Christian education.[37] James Smart said the problem with religious education is not education but theology.[38] Lois LeBar encouraged Christians to find "the answers that are inherent in the very structure of the universe" and stop when they are discovered.[39] When religious education starts with a particular structure/content there is little room for creative function, and the purpose is determined before it is considered. The purpose *is* the structure. This is the ultimate in closed system thinking.

Systemic religious education does not disparage substantive content and structure. It simply keeps them in their place. Certainly religious education has substantive content, and this content must be structured; but that is not the sole and determinative raison d'etre of religious education. Substantive content and structure lead to closed system thinking when they are reductionistically deterministic.

Summary

The design for a systemic model of religious education does not start with content and structure. Systemic religious education gives focus to purpose and to function, allowing the content and structures to develop and evolve as needed. Religious education that deals with structure first is automatically locked into a deterministic purpose and is a closed system from the outset. There is no chance for creativity, flexibility, or long-term viability in structure-oriented religious education.

RELIGIOUS EDUCATION AND THE PARADIGM OF OPEN SYSTEMS

Systemic religious education is modeled from the paradigm of open systems. By now the litany of the properties of open systems is familiar, and all that is required here is to show the particular application to religious education. As in the previous models, no simulation is attempted. What follows is a model based on the eight properties of open systems.

Holism

Reference to the definition of systemic religious education shows that the quest is for the establishment of holistic nexus. As was noted in the discussion of the phrase in chapter 4, the key is "holistic," meaning healthy and whole. The goal is not just for interconnection but for interconnection that brings life, health, and continued progress.

Religious education is especially attuned to holism because of its compound nature. It is impossible to discuss religious education without discussing both religion and education. J. M. Price noted: "Education and religion, then, are vitally interrelated. Each is incomplete without the other."[40] Even more is holism a necessary element when religion and education are fused into a new entity, religious education. Religion and education are no longer identifiable as separate parts but are interdependent elements of a new whole.

Differentiation

Without differentiation, holism degenerates into monotony. While an open system is holistic and integrative, it also has subsystems, divisions, and hierarchies. Holism and differentiation are two sides of one coin. Systemic religious education must retain differentiation while it strives for holism.

Probably the most prominent criticism of systemic religious education is that the uniqueness of religious education becomes lost in the work of religion and education. Edith Hunter encountered similar problems with her proposals: "Just as new ways in discipline, so new ways in religious education are easily misunderstood as no ways."[41] It is true that religious education gives up some of its independence through a systemic approach, but from an open systems perspective that is a sign of health. An independent, completely "differentiated" entity becomes isolated and left to die. Systemic religious education seeks to be an open system, with both uniqueness and interdependence.

Boundaries

The keys to both holism and differentiation are boundaries. Boundaries are not only the barriers which exclude but also the interfaces which connect. An open system must have boundaries which are permeable enough to allow flow-through as well as strong enough to retain identity.

Systemic religious education is bounded by the terms "search," "attempt," "create," and "transform." This quest is toward holistic nexus through a learning-adaptive process. The interface with religion and education is striking, but identity for religious education is attained through the efforts of searching, attempting, creating, and transforming. It should be clear by now that religion, education, and religious education are systemically bounded so that none stands alone. Each is systemically interrelated to the other.

Dynamism

Religion was described as binding together, education as leading out. These are terms of movement, process, and change. Religious education is searching, attempting, creating, and transforming. These too are dynamic. Systemic religious education is not a static entity but is process identifiable through time.

Gloria Durka and Joanmarie Smith worked on a dynamic expression of their theories. They wrote: "One of the basic views of the process thinkers is that the deepest Reality is not static but dynamic. In the process model, change is a positive factor in experience and not a negative one."[42] They were correct in their focus on the dynamic. The problem was their use of positive and negative. From a systemic viewpoint, change is not best experienced as positive, only as a "given." What a system does through the change can then be either healthy or unhealthy. It is the choice for healthy change that is positive.

Equifinality

The property of equifinality raises two points: one, that there is a purpose or a goal to be pursued; two, that there is a variety of ways to achieve the goal. Systemic religious education seeks to address both of these points.

Systemic religious education is teleological. It is the effort toward holistic nexus. It is present transformation of the past into a vision of the future. While never assuming that an "ideal future" can ever be a total reality, this can still be what Carl Rogers called a "vaguely transcending dream" and a "subjectively formed guiding vision."[43] The purpose of systemic religious education is ever-changing but ever-deepening progress toward holism, health, and interface.

Systemic religious education does not follow a "golden road" to the future. In truth, there is no road at all. Rather, there is growth, evaluation, and a sense of the lure toward the future[44] which can be achieved through an infinite variety of functions and structures.

Feedback

Growth, evaluation, and a sense of the lure toward the future are of such a nature as to make evaluation seem impossible. The solution to this riddle is teleology and feedback. The goal is effort toward holistic nexus. If this goal is not being achieved, if the system is not health-giving and is not achieving integration, then the functions and/or structures are in need of change.[45] The feedback received from progress (or more probably a lack of progress) toward the desired goal provides the information necessary for the implementation of healthy change. In an open system, nothing is precluded from the possibility of change. Indeed, even the purpose of the achievement of holistic nexus is not exempt from refinement, reappraisal, and reinterpretation.

James Michael Lee included in his "teaching theory"[46] the concept of feedback when he discussed the "closed-loop system":

> By closed-loop here I mean that each of the variables involved in the instructional act interacts with the other variables in a closed-loop fashion so that the effects which any single variable has on the next linked variable in the behavioral chain eventually return to the original variable to modify, reinforce, or enhance it.[47]

The only way that a learning-adaptive process can function effectively is through the kind of "closed-loop system" that Lee described. The system must have information to evaluate in order to keep itself targeted toward its goal. It is this cybernetic process that enables the system to correct and improve itself on the quest for emergent holism and integration.

Homeostasis

In order for an open system to exist, it must "be": it must have a degree of stability as it changes through time. Homeostasis is the property of an open system that describes the retention of the system's identity even as it is being transformed. Homeostasis becomes a property of systemic religious education when the effort is made to retain but transform the heritage of the past into an actualized future.

Colin Alves employed the concept of homeostasis in his own description of religious education. He defined it as follows:

> The pupil is invited to try to understand the religious heritage (or heritages, if the word can be used in the plural) of his [or her] society (or of [humankind] in general) and, having understood, to assess the significance and value of this heritage for the future of [humankind], or at least for his [or her] own future development as an individual.[48]

Religious education cannot ignore its past, but neither can it live in the past. The heritage must be known, evaluated, and transformed to meet the needs of the present as it progresses into the future.

Growth

Unfortunately, religious education has been often aligned with a fondness for the past rather than an eagerness for the future. Edith Hunter expressed her thoughts this way: "Instead of a force to control and hold back vitality, religious education ideally becomes a means of allowing this vitality to flow into the culture without distortion."[49] In similar but more pointed words, Alfred North Whitehead wrote: "The vitality of religion is shown by the way in which the religious spirit has survived the ordeal of religious education."[50] Systemic religious education looks to the future, but grows from and builds upon the wisdom of past achievement. Systemic religious education is not simply an effort to create *ex nihilo* but to transform and re-create from what has been done within its heritage.

Summary

Systemic religious education can be molded from the paradigm of open systems. As a creating, transforming, restless force it will be different from the religious education of the past. This is as it should be, from a systemic perspective. But it will not be unrelated or unrecognizable to the past efforts. It will be changed, not alien.

The full picture of systemic religious education becomes clearer when the model is put into the perspective of the systemic worldview. As was true in the previous models, systemic religious education must be fully integrated into the larger system to be functional and viable.

RELIGIOUS EDUCATION AND
THE SYSTEMIC WORLDVIEW

The vision of systemic religious education is to bring about a systemic worldview. The achievement of a systemic worldview requires systemic religious education. The two are not synonymous, but they are inextricably intertwined and interdependent. The eight characteristics of the systemic worldview are good descriptors of the values of systemic religious education.

Organismic

The chief metaphor of the systemic worldview is the organism: a holistic entity made up of interactive and interdependent parts. This organism, as an open system, is not just a conglomerate of parts or an aggregate. It is a dynamic, integrated whole with interaction and purpose. Systemic religious education is the transformational quest for holistic nexus through a learning-adaptive process. As this quest becomes actualized, the metaphor of the organism becomes clearer. The complementary nature of the systemic worldview and the systemic model allows each to develop more fully.

The organismic metaphor represents a complete reorientation of perspective from a reductionistic and mechanistic viewpoint. No longer is the goal to learn more and more about less and less. This analytic method has been (and continues to be) valuable, but any method used to an extreme becomes dangerous and unbalanced. The current need is to put the analytic material into context and interrelationship with the larger whole. The systemic perspective represents a shift of relating, of thinking, of experiencing from a molecular to a molar viewpoint.[51] Systemic religious education looks to integration and transformation rather than to exclusion and isolation.

The organismic metaphor also implies that systemic religious education is more than simply a cognitive process. Gloria Durka wrote: "The main thrust of the new substance of religious education must be a change in the way religious educators think about religious education problems."[52] Such a statement is too limited for systemic religious education. First, a systemic perspective brings into view a new and different set of problems for religious educators (and others) to consider. Second, the problems that are perceived require much more than thought. They demand widespread, creative, interactive, and cooperative action toward solution.

Relational

Systemic religious education is not merely the transmission of "facts" or "truth" about religion or theology or culture. Such activity may be used in a training exercise (more likely as indoctrination) but cannot be equated with systemic religious education. Transmission, memorization, and repetition as the entirety of religious education is absolutistic, more appropriate to a classical science worldview, and even more appropriate to a theological worldview. Religious education (so-called) that concentrates on the transmission of data and the proper recitation of the "right" answers to certain questions presupposes an external, dominant authority, eliminates the possibility of emergent purpose, and excludes authentic maturity, development, and creativity.

Systemic religious education is relational. The desire is for relationship: among information bits, among concepts and beliefs, among experiences, among persons and communities. Systemic religious education searches for, attempts at, and creates these relationships. Systemic religious education calls for interpretation, values detection, and movement toward meaning and integration. Systemic religious education is less interesting in receiving "right" answers than in asking progressively better questions.

Pluralistic

Systemic religious education seeks to find holistic nexus beyond the traditional but restrictive categories. Religious education need not be relegated to an academic discipline with neat boundaries and isolated experiments. Religious education need not be responsive to only one cultural or religious heritage. The quest is for a systemic, indeed pluralistic, perspective. It was this resistance to particularism that caused James Michael Lee to describe his macrotheory of religious instruction in this way:

> The social-science macrotheory of religious instruction avoids identification with any particular form, setting, or procedure of actual here-and-now religious instruction endeavor. . . . The social-science macrotheory necessarily avoids taking sides about which theological view is correct or which denomination is the most authentically Christian.[53]

The systemic perspective correspondingly stops short of endorsing one particular type of holistic nexus as *the* correct choice. Such a focus would be much too narrow and would disallow true integration.[54] This is not to say that systemic simulations would be difficult to create, only that the simulations would be examples of particulars and hence not of value here in describing the overall systemic perspective.

Stochastic

Determinism accepts the past, present, and future as fixed and unalterable. Change, randomness, and creativity are simply not possible in a deterministic worldview. What may appear to be creative is actually just another link in the natural (or supernatural) chain of cause and effect.

Stochasticity understands the future to be undetermined, unformed, and bifurcative.[55] The future is simply "not yet," else it would not be the future. The future can be affected from the present—the existential point of bifurcation. It is the hope and vision of this more desirable future to be created which provides the motivation for systemic religious education.

Systemic religious education is stochastic in that it accepts the heritage of the past but does not allow the past to dictate what course the future must take. The heritage of the past is to be used and transformed existentially to actualize a desired future. The future is not allowed to "happen," but is created, guided, and controlled to whatever extent is possible. Regardless of the efforts of a planning process, however, the future is always respected as capricious and surprising. This is the reason for the development of a learning and adapting process that is able to adjust to the presently unknown future.

Dynamic

The systemic worldview perceives reality as processive and dynamic. Shirley Heckman made this comment on the different view of life:

> In the shift from Newton to Einstein, we moved from believing the world to be static with absolute definitions and answers about how to live. We now know life to be dynamic. Life flows around and through us in a variety of ways. Change is constantly occurring at a rate we find difficult to comprehend.[56]

In like manner, systemic religious education perceives reality dynamically. For that reason, systemic religious education is process: a ceaseless activity of searching, attempting, creating, and transforming.

Negentropic

Since negentropy is the tendency toward order, growth, and complexity, then systemic religious education is in every sense negentropic. The overall goal of systemic religious education is to achieve holistic nexus, and by all standards this is an effort toward order, growth, and complexity. In dramatic terms, systemic religious education is a participant in the quest to overcome death (entropy) and to develop life (negentropy). This quest is not just for the academic viability of religious education, but for societal survival.

The order, growth, and complexity reflective of an open system is a result of an interaction of the elements of the system with each other and with the environment. In other words, the order that develops is *emergent* from within the system as it interrelates with its environment. Order is not imposed or imported externally. It is an evolutionary, creative, and transformational process of the system. Systemic religious education, then, does not receive its order or structure from some external authority or discipline,[57] but searches for, attempts at, and creates order and structure systemically through interaction and interrelationship with the environment.

Holistic

The systemic worldview, with its emphasis on holism and integration, can find actualization in the work of systemic religious education. Systemic religious education is not just a good idea, or merely a diversionary activity. Systemic religious education is an essential and crucial contributor to the work of insuring the continued life of the biosphere. The task of systemic religious education is to help find ways to put life together; without the integrative influence of systemic religious education (along with other integrative efforts) chaos and disintegration will take over. Systemic religious education seeks to facilitate holism and organicism.

The systemic worldview transcends dualities to find integration and interaction. Leon McKenzie wrote: "Reality may be perceived to be bifurcated into the realms of the sacred and the profane by those who look at reality from behind Platonic spectacles, but such a dichotomy of being, ontologically, is unintelligible."[58] The systemic worldview removes the inappropriate lenses (to continue McKenzie's analogy) but does not leave the seeker unaided. The systemic worldview provides a different set of spectacles. From a systemic perspective, wholes become apparent with their interaction, interrelationships, and interdependence. What appear to be unrelated and isolated pieces from a molecular viewpoint become interconnected, synergistic elements of a dynamic system from a molar perspective.

Cybernetic

The function of cybernetics is fundamental to systemic religious education. The teleological design of open systems allows purpose to emerge from the interaction of the elements of the system with each other and with the environment. Such dynamic, evolutionary purpose (as distinct from imposed, external purpose) requires the open system to receive continual feedback on its movement toward maturity and complexity. Systemic religious education does not seek nexus, but holistic nexus; it does not seek the future, but an ideal future. The cybernetic characteristic of the systemic worldview is well-suited for regulating and evaluating the flow of information, which is necessary to keep the vision of systemic religious education in focus.

Summary
Systemic religious education and the systemic worldview are integrally related and complementary. Systemic religious education is made functional within the context of the systemic worldview. The systemic worldview is actualized through the development of systemic religious education.

One further aspect of systemic religious education needs attention. It must be put in its environmental context of other theoretical approaches. In the following section, systemic religious education gains further actualization as it is seen in relief of various other proposals for religious education.

SYSTEMIC RELIGIOUS EDUCATION IN ENVIRONMENTAL PERSPECTIVE

It remains to put systemic religious education within the environmental perspective of contemporary approaches to religious education. This can be done briefly by employing the categories and discussions from chapter 1 that described the various perspectives. It is appropriate to return to the starting point of the book to show the full cycle. In light of the previous treatment all that needs to be done is to relate the systemic approach to the approaches already presented. Two sections follow. The first examines the relationship of systemic religious education to historical and theoretical perspectives. The second shows the correspondence between systemic religious education and selected individual perspectives.

Historical and Theoretical Perspectives
The three divisions used in chapter 1 to express the historical and theoretical dimensions of religious education were from the work of Harold William Burgess, Ian P. Knox, and Kendig Brubaker Cully. These three are again employed to locate the position of religious education from a systemic perspective.
Harold William Burgess. It was Harold William Burgess who

proposed that contemporary religious education could be categorized into four theoretical approaches: the traditional theological approach, the social-cultural approach, the contemporary theological approach, and the social-science approach. He believed the best hope for religious education resided in the social-science approach since the other three were primarily theological in nature.[59] The social-science approach does not start with theological concerns but with a desire to do religious education more effectively.[60] The focus is on holism and process rather than on the mere transmission of content.

The systemic perspective on religious education is one way of doing the social-science approach. Close examination of the categories Burgess developed reveals that fundamentally only two options exist: a theological approach and a social-science approach. This has been pointed out repeatedly by James Michael Lee and others.[61] The systemic perspective as a participant of the social-science approach is much broader and more foundational than a theological approach by virtue of its attention to the fundamental construction elements, such as paradigms and worldviews. The systemic perspective may be interactive with theology but is neither determined by it nor subservient to it.

Ian P. Knox. Like Harold William Burgess, Ian Knox proposed theoretical catgories for understanding the field of religious education. He discussed three possible positions: the transcendist position, the immanentist position, and the integrationist position.[62] From the sound of this terminology, the integrationist position would seem to be most compatible with the systemic perspective. On reflection, however, this is not the case. The problem is that Knox was not able to develop, define, or defend the integregationist position with any precision or clarity. Although it sounds like a good compromise possibility, in reality it has no substance. By Knox's own admission, the candidates he proposed for the integrationist position did not fit the category.[63] The lack of distinction for the integrationist position precludes it from being a viable alternative.

The two positions left, then, are the transcendist and the immanentist. There is little doubt as to which is most descriptive of the systemic perspective. One of the primary considerations of the systemic perspective is the emergence of purpose from the interaction of the elements of the system with each other and with the environment. Such teleology is not imposed from "above" but is generated from "within." The systemic perspective is clearly immanentist.[64]

Kendig Brubaker Cully. It was Kendig Brubaker Cully's contribution that the recent history of religious education could be divided up into two historical eras. From the early days of the twentieth century until about 1940, religious education was based on a liberal theology. From 1940 Cully believed that neo-orthodox theology took over as the primary base. At the time of his writing (1965), Cully was probably accurate. Since that time it appears that another phase has dawned.

The social-science approach first appeared in book form in 1970, with articles in journals preceding.[65] The development of the social-science approach has been advanced chiefly through the work of James Michael Lee. This approach rejects theology as the sole foundation for religious education and moves on to social science for the construction of theory in religious education. The systemic perspective is a part of the social-science approach which declines the pure theological argument. The "search for a religious education since 1965" appears to be oriented more toward scientific and theoretical underpinnings than toward theological structures. The systemic perspective has been designed to be at least a partial answer in the current search for an adequate base for religious education.

Individual Perspectives

A survey of every recent religious educator is certainly not possible, and it is not needed. Again retracing the work of chapter 1, four examples from the field of religious education are adequate to place the systemic perspective in context. The educators chosen are James Smart, Randolph Crump Miller, James Michael Lee, and John Westerhoff.

James D. Smart. James D. Smart was primarily a theologian and biblical interpreter who also gave attention to religious education. His attempts to relate theology and religious education found respect among scholars in both fields and provided religious education with some much-needed academic respectability. Since he tried to make religious education more palatable to the theological community, it is no surprise that Smart portrayed religious education as a part of the theological process. Smart's self-appointed task was to put religious education on an adequate and substantial theological base.

The contribution of James Smart to the systemic perspective was his insistence on the unity and integration of the church's ministry. He believed the "rebirth of ministry" would come when the heritage of the apostolic ministry was reinstituted as the unifier for the work of the church.

This stance was also that which distinguished Smart from the systemic perspective. Smart's final conclusion was that the real problem was a theological problem.[66] The way to achieve unity was to return to a distinctly Christian, actually neo-orthodox, theological position, and then the religious education problem would solve itself. Though the systemic perspective does see theology as problematic, theology is neither the root of the problems of religious education nor is it the solution to the problems of religious education. Theology may be interactive with systemic religious education, but theology is not the determining factor for systemic religious education. To begin construction with a theological, structural design is to produce a deterministic, closed system.

Randolph Crump Miller. Randolph Crump Miller remained convinced that theology was the "clue" to religious education. Even if his theology was processive ("truth about God in relation to [humans]"[67]) and hidden ("grace in the foreground, theology in the background"[68]), Miller still could say regarding religious education: "It is primarily a theological endeavor."[69] It should be obvious by now that systemic religious education differs from this conceptualization.

James Michael Lee. The social-science approach as developed by James Michael Lee has much in common with the systemic perspective. The social-science approach begins from a modern science, actually an empirical, viewpoint. It is an effort in theory derived from practice. Indeed, Lee even acknowledged his work as "macrotheory," which is the "integrating of the various theories and sub-theories involved"[70] to explain all particularistic practice. Most relevantly, Lee wrote: "Fundamentally this approach is a worldview, a way in which a person meets, interprets,

and integrates reality."[71] This is precisely the intent of the systemic perspective.

The difference between systemic religious education and Lee's
work is a matter of focus. Systemic religious education is focused
on the broadest interpretation of the field of religious education.
James Michael Lee has focused instead on religious instruction,
as he emphasized in the epilogue to his trilogy of books on the
social-science approach to religious instruction:

> The trilogy both in its sum and in its parts does not deal with the
> entire range of intentional religious education. It deliberately ex-
> cludes from its purview two of the three basic constituents of inten-
> tional religious education, namely religious counseling and the ad-
> ministration of religious education activities. The focus of the tril-
> ogy is squarely on the third of these three fundamental components
> of intentional religious education, namely religious instruction.[72]

There is no delusion that the entirety of systemic religious education could be discussed in this book. What appears here is an
introduction to the theory of systemic religious education. If Lee
could refer to his monumental trilogy as a "work for beginners"
and "nothing more than an introduction to the field of religious
instruction,"[73] then surely this one volume is not an exhaustive
treatment of all of systemic religious education.

The most productive understanding of systemic religious education is to take it as complementary to the work of James Michael Lee. Both are constructed from the social-science approach.
Lee emphasized one of the three "fundamental components" of
religious education, and systemic religious education provides a
theoretical perspective for the entire field.

John H. Westerhoff III. John Westerhoff has many strengths,
but even as he has observed, permanent and unified theoretical
construction is not one of them.[74] Westerhoff is eclectic rather
than systemic, so that he is of no direct help in a comparison with
the systemic approach. He has emphasized two pivotal ideas,
however, that are of importance in systemic religious education.

First, Westerhoff used the term "paradigm" similar to the way
it has been used in this book. While he did not recognize that a
paradigm is a reflection of a worldview, he did see it as a pattern

for construction of models. Westerhoff planted a seed for religious education with this discussion of paradigms.[75]

Second, Westerhoff has given increasing support to the role of socialization in religious education. While certainly not alone in this type of consideration, he has been one to keep that dimension of cultural transmission visible.[76] The systemic approach to religious education incorporates this idea in its emphasis on the transformation of the heritage of the past, on the importance of relationships and interconnections, and on the awareness of the pervasive influence of the environment.[77] However, the systemic approach is not restricted to socialization but often goes beyond it to achieve holistic, free goals and structures.

John Westerhoff's charming capriciousness allows him to combine ideas in unique if not contradictory fashion. For example, Westerhoff has espoused both socialization and liberation theology, two seemingly opposed positions.[78] Westerhoff is one of those creative persons who continually throws off interesting but undeveloped ideas. Such persons are of value to the future of religious education, using their fertile imaginations to explore new areas of inquiry. The additional, and crucial, need is the difficult and serious work of developing these creative ideas into testable, workable theory. This lack of attention to theory has hampered the maturity of religious education. The desire to construct a theory that would improve the health and viability of the field has provided the motivation for the development of a systemic perspective for religious education.

CONCLUSION

The purpose of this chapter was to show how a systemic model of religious education could be constructed. The model outlined was not "the" model, nor was it a concrete simulation. It was but one search for, attempt at, and creation of holistic nexus.

It would be wrong to think that it was only in this chapter that religious education was addressed. In a real sense the entire book has been an experience in systemic religious education. How can religious education be done better? The answer is found to some degree on each page of this book.

NOTES

1. William Wordsworth, "My Heart Leaps Up," in *Poems of Wordsworth,* ed. Matthew Arnold (New York: Thomas Y. Crowell, 1892), p. 111.

2. Gregory Bateson, *Steps to an Ecology of Mind: A Revolutionary Approach to Man's Understanding of Himself* (New York: Ballantine Books, 1972), p. xvii.

3. Leon McKenzie, *The Religious Education of Adults* (Birmingham, Ala.: Religious Education Press, 1982), p. 2.

4. This confusion is reflected in a compilation commemorating the 75th anniversary of the Religious Education Association. See John H. Westerhoff III, ed., *Who Are We?: The Quest for a Religious Education* (Birmingham, Ala.: Religious Education Press, 1978).

5. Erik Erikson, *Childhood and Society,* 2nd ed. (New York: W. W. Norton, 1963), p. 261.

6. Iris Cully, "What Killed Religious Education?" *Religion in Life* 40 (Autumn, 1971), pp. 404-411.

7. James Michael Lee, *The Shape of Religious Instruction: A Social Science Approach* (Birmingham, Ala.: Religious Education Press, 1971), p. 6.

8. Ibid. Also see James Michael Lee, *The Content of Religious Instruction: A Social Science Approach* (Birmingham, Ala.: Religious Education Press, 1985), p. 746.

9. For a discussion of this point, see Jack L. Seymour, "Approaches to Christian Education," in *Contemporary Approaches to Christian Education*, ed. Jack L. Seymour et. al. (Nashville: Abingdon Press, 1982), p. 20.

10. See Westerhoff, "Risking an Answer: A Conclusion," in *Who Are We?*, p. 268.

11. John H. Westerhoff III, "A Discipline in Crisis," *Religious Education* 74 (January-February, 1979), p. 10.

12. Westerhoff, "Risking an Answer: A Conclusion," in *Who Are We?*, p. 269.

13. This has been described variously, but one of the best is Gwen Kennedy Neville and John H. Westerhoff III, *Learning Through Liturgy* (New York: Seabury Press, 1978), especially Part II, "The Christian Life in Liturgical Context," pp. 89-181.

14. Actually, this kind of dogmatism is even more reflective of catechism than catechesis.

15. Westerhoff, "Risking an Answer: A Conclusion," in *Who Are We?*, p. 270. The particularism is obvious in this quote. It is difficult to imagine, for example, Jewish educators accepting a word that means "being Christian together." The term "catechesis" has such a long and strong Christian association that there seems little hope for ecumenical acceptance.

16. Lois LeBar, *Education That Is Christian,* rev. ed. (Old Tappan, N.J.: Fleming H. Revell, 1981), p. 20.

17. Ibid. This rigid, dualistic type of thinking is what James Michael Lee called "spookification": "By spookification I mean the unwarranted attempt to explain empirical phenomena in religious instruction by resorting to high-sounding but fundamentally meaningless spectral explanations of these phenomena . . . while at the same time rejecting as insufficiently religious and un-Godlike those empirical explanations which adequately and parsimoniously account for the nature and workings of these phenomena." James Michael Lee,

"Lifework Spirituality and the Religious Educator," in *The Spirituality of the Religious Educator*, ed. James Michael Lee (Birmingham, Ala.: Religious Education Press, 1985), p. 29, note 63.

18. LeBar, *Education That Is Christian*, p. 79.

19. Ibid., p. 208.

20. Thomas Groome's definition of religious education was: "Religious education activity is a deliberate attending to the transcendent dimension of life by which a conscious relationship to an ultimate ground of being is promoted and enabled to come to expression." Thomas H. Groome, *Christian Religious Education: Sharing Our Story and Vision* (San Francisco: Harper & Row, 1980), p. 22. Compare this with Groome's definition of Christian religious education on page 25.

21. Ibid., p. 24.

22. Ibid., p. 26. Also see use of this terminology in Mary Elizabeth Moore, *Education for Continuity and Change: A New Model for Christian Religious Education* (Nashville: Abingdon Press, 1983).

23. Marvin J. Taylor, "Introduction," in *Foundations for Christian Education in an Era of Change*, ed. Marvin J. Taylor (Nashville: Abingdon Press, 1976), p. 5.

24. Ibid., pp. 7-8.

25. For example, see Norma H. Thompson, "The Role of Theology in Religious Education," in *Religious Education and Theology*, ed. Norma H. Thompson (Birmingham, Ala.: Religious Education Press, 1982), p. 15; also see Westerhoff, "Risking an Answer: A Conclusion," in *Who Are We?*, pp. 264-268.

26. This theme is throughout Chave's book, mentioned on the first page of the introduction and variously from there. See Ernest J. Chave, *A Functional Approach to Religious Education* (Chicago: University of Chicago Press, 1947), p. v and elsewhere.

27. Ibid., pp. 126-127.

28. Mary K. Cove and Mary Louise Mueller, *Regarding Religious Education* (Birmingham, Ala.: Religious Education Press, 1977), p. 24.

29. James Michael Lee, *The Flow of Religious Instruction: A Social Science Approach* (Birmingham, Ala.: Religious Education Press, 1973), pp. 17-18.

30. Lee, *The Content of Religious Instruction*, p. 25. I have already referred to Lee's concept briefly in chapter 1.

31. Shirley J. Heckman, *On the Wings of a Butterfly: A Guide to Total Christian Education* (Elgin, Ill.: The Brethren Press, 1981), p. 13. One major difference here is that Heckman calls for us "to anticipate the future." Systemic religious education creates the future through a learning-adaptive process.

32. Lee, *The Shape of Religious Instruction*, pp. 10-11.

33. Ibid.

34. Chave, *A Functional Approach to Religious Education*, p. 131.

35. McKenzie, *The Religious Education of Adults*, pp. 5-6.

36. Carl R. Rogers, *On Becoming a Person: A Therapist's View of Psychotherapy* (Boston: Houghton Mifflin, 1961), p. 122.

37. Randolph Crump Miller, *The Clue to Christian Education* (New York: Charles Scribner's Sons, 1950), p. 15.

38. James D. Smart, *The Teaching Ministry of the Church* (Philadelphia: Westminster Press, 1954), p. 205.

39. LeBar, *Education That Is Christian*, p. 182.

40. J. M. Price, "Nature and Scope of Religious Education," in *A Survey of Religious Education,* ed. J. M. Price et al., 2d ed. (New York: Ronald Press Company, 1959), p. 6.

41. Edith F. Hunter, *The Questioning Child and Religion* (Boston: Starr King Press, 1956), p. 17.

42. Gloria Durka and Joanmarie Smith, *Modeling God: Religious Education for Tomorrow* (New York: Paulist Press, 1976), p. 63.

43. Carl R. Rogers, *A Way of Being* (Boston: Houghton Mifflin, 1980), p. 238.

44. See this phrase in the context of Alfred North Whitehead, *Process and Reality: An Essay in Cosmology,* ed. David Ray Griffin and Donald W. Sherburne, cor. ed. (New York: The Free Press, 1978), pp. 346, 413.

45. It should be noted that terms such as "health" and "integration" are process terms, meaning that even the teleology of systemic religious education continues to be refined and shaped. All the interactive elements of an open system are subject to change and transformation.

46. This was Lee's term for his theory. See this in the context of the other theories he described in Lee, *The Flow of Religious Instruction,* pp. 149-205.

47. Ibid., p. 199.

48. Colin Alves, "Why Religious Education?", in *New Movements in Religious Education,* ed. Ninian Smart and David Horder (London: Temple Smith, 1975), p. 28.

49. Hunter, *The Questioning Child and Religion,* p. 191.

50. Alfred North Whitehead, "The Rhythmic Claims of Freedom and Discipline," in Alfred North Whitehead, *The Aims of Education and Other Essays* (New York: Macmillan Company, 1929; reprint edition; New York: The Free Press, 1967), p. 39.

51. It is crucial to have clarity on this point. The systemic perspective does *not* call a halt to analysis. The systemic perspective seeks to balance analysis with integrative and environmental considerations. The choice is not one of either-or, but instead is an effort toward a both-and complementarity.

52. Gloria Durka, "Modeling Religious Education for the Future," in *The Religious Education We Need: Toward the Renewal of Christian Education,* ed. James Michael Lee (Birmingham, Ala.: Religious Education Press, 1977), p. 96.

53. Lee, *The Content of Religious Instruction,* p. 753.

54. Just as there is danger in being narrow and particularistic, there is also the danger of being nonevaluative. The criteria of health, growth, and maturity for the system must be kept primary.

55. A bifurcative future refers to the present as the bifurcation point, with a multitude of possibilities for the future. See this idea expressed in John A. Dillon, Jr., *Foundations of General Systems Theory* (Louisville, Ky.: University of Louisville, 1982), pp. 162 ff. Also see Ilya Prigogine and Isabelle Stengers, *Order Out of Chaos: Man's New Dialogue with Nature* (New York: Bantam Books, 1984), pp. 160-176.

56. Heckman, *On the Wings of a Butterfly,* pp. 31-32.

57. James Michael Lee terms such conceptions of religious instruction as "messenger boy" and "translator" stages. See Lee, "The Authentic Source of Religious Instruction," in *Religious Education and Theology,* pp. 156-165.

58. McKenzie, *Religious Education of Adults,* p. 18.

59. Harold William Burgess, *An Invitation to Religious Education* (Birming-

ham, Ala.: Religious Education Press, 1975), p. 168.

60. Ibid., p. 169.

61. For example, see Lee, *The Content of Religious Instruction,* pp. 1-12. This discussion is not a reintroduction of dualism, where the choice is either theology or social-science. The debate concerns how theology and social science relate.

62. These are described in Ian P. Knox, *Above or Within?: The Supernatural in Religious Education* (Birmingham, Ala.: Religious Education Press, 1976).

63. Ibid., p. 143. For example, Randolph Crump Miller is better understood as an immanentist, while Marcel van Caster is better interpreted as a transcendist.

64. These terms (immanentist and transcendist) are not words of my choice, since they are reflective of absolutistic and dualistic world views. They are considered here only for the purpose of relating systemic religious education to earlier work.

65. For a good summary of this history, see Burgess, *An Invitation to Religious Education,* pp. 127-129.

66. James D. Smart, *The Teaching Ministry of the Church* (Philadelphia: Westminster Press, 1954), p. 205.

67. Randolph Crump Miller, *The Clue to Christian Education* (New York: Charles Scribner's Sons, 1950), p. 5.

68. Ibid., p. 7.

69. Randolph Crump Miller, *The Theory of Christian Education Practice* (Birmingham, Ala.: Religious Education Press), p. 1.

70. James Michael Lee, "To Basically Change Fundamental Theory and Practice," in *Modern Masters of Religious Education,* ed. Marlene Mayr (Birmingham, Ala.: Religious Education Press, 1983), p. 299.

71. Lee, *The Shape of Religious Instruction,* p. 3.

72. Lee, *The Content of Religious Instruction,* p. 746.

73. Ibid., p. 750.

74. See John H. Westerhoff III, "A Journey into Self-Understanding," in *Modern Masters of Religious Education,* pp. 115-117.

75. This concept is discussed throughout John H. Westerhoff III, *Will Our Children Have Faith?* (New York: Seabury Press, 1976).

76. See especially John H. Westerhoff III, and Gwen Kennedy Neville, *Generation to Generation: Conversations on Religious Education and Culture* (Philadelphia: United Church Press, 1974).

77. John Westerhoff is closer to a theological approach than to a social-science approach, so it is well to keep in mind what Harold William Burgess said about the theological approach and the environment. See, for example, Burgess, *An Invitation to Religious Education,* pp. 50-51.

78. For example, see Westerhoff, *Will Our Children Have Faith?* pp. 16-19; 30-32.

Afterword

Do not go gentle into that good night,
Old age should burn and rave at close of day;
Rage, rage against the dying of the light.

Though wise men at their end know dark is right,
Because their words had forked no lightning they
Do not go gentle into that good night.[1]

Dylan Thomas

If the words in this book have "forked no lightning," then they are a failure. There is more than sufficient opportunity for light to shine in a future filled with the shadows of fascism and bigotry, of stultifying indifference to human and environmental needs, and even the final darkness of a nuclear winter. Religious education must not become just one more isolated field that concentrates on minutiae and esoterica. Religious education must become systemic, participating in a process that creates, permeates, and revolutionizes the future as surely as the yeast that transforms the inert dough.

This book was written to portray religious education from a systemic perspective. These paragraphs signal only the end of the beginning for the development of systemic religious education and by no means the beginning of the end. The growth and maturity of religious education is an evolutionary process that is continually searching for better forms of expression. The present situation of religious education is remarkably similar to that of a client who once told Carl Rogers:

I haven't finished the job of integrating and reorganizing myself, but that is only confusing, not discouraging, now that I realize this is a continuing process. . . . It's exciting, sometimes upsetting, but deeply encouraging to feel yourself in action, apparently knowing where you are going even though you don't always consciously know where that is.[2]

If religious education is to grow and mature, then religious education will have to experience the excitement, the confusion, the upset, and the enthusiasm that is inherent in the process.

The future of religious education is yet to be created. What are some ways to bring it about? While there are any number of ways to answer such a question, it is instructive to point out a few of the growing edges of systemic religious education.

One area that needs attention is the production of systemic simulations. This book has been a theoretical work, describing ways that religious education can be conceptualized and modeled from a systemic perspective. It is now necessary to translate these models into actual, integrative simulations. The models outlined in the final chapters of this book will receive refinement, correction, and adaptation when simulations are constructed and implemented. The task of developing and evaluating simulations will enflesh the systemic theory and will generate activity and energy for the field of religious education.

It may go without saying that the entire proposal for a "systemic perspective" needs discussion and assessment. This book has proposed the theoretical constructs of paradigm, worldview, model, and simulation as components of the systemic perspective. This proposal, as well as the way these components are developed, required serious evaluation and feedback. A perspective created, delineated, and espoused by one person is hardly systemic. An authentically "systemic" perspective demands diverse participation. This book is less interested in specifying certain "rules" to play by than it is committed to suggesting a different perspective whereby a new "game" may emerge.

The continued development of systems theory holds vast potential, not just for religious education, but for the entire society. Research and development in the area are expanding at exponential rates, but systems theory still has many areas of application yet untouched. This book is one attempt to break new ground for its use. Systems theory must not be allowed to rigidify and ossify; it must continue to be stretched, tested, and employed as a means toward integration and wholeness.

One of the most exciting but elusive opportunities for further inquiry is investigation into the presuppositions, fundamental beliefs, and guiding values that have been identified by the term "worldviews" in this book. Disagreement and controversy over particular issues receive much more understanding and clarity when put in the context of a broader perspective. This book has suggested that a new worldview is emerging. What role can religious education play in this nascent worldview?

In summary, the argument of this book is that religious education must be recast and revitalized from a systemic perspective in order to contribute to the task of actualizing holistic nexus. Fragmentary, eclectic, and isolationist approaches to religious education (along with other areas) are not only inadequate and misleading, but they are ultimately dangerous and life-threatening. However it is constructed, systemic religious education must lead to health, integration, and life. If it does not, it is an accomplice to disease, disintegration, and death. Religious education has a viable, legitimate, and essential role in the emerging systemic worldview if it becomes a learning-adaptive process that searches for, attempts at, and creates a more desirable future. Anything less is an abdication of responsibility and would rightly cause the death of religious education.

NOTES

1. Dylan Thomas, "Do Not Go Gentle into That Good Night," in *The Norton Anthology of Poetry,* ed. Alexander W. Allison et al., 3rd ed. (New York: Norton, 1983), p. 1181.

2. Carl R. Rogers, *On Becoming a Person: A Therapist's View of Psychotherapy* (Boston: Houghton Mifflin, 1961), p. 122.

Index of Names

245

Index of Subjects

Universe *(cont.)*
  heliocentric, 77, 84, 89, 91
  static, 94-95, 103, 110-111
University, 196, 199
Utopianism, 59, 116

Validity, 79, 127
Values, 63, 79, 82, 132, 141,
  146, 150, 156, 157, 162, 163,
  173, 183, 192, 212, 225, 227,
  243
Variables, 10, 11, 57, 93, 109,
  224
Variants, structural, see
  Structural variants
Variety, 10, 49, 69, 140, 145,
  151-152, 155, 158, 161, 165,
  173, 174, 189, 190, 193-194,
  223-224
  See also Differentiation;
    Diversity
Venus, 77, 78
Village, global, see Global
  village
Vitalism, 48, 62, 70
Vitalists, 53, 97, 114, 123

War, 14, 82, 132, 139, 174
  See also World War
Water, 85, 111, 154

Weapons, nuclear, see Nuclear
  weapons
Weltanshauung, 37
Wholeness, 146, 163, 243
Wisdom, 62, 196-197, 199
World, 77-78, 144
  evolving, 132
  postmodern, 158
World community, 133
World hypothesis, 37, 39-40
World Machine, 91-92, 124
World order, 144, 158, 163
World solidarity, 150-151, 156
Worldview, 3, 25, 34, 37, 39,
  59, 60, 74-119, 127, 160-164,
  198-202, 211-212, 226-232,
  234
  classical science, 84
    89-99, 104-106, 121
    176, 183, 203, 227
  Newtonian, 89, 183
  orientation to, 75-81
  ruined, 118
  static, 172
  systemic, 3, 84,
    98-119, 160-164,
    198-202, 226-231
  theological, 84-89,
    98-99, 121, 227
World War, 14, 15, 66
Worship, 150

524 387